POLITICAL CULTURE AND COMMUNIST STUDIES

St Antony's/Macmillan Series

General editor: Archie Brown, Fellow of St Antony's College, Oxford

Roy Allison FINLAND'S RELATIONS WITH THE SOVIET UNION 1944–84
Said Amir Arjomand (editor) FROM NATIONALISM TO REVOLUTIONARY ISLAM
Anders Åslund PRIVATE ENTERPRISE IN EASTERN EUROPE
Archie Brown (editor) POLITICAL CULTURE AND COMMUNIST STUDIES
Archie Brown and Michael Kaser (editors) SOVIET POLICY FOR THE 1980s
S. B. Burman CHIEFDOM POLITICS AND ALIEN LAW
Renfrew Christie ELECTRICITY, INDUSTRY AND CLASS IN SOUTH AFRICA
Robert O. Collins and Francis M. Deng (editors) THE BRITISH IN THE SUDAN, 1898–1956
Wilhelm Deist THE *WEHRMACHT* AND GERMAN REARMAMENT
Julius A. Elias PLATO'S DEFENCE OF POETRY
Ricardo Ffrench-Davis and Ernesto Tironi (editors) LATIN AMERICA AND THE NEW INTERNATIONAL ECONOMIC ORDER
David Footman ANTONIN BESSE OF ADEN
Bohdan Harasymiw POLITICAL ELITE RECRUITMENT IN THE SOVIET UNION
Neil Harding (editor) THE STATE IN SOCIALIST SOCIETY
Richard Holt SPORT AND SOCIETY IN MODERN FRANCE
Albert Hourani EUROPE AND THE MIDDLE EAST
Albert Hourani THE EMERGENCE OF THE MODERN MIDDLE EAST
J. R. Jennings GEORGES SOREL
Bohdan Krawchenko SOCIAL CHANGE AND NATIONAL CONSCIOUSNESS IN TWENTIETH-CENTURY UKRAINE
A. Kemp-Welch (translator) THE BIRTH OF SOLIDARITY
Paul Kennedy and Anthony Nicholls (editors) NATIONALIST AND RACIALIST MOVEMENTS IN BRITAIN AND GERMANY BEFORE 1914
Richard Kindersley (editor) IN SEARCH OF EUROCOMMUNISM
Gisela C. Lebzelter POLITICAL ANTI-SEMITISM IN ENGLAND, 1918–1939
Nancy Lubin LABOUR AND NATIONALITY IN SOVIET CENTRAL ASIA
C. A. MacDonald THE UNITED STATES, BRITAIN AND APPEASEMENT, 1936–1939
Robert H. McNeal TSAR AND COSSACK, 1855–1914
David Nicholls HAITI IN CARIBBEAN CONTEXT
Patrick O'Brien (editor) RAILWAYS AND THE ECONOMIC DEVELOPMENT OF WESTERN EUROPE, 1830–1914
Roger Owen (editor) STUDIES IN THE ECONOMIC AND SOCIAL HISTORY OF PALESTINE IN THE NINETEENTH AND TWENTIETH CENTURIES
D. C. M. Platt and Guido di Tella (editors) ARGENTINA, AUSTRALIA AND CANADA
Irena Powell WRITERS AND SOCIETY IN MODERN JAPAN
T. H. Rigby and Ferenc Fehér (editors POLITICAL LEGITIMATION IN COMMUNIST STATES
Marilyn Rueschemeyer PROFESSIONAL WORK AND MARRIAGE
A. J. R. Russell-Wood THE BLACK MAN IN SLAVERY AND FREEDOM IN COLONIAL BRAZIL
Aron Shai BRITAIN AND CHINA, 1941–47
Lewis H. Siegelbaum THE POLITICS OF INDUSTRIAL MOBILIZATION IN RUSSIA, 1914–17
David Stafford BRITAIN AND EUROPEAN RESISTANCE, 1940–1945
Nancy Stepan THE IDEA OF RACE IN SCIENCE
Marvin Swartz THE POLITICS OF BRITISH FOREIGN POLICY IN THE ERA OF DISRAELI AND GLADSTONE
Guido di Tella ARGENTINA UNDER PERÓN, 1973–76
Rosemary Thorp (editor) LATIN AMERICA IN THE 1930s
Rosemary Thorp and Laurence Whitehead (editors) INFLATION AND STABILISATION IN LATIN AMERICA
Rudolf L. Tökés (editor) OPPOSITION IN EASTERN EUROPE

POLITICAL CULTURE AND COMMUNIST STUDIES

Edited by
Archie Brown

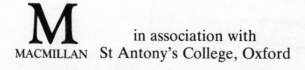

MACMILLAN   in association with
St Antony's College, Oxford

First published 1984

Published by
THE MACMILLAN PRESS LTD
Houndmills, Basingstoke, Hampshire RG21 2XS
and London
Companies and representatives
throughout the world

Typeset by
Wessex Typesetters Ltd
Frome, Somerset

Printed in Great Britain by
The Pitman Press
Bath

British Library Cataloguing in Publication Data
Political culture and communist studies.
1. Communist state   2. Communist countries
—Politics and government
I. Brown, Archie, *1938–*
320.9171'7   JC474
ISBN 0–333–31993–1
ISBN 0–333–38631–0 Pbk

710 002895 –1

Contents

Tables   vi
Notes on the Contributors   vii
Preface   xi

1 Introduction   1
  Archie Brown

2 Political Culture and Communist Politics: One Step
  Forward, Two Steps Back   13
  Mary McAuley

3 Political Culture: Some Perennial Questions Reopened   40
  John Miller

4 Soviet Political Culture Reassessed   62
  Stephen White

5 Soviet Political Culture through Soviet Eyes   100
  Archie Brown

6 Czechoslovak Political Culture: Pluralism in an
  International Context   115
  H. Gordon Skilling

7 Czechoslovakia's Political Culture Reconsidered   134
  David W. Paul

8 Conclusions   149
  Archie Brown

Index   205

Tables

3.1 Party membership and specialist education, 1970   51

4.1 The establishment of constitutional and parliamentary regimes   69

4.2 Extension of the franchise in selected countries   70

4.3 The development of electoral participation in selected countries (1850–1975)   72

Notes on the Contributors

Archie Brown is a Fellow of St Antony's College, Oxford, and Lecturer in Soviet Institutions at Oxford University. After studying as an undergraduate and graduate student at the London School of Economics (University of London), he was a Lecturer in Politics at Glasgow University from 1964 until 1971 when he moved to Oxford. He has been Visiting Professor of Political Science at the University of Connecticut and at Yale University and he gave the 1980 Henry L. Stimson Lectures at Yale. Mr Brown, who has made a number of study-visits to the Soviet Union and Eastern Europe, is a former Convener of the Communist Politics Group of the Political Studies Association of the U.K. He is the author of *Soviet Politics and Political Science* (1974) and *Political Change within Communist Systems* (forthcoming) and co-editor of and contributor to *The Soviet Union since the Fall of Khrushchev* (with Michael Kaser, 1975; 2nd enlarged, edn, 1978), *Political Culture and Political Change in Communist States* (with Jack Gray, 1977; 2nd edn, 1979), *Authority, Power and Policy in the USSR* (with T. H. Rigby and Peter Reddaway, 1980), *The Cambridge Encyclopedia of Russia and the Soviet Union* (with John Fennell, Michael Kaser and H. T. Willetts, 1982) and *Soviet Policy for the 1980s* (with Michael Kaser, 1982).

Mary McAuley is Senior Lecturer in Government at the University of Essex. After studying at Oxford University as an undergraduate and graduate student, she taught at Glasgow University (where she was Assistant Editor of *Soviet Studies*) and York University before moving to Essex in 1969. She has made numerous study-visits to the Soviet Union, including an eighteen-month stay at Leningrad University. She is a former Convener of the Communist Politics Group of the Political Studies Association of the U.K. Dr McAuley, who has held visiting professorships at the University of Wisconsin (1976–7) and University of California at Berkeley (1983) is the author of *Labour Disputes in Soviet Russia 1957–65* (1969) and *Politics and the Soviet Union*

(1977). She is currently writing a social and political history of Leningrad.

John Miller is Senior Lecturer in Politics at La Trobe University, Melbourne. After studying as an undergraduate at Cambridge, he made extended cultural-exchange visits as a graduate student to Bulgaria (1963) and the Soviet Union (1967–8) and also pursued graduate studies at Glasgow University. From 1968 until 1972, when he moved to his present post in Australia, he was Lecturer in the Institute of Soviet and East European Studies at Glasgow. In 1976 and in 1980–1 he was a visiting Senior Associate Member of St Antony's College, Oxford. Mr Miller is the author of several major articles and contributions to symposia and of a forthcoming monograph on the relationship between party and society in the Soviet Union.

David W. Paul took his first degree at Carleton College, a master's degree at Johns Hopkins, and his doctorate at Princeton before moving to the University of Washington at Seattle as an Assistant Professor of Political Science. He has travelled extensively in Eastern Europe and has taken a particular interest in Czechoslovakia. Dr Paul is the author of *The Cultural Limits of Revolutionary Politics: Change and Continuity in Socialist Czechoslovakia* (1979) and *Czechoslovakia: Profile of a Socialist Republic at the Crossroads of Europe* (1981); he is also editor of *Politics, Art and Commitment in the East European Cinema* (1984).

H. Gordon Skilling is Emeritus Professor of Political Science at the University of Toronto. After taking his first degree at the University of Toronto, Gordon Skilling studied at Oxford from 1934 until 1936 as a Rhodes Scholar before taking his doctorate at the University of London. He went on to teach political science at the University of Wisconsin, at Dartmouth College and, from 1959, at the University of Toronto. From 1963 until 1975 Professor Skilling was Director of the Centre for Russian and East European Studies at Toronto. He has been a Senior Fellow and later Visiting Professor at the Russian Institute of Columbia University in New York and a Visiting Fellow of St Antony's College, Oxford. In 1982 he was awarded an honorary doctorate of law by the University of Toronto and he is a Fellow of the Royal Society of Canada. Professor Skilling has been a pioneer in the study of comparative communism and the foremost specialist on Czechoslovakia among Western political scientists. A frequent traveller to Eastern Europe, he first visited Czechoslovakia in 1937 and most recently in 1984. His publications include the following books: *Communism National and International* (1964), *The Governments of Communist East Europe* (1966), *Interest Groups in Soviet Politics* (co-editor with Franklyn Griffiths, 1971), *The Czech Renascence of the Nineteenth Century* (co-editor with Peter Brock, 1970), *Czechoslovakia's Interrupted Revolution* (1976) and *Charter 77 and Human Rights in Czechoslovakia* (1981).

Stephen White is Lecturer in Politics at Glasgow University and is currently the Convener of the Communist Politics Group of the Political Studies Association of the UK. After graduating from Trinity College, Dublin, in 1968, he was a post-graduate student at the Institute of Soviet and East European Studies of Glasgow University, where he took his doctorate. Immediately before taking up his Lectureship at Glasgow in 1971, he spent an academic year in Moscow University on a cultural exchange studentship and he has subsequently been a frequent visitor to the Soviet Union. His publications include *Political Culture and Soviet Politics* (1979), *Britain and the Bolshevik Revolution* (1980), *Communist Legislatures in Comparative Perspective* (co-editor with Daniel Nelson, 1982), *Communist Political Systems* (co-author with John Gardner and George Schöpflin, 1982) and *The Party Rules of the Communist World* (co-editor with William B. Simons, 1984).

Preface

This book had its origins in a panel on 'Political Culture and Communist Studies' which I convened at the Second World Congress for Soviet and East European Studies, held at Garmisch-Partenkirchen in the Federal Republic of Germany in early October 1980. Three of the eight chapters – those of Mary McAuley, Gordon Skilling and Stephen White – were presented to that Congress and no attempt has been made to update them beyond 1981 when they were submitted in their final form. This publication is not, however, and was never intended to be, a 'conference proceedings' volume. From the outset the aim has been to produce an integrated and coherent book; it will be for the reader to decide how far we have succeeded.

The process of writing and editing, interrupted as it was by too many other commitments on the part of the editor, took substantially longer than either I or the contributors expected. I am therefore extremely grateful to those who were first to finish – Dr McAuley, Professor Skilling and Dr White – for the patience and tolerance they have shown while awaiting the publication of the book. (Though Chapters 3, 5 and 7 had their embryonic form in their authors' discussants' notes on Chapters 2, 4 and 6, they were only later written as full-fledged chapters. Chapters 1 and 8 were, of course, written in their entirety well after the Congress and specially for this book.) Since the final chapter has just been completed, as I write these words, in the summer of 1984, it is worth emphasising that I had the opportunity there to refer to publications which had still not seen the light of day when some of the other chapters were written. However, unlike discussions of Communist leadership politics, the themes of this volume are not ones which are likely to become out of date as a result of developments in day-to-day politics. Indeed, it is fair to say that none of the arguments which were first aired at Garmisch have been overtaken by subsequent writing or events.

The first chapter to be completed, in its conference paper form, was that by Mary McAuley. Partly for that reason, but also and more importantly because of the challenge it presented to all who had used the concept of political culture in the context of Communist studies, it is a recurring point of reference throughout the volume. Though many of the points raised in McAuley's critique are taken up in subsequent chapters, not all of them receive detailed consideration. On that score at least no apologies are due, since McAuley poses enough interesting questions to keep an entire graduate school busy for a decade. Moreover, the other contributors present their own views on what the major problems are and concerning the evidence which may be brought to bear on them.

Apart from my indebtedness to all the contributors of chapters for their friendly co-operation, there are a number of other people whom I am glad of this opportunity to thank. For very useful discussions, including some invaluable bibliographical suggestions, I am most grateful to Diana Forsythe and Renée Hirschon (in anthropology) and to Michael Argyle and Joseph Jaspars (in social psychology). For kindly reading most of what I have written in draft, and for their helpful comments, I am greatly indebted to Robert E. Lane, Michael Lessnoff and Kathy Wilkes. None of these scholars bears any responsibility for what I ultimately wrote and for such deficiences as the reader may find in the final product.

If this book is appearing later than its planned target, that is no fault of its British or American publishers. I am, indeed, much indebted to them for the speed and efficiency with which the book has proceeded through production and especially grateful in that connection to Tim Farmiloe and Keith Povey. In the preparation of the manuscript for publication, I have been fortunate indeed in having access to the outstanding secretarial skills of Jackie Willcox. My greatest debt I leave to the last. It is to my wife, Pat, who has not only tolerated the inroads upon family life made by the periods of Stakhanovite activity which have characterised my work on this volume, but has made an important contribution to the book itself by compiling the index.

Oxford   ARCHIE BROWN

1 Introduction

ARCHIE BROWN

Some of the ideas embodied in the concept of political culture are to be found already in Plato and Aristotle,[1] but the terminology, 'political culture', would appear to have been first used by Herder in the late eighteenth century.[2] It is of some interest in the context of the present volume that the term cropped up in nineteenth-century Russian historical writing,[3] and that it was used by Lenin in 1920.[4] However, its elaboration as a concept of modern political science – and the debate concerning its scope and usefulness – dates only from the 1950s.

Those who first developed the concept and made use of it in research (among whom a pioneering role was played by Gabriel Almond) did so under the influence of Weberian and Parsonian sociology, of innovative work in social psychology (not least that of Paul Lazarsfeld) and of studies in both social and cultural anthropology (from the work of Bronislaw Malinowski to that of Ralph Linton).[5] The development of new research techniques, making possible more sophisticated sample surveys was also a stimulus (indeed, Almond goes so far as to describe it as the 'catalytic agent') to the empirical studies of the 1960s on political culture by such scholars as Almond, Coleman, Powell, Pye and Verba.[6]

Many questions have subsequently been raised concerning both the methodological and the ideological foundations of much of that work.[7] In particular, it was unfortunate that many studies conducted in the 1960s tied the concept of political culture to the notion of 'political development', a concept which one of its early proponents, Samuel Huntington, has more recently correctly acknowledged to be 'rather diffuse, controversial and value-laden'.[8] In the literature of the 1960s, as I have noted elsewhere,[9] the characteristics of a developed political system frequently bore an uncanny resemblance to the principal features of the American polity, though often in a somewhat idealised form.

1

Yet, in spite of their disagreements with arguments and assumptions to be found in the 'political culture and political development' literature, much of the earlier writing on Communist political cultures, such as that of Frederick Barghoorn,[10] Richard R. Fagen,[11] Richard H. Solomon,[12] Robert C. Tucker,[13] and the present author,[14] undoubtedly owed something to the stimulus of the works of Almond, Pye and Verba and others. Increasingly, the study of 'political culture' (even in the hands of its progenitors) became separate from the highly questionable idea of unilinear 'political development', though in the process definitions of political culture multiplied. A 1976 study counted more than thirty different ways of defining the concept,[15] and the burgeoning literature on Communist political cultures not only reflected but also added to the variety of definition and interpretation.[16]

The main division of opinion concerning the scope of the concept is, however, between those who wish to restrict it to subjective orientations to the political system and those who would include overt political behaviour as a part of political culture. It may be useful to take two representative definitions from each side. Huntington and Dominguez, in their contribution to the volume on Macropolitical Theory of the *Handbook of Political Science*, defined 'the political culture of a society' as consisting of 'the empirical beliefs about expressive political symbols and values and other orientations of the members of the society toward political objects',[17] and in my introduction to the first book to attempt to study Communist political cultures comparatively, I proposed that the concept be understood as 'the subjective perception of history and politics, the fundamental beliefs and values, the foci of identification and loyalty, and the political knowledge and expectations which are the product of the specific historical experience of nations and groups'.[18] Taking the broader view, David W. Paul has defined political culture as 'the configuration of values, symbols, and attitudinal and behavioural patterns underlying the politics of a society',[19] while for Stephen White, 'political culture may be defined as the attitudinal and behavioural matrix within which the political system is located'.[20]

Earlier influential uses of political culture in the broader sense (embracing behaviour as well as beliefs, values, political knowledge, etc.) include, notably, those of Tucker[21] and Fagen,[22] though both eschew definitions of political culture. Indeed Tucker prefers to speak of a 'cultural approach to politics'[23] and of the desirability of viewing 'the political system of a society in cultural terms, i.e., as a complex of real and ideal culture patterns, including political roles and their interrelations, political structures, and so on'.[24] Fagen, like Tucker, favours what he regards as a more anthropological approach than that adopted by most political scientists, suggesting that 'anthropologists interested in planned change do not limit their definition of culture to psychological variables; they include patterned ways of life and action as well as the states of mind that sustain and condition these patterns'.[25] This, however – and it is a point to which I shall return in the concluding chapter – oversimplifies considerably what is happening in modern anthropology.

It is an interesting fact that whereas a majority of political scientists employing the concept of political culture have favoured a narrower 'subjective' definition, most of those among them who have applied the concept to the study of Communist systems have favoured a broad definition which includes behaviour. It is never easy to get agreement among diverse and independent-minded scholars to use the same concept in the same way even within the confines of a single volume. While *Political Culture and Political Change in Communist States* came closer than many collective works to attaining that goal, I noted in the Preface to the first edition that while 'a high level of agreement in principle on a particular common approach to the study of political cultures of Communist societies was achieved . . . it was not always possible to apply this as fully in practice as we would have wished.'[26] Indeed, it became evident that the acceptance of the definition of political culture which I used in that work was more a reflection of the wishes of the contributors to maximise the comparative component of the study than of complete agreement on the part of all of them with the subjective demarcation of the concept. Stephen White's adoption of a broader definition (cited earlier) in his own subsequent book is a clear indication of this.

Gabriel Almond, in his review of White's book,[27] has remarked that 'it is a matter of interest that specialists on communist countries . . . criticise the definition of political culture which confines it to subjective properties as in the work of Pye, Verba and Almond'.[28] Where, as in the present volume, no attempt has been made to achieve consensus on the use of terms since the very purpose of the volume is to draw out disagreements and problems, I am probably in a minority of one in holding to the view that quite enough has already been brought under the umbrella of political culture in the 'subjective' definition and that to broaden its scope further reduces its analytical usefulness. The problem of the scope of the concept is one of the recurring issues in this book, though for Almond, 'why this polemic should have developed is something of a mystery, since it would seem elementary that one of the main questions one would ask about these phenomena is how the two – attitude and behaviour – relate to and affect each other'.[29]

A major reason for the preference of a majority of students of Communist systems for the broader definition is the difficulty of conducting research on the values and beliefs, political knowledge and expectations of citizens within a Communist system, especially by social scientists from Western countries (notwithstanding the fact that much can be made of the survey data, when they are studied and used discriminatingly, of the indigenous scholarship of the Soviet Union and Eastern Europe). To delineate concepts in such a way that they will be conducive to productive research is a respectable reason for settling on a particular definition. Those, however, who wish to use the concept of political culture to embrace political behaviour have to face the problem either of taking all political behaviour within a Communist system at its face value or of making a distinction between certain behaviour which reflects basic beliefs and other behaviour which results from threats of sanctions or from more subtle social pressures.

Probably few well-informed Western scholars would wish to accept 99 per cent votes for the candidate of the Communist Party in, say, Estonia or Czechoslovakia as accurately reflecting the fundamental beliefs and values of Estonians, Czechs or Slovaks. Such turnouts may be a more accurate measure of the mobilisational capacity of these established Communist systems. Indeed, if a problem of the 'subjective' definition of political culture is that it is precisely in authoritarian regimes that it is hardest to get at the beliefs and values of citizens, it is equally a problem of these societies that the gulf between beliefs on the one hand, and behaviour on the other, may be an especially wide one, and that much overt political behaviour (of which voting behaviour is a clear example) may owe a lot to the price which non-conformists must pay for their non-conformity. Once, however, we begin to make distinctions between certain political behaviour which reflects the beliefs and values of those involved and political behaviour which may not reflect these, we come up against the need to discuss the relationship between beliefs and behaviour, the need to analyse the interaction between the two. While this is at no time an easy task, it is made even harder when no clear conceptual distinction is made between the complex of subjective orientations on the one hand, and overt behaviour on the other.

It can be objected that 'political culture' is not the most appropriate terminology to embrace the subjective orientation to politics of nations and groups. Provided it is recognised that popular perceptions of history and politics, fundamental beliefs and values, foci of identification and loyalty, and political knowledge and expectations are actually important objects of study and that Communist countries provide interesting testing-ground of the ease or difficulty with which such subjective orientations may be altered, it does not matter greatly whether the term, 'political culture', is or is not used as the conceptual umbrella under which the various subjective factors are grouped. There are grounds of convenience for using the concept in this way, however. Not only is it a useful 'shorthand' which obviates the need to reproduce long lists of subjective variables when they are being discussed collectively but it already has a lineage in political science which has proved more robust than the theories of 'political development' and 'modernisation' with which political culture was originally linked.

The argument that students of the politics of large-scale, complex societies should follow the example of many earlier anthropologists in their use of the concept of culture is not very persuasive. There is, in the first place, the difficulty that 'culture' for anthropologists carries far more different meanings than does 'political culture' for political scientists. Well over a hundred different definitions of culture in anthropology had already been counted by 1952.[30] There are anthropologists who regard the term as so broad as to be useless as a category of analysis.[31] This may have been an unduly harsh judgement, but the conceptual breadth of culture for the 'traditional' anthropologist has perhaps only been 'operationally' viable because of the spatial narrowness which has generally characterised its application. As David Kaplan and Robert A. Manners have noted, the usual practice has been for an anthropologist to 'select a linguistic, geographic, or cultural unit that was somewhat manageable (manageable in terms of field research that could be carried on by a single anthropologist) identify it as culture X, and proceed to analyze this arbitrarily defined unit as though it were a "system" '.[32] The generalisations made by anthropologists on such a basis have often extended far beyond the narrow geographic area examined, but they have been of correspondingly uncertain validity. In the words of Kaplan and Manners: 'It was generally assumed that the part studied stood for the whole; that if you had seen one or a selected few segments of tribe X, you had seen them all; and that whatever you were able to report for the microcosm within which you had lived would hold as well for the rest of the society'.[33] Yet, even among the preliterate social groupings traditionally favoured by anthropologists as objects of study, there are many cases where 'the whole is greater – or at least different – than the sum of its parts'.[34] When the object of study is not the Trobriand Islanders but the peoples of the Soviet Union, the problem of microcosm and macrocosm assumes truly daunting dimensions. Among anthropologists – not least among those who have turned their attention to literate, industrial societies – there has been a growing awareness of this general problem. In the final chapter of the present volume I shall devote some attention to this newer body of anthropological literature which favours a delimitation of the concept of culture in a way which parallels the 'subjective' definition of political culture.

If the concept of *culture* in the hands of many anthropologists has, nevertheless, involved both a very wide-ranging definition of the term and a holistic approach to the study of a small segment of society, the concept of *political culture* in the hands of political scientists has tended to be used to explore a more restricted range of problems, though generally on a state-wide or nation-wide basis.[35] If the 'political' concerns of 'political culture' have, on the one hand, led scholars to focus their attention on an entire polity, a strict interpretation of the 'political' does, on the other hand, enable them (if they wish) to filter out phenomena which may be regarded as belonging more properly to the province of the anthropologist or sociologist. Of course, not all students of politics wish to be so circumscribed or so circumspect. Thus, for example, Volker Gransow, in a paper devoted to 'Political Culture in the German Democratic Republic' includes a table on the incidence of 'Female Orgasms in the GDR'.[36] Problems of the reliability of the research findings aside, it is doubtful if anything is to be gained by stretching the concept of political culture to make it synonymous with 'culture' in the broadest possible sense.[37]

While the argument over the conceptual scope of 'political culture' for particular purposes (like the debate over the concept of culture among anthropologists)[38] is a serious one, it should be recognised that interesting and illuminating work can be produced by scholars who proceed from different definitional starting-points. Thus, one of the fathers of the 'subjectivist' definition of political culture, Gabriel Almond, has no difficulty in finding much of value in the writings of Tucker and White, notwithstanding their professed attachment to a more 'anthropological' approach to the study of political culture.

Indeed, with Almond's recent writings, the wheel has come full circle.[39] One reason why a study of the difficulties involved in the use of the concept of political culture in general and its application in Communist studies in particular – together with discussion of what has or has not been achieved so far and of where we should go from here – is especially timely is that those who originally made use of the concept in their studies of the 'first' and 'third' world are now citing political cultural analyses of the 'second' (Communist) world as 'a test of the explanatory power of political culture theory'.[40]

In *Political Culture and Political Change in Communist States*, I argued that, as compared with studies of, say, Britain or the United States:

> the possibilities of discussing sensibly the harmony or dissonance between values, on the one hand, and political structures, on the other, are perhaps greater in the case of Communist societies where there have been (a) a radical break in the continuity of political institutions, and (b) an unusually overt and conscious attempt to create new political values and to supplant the old.[41]

Citing this and other passages from the introduction to that volume and a number of Jack Gray's concluding observations, Gabriel Almond himself draws the conclusion in *The Civic Culture Revisited* that 'it would thus appear, not that political culture is an intractable variable, but that there are limits to its plasticity, and inherent propensities of a modestly encouraging sort'.[42]

More recently, in an article devoted to 'Communism and Political Culture Theory', Almond puts the point thus:

> What the scholarship of comparative communism has been telling us is that political cultures are not easily transformed. A sophisticated political movement ready to manipulate, penetrate, organize, indoctrinate, and coerce and given an opportunity to do so for a generation or longer ends up as much or more transformed than transforming. But we have to be clear about what kind of a case we are making for political culture theory. We are not arguing at all that political structure, historical experience, and deliberate efforts to change attitudes have no effect on political culture. Such an argument would be manifest foolishness.[43]

In the chapters that follow, these and other issues are argued out. In order that the discussion will not remain merely at an abstract level, but that the relevance or potential relevance of the concept of political culture to the problem of continuity and change within Communist systems will be kept to the fore, particular attention is paid to two cases – that of the Soviet Union and that of Czechoslovakia – although several of the chapters draw also on the experience of other Communist countries.

Mary McAuley is much less satisfied than is Gabriel Almond with the writings on political culture of Communist politics specialists hitherto. In a characteristically stimulating chapter, she usefully sharpens many of the issues underlying these studies which have been inadequately considered up to the present. In several of the subsequent chapters the challenge of McAuley's critique is taken up and in varying degrees supported, expanded, qualified or rebutted.

Chapters 2–7 are 'paired'. Thus, John Miller, in Chapter 3, addresses the problems of the status and application of the concept of political culture raised by McAuley in the previous chapter. He takes up the difficult question of the transmission and evocation of values in Communist countries and pays particular attention to the Soviet case.

Chapters 4 and 5 are specifically devoted to the Soviet Union. Stephen White, in the first of these, not only brings further extensive evidence to bear on the problem of Soviet political culture but also replies to a number of Mary McAuley's criticisms of his earlier work. In the following chapter, I take up some of the points raised, or but lightly touched upon, by White, but devote particular attention to the body of *Soviet* writing on Soviet political culture which has been growing apace in recent years.

While all the countries of Eastern Europe have had different historical experience from that of the Soviet Union (although there are also, of course, vast differences *within* the USSR) Czechoslovakia makes a particularly interesting juxtaposition, for it went through a period of more unambiguous liberal democracy (or, in Marxist–Leninist terms, 'bourgeois democracy') than any of the other Communist states. Certainly the First Czechoslovak Republic represents a sharp contrast not only with the Soviet Union in those years (1918–38) but with the pre-Soviet experience of authoritarian rule.

The relevance of this experience for Communist Czechoslovakia is, however, a matter of debate. H. Gordon Skilling, in Chapter 6, takes up the issue of continuity and discontinuity and lays particular stress on the international context. David W. Paul, in Chapter 7, reassesses his own and other writing on the political culture of Czechs and Slovaks and also responds to Skilling's analysis.

The final chapter of this somewhat argumentative book does not purport to set out agreed conclusions – only those of the present author. An attempt is made to draw together some of the major points of the earlier chapters and the opportunity is taken to disagree with some of them. At the same time, since I share at least some of the dissatisfaction with what has been achieved in Communist political cultural studies up to now, I suggest a few ways (which are partly a response to, and partly independent of, the earlier chapters in the volume) in which the study of political culture in the Communist context may move forward without, it is earnestly to be hoped, taking two steps back.

NOTES AND REFERENCES

1. As noted, for example, by Gabriel Almond, 'The Intellectual History of the Civic Culture Concept', in Gabriel A. Almond and Sidney Verba (eds), *The Civic Culture Revisited* (Boston, Mass., 1980) pp. 1–36, esp. pp. 2–4.

2. F. M. Barnard, 'Culture and Political Development: Herder's Suggestive Insights' in *American Political Science Review*, vol. LXIII, no. 2, June 1969, pp. 379–97, at p. 392.

3. V. I. Ger'e, 'Respublika ili monarkhiya ustanovitsya vo Frantsii?' in V. M. Bezobrazov (ed.) *Sbornik gosudarstvennykh znaniy*, vol. III, 1877, p. 165. (I am grateful to my colleague, Richard Kindersley, for this reference.)

4. V. I. Lenin, *Polnoe sobranie sochineniy* (Moscow, 1963) vol. 41, p. 404.

5. Almond, 'The Intellectual History of the Civic Culture Concept', in *The Civic Culture Revisited*, mentions these and many other writers who influenced thinking about what has come to be known as 'political culture', though, surprisingly, he excludes from his list of anthropologists the name of Clyde Kluckhohn.

6. For representative examples of the political culture writing of the 1960s, see Gabriel A. Almond and James S. Coleman (eds) *The Politics of the Developing Areas* (Princeton, New Jersey, 1960); Gabriel A. Almond and Sidney Verba (eds) *The Civic Culture* (Princeton, New Jersey, 1963). Lucian W. Pye and Sidney Verba (eds) *Political Culture and Political Development* (Princeton, New Jersey, 1965) and Gabriel A. Almond and G. Bingham Powell, Jr. *Comparative Politics: A Developmental Appraoch* (Boston, Mass., 1966).

7. See, for example, Brian Barry, *Sociologists, Economists and Democracy* (London, 1980), Carole Pateman, 'The Civic Culture: A Philosophic Critique' and Jerzy J. Wiatr, 'The Civic Culture from a Marxist–Sociological Perspective' both in Almond and Verba (eds) *The Civic Culture Revisited*.

8. Samuel P. Huntington and Jorge I. Dominguez, 'Political Development', in Fred I. Greenstein and Nelson W. Polsby (eds) *Handbook of Political Science, vol. III: Macropolitical Theory* (Reading, Mass., 1975) p. 47.

9. In the Introduction to Archie Brown and Jack Gray (eds) *Political Culture and Political Change in Communist States* (London and New York, 1977) (2nd edn, 1979) p. 3.

10. Frederick C. Barghoorn, 'Soviet Russia: Orthodoxy and Adaptiveness', in Pye and Verba (eds) *Political Culture and Political Development*, pp. 450–511.

11. Richard R. Fagen, *The Transformation of Political Culture in Cuba* (Stanford, 1969).

12. Richard H. Solomon, *Mao's Revolution and the Chinese Political Culture* (Berkeley, 1971). This major study makes only limited use of the categories developed by Almond and Verba, but the author acknowledges his debt to Lucian Pye.

13. Robert C. Tucker, 'Culture, Political Culture and Communist Society' in *Political Science Quarterly*, vol. 88, no. 2, June 1973, pp. 173–90; and Tucker, 'Communist Revolutions, National Cultures and the Divided Nations' in *Studies in Comparative Communism*, vol. VII, no. 3, Autumn 1974, pp. 235–45.

14. A. H. Brown, 'Political Change in Czechoslovakia' in *Government and Opposition*, vol. 4, no. 2, Spring 1969, pp. 169–94, esp. pp. 189–94 on 'Political Culture and Political Change'; and Brown, *Soviet Politics and Political Science* (London, 1974) esp. Ch. 4, 'Political Culture', pp. 89–104 and 124–8.

15. G. Patrick, *The Concept of 'Political Culture'*, International Studies Association Working Paper no. 80 (cited by Dennis Kavanagh, *Political Science and Political Behaviour* (London, 1983) pp. 50 and 213.

16. See, for instance, Kenneth Jowitt, 'An Organizational Approach to the Study of Political Culture in Marxist–Leninist Systems' in *American Political Science Review*, vol. LXVIII, no. 3, September 1974, pp. 1171–91; Alan P. Liu, *Political Culture and Group Conflict in Communist China* (Santa Barbara, 1976); Lowell Dittmer, 'Political Culture and Political Symbolism: Toward a Theoretical Synthesis' in *World Politics*, vol. XXIX, no. 4, July 1977, pp. 552–83; Dittmer, 'Comparative Communist Political Culture' in *Studies in Comparative Communism*, vol. XVI, nos 1 and 2, Spring/Summer 1983, pp. 9–24; Brown and Gray (eds) *Political Culture and Political Change in Communist States*; Robert C. Tucker (ed.) *Stalinism: Essays in Historical Interpretation* (New York, 1977); David W. Paul, *The Cultural Limits of Revolutionary Politics: Change and Continuity in Socialist Czechoslovakia* (New York, 1979); and Stephen White, *Political Culture and Soviet Politics* (London and New York, 1979).

17. In Greenstein and Polsby (eds) *Handbook of Political Science, vol. III: Macropolitical Theory*, p. 15.

18. Brown and Gray (eds) *Political Culture and Political Change in Communist States*, p. 1.

19. Paul, *The Cultural Limits of Revolutionary Politics*, p. 3.

20. White, *Political Culture and Soviet Politics*, p. 1.

21. Tucker, 'Culture, Political Culture and Communist Society', esp. pp. 176–9; and Tucker, 'Communist Revolutions, National Cultures and the Divided Nations', esp. pp. 239–41.

22. Fagen, *The Transformation of Political Culture in Cuba*, esp. pp. 4–6.
23. Tucker, 'Culture, Political Culture and Communist Society', p. 182.
24. Ibid.
25. Fagen, *The Transformation of Political Culture in Cuba*, p. 5.
26. Brown and Gray (eds) *Political Culture and Political Change in Communist States*, p. xiii.
27. *Soviet Studies*, vol. XXXIII, no. 2, April 1981, pp. 307–8.
28. Ibid, p. 307. In placing my name alongside that of White and Gray (as well as those of Fagen, Jowitt and Tucker) Almond seems, however, to have been temporarily afflicted by colour blindness. For though I have criticised the intellectual context in which the concept of political culture was employed in the 1960s, I have favoured the non-behavioural definition. Apart from some of the contributors to *Political Culture and Political Change in Communist States*, another of the minority of Communist politics specialists who appears to favour the subjective definition of political culture is Zvi Gitelman. It is with values and attitudes that he is concerned in his interesting article, based on survey research among Soviet emigrants to Israel, 'Soviet Political Culture: Insights from Jewish Emigrés' in *Soviet Studies*, vol. XXIX, no. 4, October 1977, pp. 543–64.
29. Almond, *Soviet Studies*, vol. XXXIII, no. 2, April 1981, p. 307.
30. David Kaplan and Robert A. Manners, *Culture Theory* (Englewood Cliffs, New Jersey 1972) p. 3 (citing A. L. Kroeber and Clyde Kluckhohn, 'Culture: A Critical Review of Concepts and Definitions' in Harvard University, *Papers of the Peabody Museum of American Archaeology and Ethnology*, 1952, vol. 47).
31. Thus, for instance, Kaplan and Manners write: '*Culture* is admittedly an omnibus term. Many investigators have suggested that it is too omnibus to be useful as an analytical tool' (*Culture Theory*, p. 3). Alfred G. Meyer has written of 'the concept of culture' having 'fallen into disuse, if not disrespect', among anthropologists (Meyer, 'Communist Revolutions and Cultural Change' in *Studies in Comparative Communism*, vol. V, no. 4, Winter 1972, pp. 345–70, at p. 355). Yet, as the Kaplan and Manners review of the anthropological literature published in the same year reveals, there is still plenty of life in the anthropological use of the concept, if little agreement among anthropologists as to its precise scope. On these points, see also Clyde Kluckhohn, *Culture and Behavior* (New York, 1962) esp. Ch. 2, 'The Concept of Culture', pp. 19–73, and the discussion in Chapter 8 of the present volume.
32. Kaplan and Manners, *Culture Theory*, p. 191.
33. Ibid, p. 192.
34. Ibid.
35. The more careful scholars among the latter, however, do not make *a priori* assumptions on the extent to which there is a unified, dominant, dichotomous or fragmented political culture, on whether or not important political sub-cultures may be said to exist, but regard these as matters for empirical investigation.
36. Volker Gransow, 'Political Culture in the German Democratic Republic: Propositions for Empirical Research' (paper presented to the Fifth

International Symposium on the German Democratic Republic, at Conway, New Hampshire, June 1979) p. 11.

37. On 'conceptual stretching', see Giovanni Sartori, 'Concept Misformation in Comparative Politics', *American Political Science Review*, vol. LXIV, no. 4, December 1970, pp. 1033–53.

38. In addition to Kluckhohn, *Culture and Behavior*, and Kaplan and Manners, *Culture Theory*, see also, for example, Clifford Geertz, *The Interpretation of Cultures* (New York, 1973), to which some attention will be paid in the concluding chapter of this book.

39. See, in particular, Almond, 'The Intellectual History of the Civic Culture Concept' in Almond and Verba (eds) *The Civic Culture Revisited*, esp. pp. 30–2 and 36; and Gabriel A. Almond, 'Communism and Political Culture Theory' in *Comparative Politics*, vol. XVI, no. 1, January 1983, pp. 127–38.

40. Ibid, p. 127.

41. Brown and Gray (eds) *Political Culture and Political Change in Communist States*, p. 12.

42. Almond, 'The Intellectual History of the Civic Culture Concept', p. 32.

43. Almond, 'Communism and Political Culture Theory', p. 137.

2 Political Culture and Communist Politics: One Step Forward, Two Steps Back

MARY McAULEY

What is the relationship between the way people view the world and the political orders that exist or come into being? This is hardly a new question. However, for a number of reasons, it is time to ask it again with the focus on Communist-party states. First, the political culture approach of the 1960s has gained its adherents among those who study politics in Communist-party states. There are now a number of studies of the political culture of these countries. Second, some of the East-European Marxists have recently discussed aspects of ideology, of culture, and social attitudes in their societies in novel and interesting ways. And, third, some scholars in Western Europe, mainly Marxists, have begun to re-examine the question of ideology in general and to suggest new methods of analysis. They have tended to ignore Communist-party states but we can (and should) see whether their work sheds light on political ideas and values in such states. Indeed to deal with the topic satisfactorily, we have to think comparatively and historically. How do political perceptions arise? How do we explain those that exist in Communist-party states? Inevitably we start thinking about the relationship between past sets of values and the present. Furthermore, if we wish to offer explanations for the types of political perceptions held in certain societies, we have to ask whether the political order in those societies is a relevant factor – and this can only be answered by comparison with societies which possess different types of political organisation.

But if the questions are exceedingly interesting and important,

13

answering them is correspondingly difficult. This chapter makes no attempt to do that. It limits itself to dealing with some of the problems that such an endeavour encounters, and it does this by examining the political culturalists' approach. A negative chapter is never very satisfactory but it is only by struggling through the brambles that we can find the beginning of the steep and rocky path to the summit below which, at last, the countryside spreads out before us. The political culturalists have done us a service by reminding us of the countryside to be surveyed but, I would argue, their endeavours to map it leave them and us hopelessly tangled in the brambles at the foot of the mountain.

The political culturalists are divided between those who are interested in 'the subjective perception of history and politics, the fundamental beliefs and values, the foci of identification and loyalty, and the political knowledge and expectations which are the product of the specific historical experience of nations and groups'[1] and those who argue for a definition of political culture which embraces behaviour as well. The most explicit advocates of the first position are the contributors to the Brown–Gray volume on political culture in Communist-party states. They ask 'the large and important question . . . how successful have the holders of institutional power been in *changing* political culture – in replacing traditional values and creating a "new man"?' (p. 18). They suggest that since, in these societies, there has been 'a radical break in the continuity of political institutions' followed by conscious attempts to create new values, we can see whether political values are 'malleable' or whether they persist despite attempts to change them (p. 12). They are concerned to examine 'the relationship between political culture and political change' (p. 19) with the main focus on what has happened to values and attitudes. The leading exponent of the other, wider, definition of political culture is Tucker:

Political culture, *politics as a form of culture* (my italics), and politics as an activity related to the larger culture of society, might in other words be taken as the central subject matter of the discipline. Instead of treating political culture as an attribute of a political system, we would then view the political system of society in cultural terms, i.e. as a complex of real and ideal culture patterns, including political roles and their interrelations, political structures and so on.[2]

Given that we are interested in identifying and explaining political perceptions, it is the work of the first group, the subjectivists let us call them, on which we shall concentrate here, and we limit the discussion to a few key questions. How do we identify subjective beliefs, particularly in bygone societies but also today? How should we analyse the relationship between past and present beliefs? We then turn to the question of analysing or interpreting responses to surveys and, finally, to official culture. In each case, we contend, the subjectivists' answers are unsatisfactory. There is not space to complement the criticism with constructive analysis; all we can do is to raise a few signposts pointing in the right direction.

THE IDENTIFICATION OF BELIEFS

If we are to analyse political perceptions and to try to explain them, we must first be able to identify them. Let us start with what seems a simple task: a comparison of contemporary attitudes in Communist-party states with their pre-revolutionary counterparts. For the contemporary period the contributors to the Brown–Gray volume – Archie Brown, David A. Dyker, Jack Gray, George Kolankiewicz, Francis Lambert, George Schöpflin, Ray Taras, Stephen White and Gordon Wightman – rely, where they can, on survey data of political knowledge, of views towards the country's past and present, of moral values or attitudes to socially desirable behaviour. If survey data are something of a problem for the contemporary period, comparable data for the pre-revolutionary periods only exist for Czechoslovakia for 1946. The other authors have to discover the pre-revolutionary 'political culture' of their societies by different means. Their attempts demonstrate the difficulties and lead us to see that it is no easy matter to identify even contemporary views.

Schöpflin gives us a brief history of the Hungarian state, of government practices and social behaviour which he then terms Hungarian 'political experience' or 'political tradition'; Gray provides an elegant account of conflicting strains within Confucianism and reminds us how little we know of peasant values apart from the existence of rebellions aimed either at 'social justice within the system' or at millenial transformations. Kolankiewicz and Taras move almost immediately to contemporary perceptions of the past, ignoring past views themselves. From Dyker we have a description of many features of Yugoslav society, reference to folk myths or intellectual portrayals of them. All this may be fair enough in itself (it sounds suspiciously Tuckerite at times) but none of it tells us what 'the subjective perception of history and politics, the fundamental beliefs and values . . . .' within society, at that time, were.

White's attempt to identify Tsarist political culture demonstrates the problem most clearly, perhaps because he devotes most attention to it. In the Brown–Gray volume he tries (it seems) to limit himself to talking of attitudes but, when he describes the 'essential features' of traditional Russian political culture, he mentions weak representative institutions; low levels of participation; a centralised, bureaucratic, authoritarian governing style; personalised attachment to authority; little political knowledge or experience, 'broad scope of government . . .' etc.[3] In effect his political culture includes government behaviour, citizen behaviour and attitudes, and even political institutions. This lands him with the problem of retaining 'political culture' as something separate, distinguishable, from 'the way the system works'.[4] The subjectivists might well argue that the unsatisfactory situation in which White finds himself is the consequence of his having polluted the pure air of political perceptions with behaviour. Maybe, but their descriptions of traditional political culture contained references to behaviour too. How then should one set about discovering the perceptual world of a past social order? Again let us look at White.

After describing the autocratic nature of Tsarist rule, he concludes 'One consequence of the weak articulation of representative institutions was a highly *personalised attachment to political authority* . . .' (p. 29). He notes how peasant risings would claim the Tsar as their protector and quotes Avrich on the myth of the Just Tsar. He repeats the point again – given little experience of representative democracy, 'levels of attachment to representative institutions were correspondingly low' (p. 31). He continues with a description of legal practice, of government control over the courts, of government concern for moral welfare, church–state co-operation and suggests that the formula '*Samoderzhavie, Pravolslavie, Narodnost*'' expressed these practices. This he describes as being 'in many ways the most distinctive contribution of the old regime to the political culture of the Soviet regime which succeeded it' (p. 34). The new regime inherited 'a distinctive and deeply-rooted pattern of orientations to government which we shall term the "traditional Russian" political culture' (p. 34).

Now I find this a quite unsatisfactory description of the political beliefs and attitudes towards authority of the late Tsarist period, an extraordinary description in fact. It seems to ignore a whole array of other behaviour, opinions and beliefs. There was peasant individualism as well as collectivism, strong anarchist notions against any 'state', repeated demands for and attempts to introduce representative institutions, criticisms of censorship, religious sects practising autonomy, generals complaining bitterly of the lack of nationalist and religious feelings among the troops. Neither the demands of 1905 nor those of 1917 put to the Congress of Soviets bear many traces of White's 'distinctive and deeply-rooted pattern of orientations'. And the myth of the Just Tsar was collapsing by the turn of the century, despite the autocratic system. Why? *'Samoderzhavie'* may have represented the views of latter-day Tsarist circles, a political order under threat from society and struggling to maintain its slipping grasp – but, as such, it represented a notion of authority and political order that had *little support* in society. It seems, at the very least, that we should talk of a clash of political cultures in late nineteenth- and early twentieth-century Russia. The Bolsheviks did *not* inherit a 'distinctive set of orientations'; they inherited (and let us remember that their ideas too were a product of the old society) a most extraordinarily rich, jumbled and contradictory set of political perceptions:

in a country like yours, where modern large-scale industry has been grafted onto the primitive peasant commune and where, at the same time, all the intermediate stages of civilisation coexist with each other, in a country which, in addition to this, has been enclosed by a despotism with an intellectual Chinese wall, in the case of such a country one should not wonder at the emergence of the most incredible and bizarre combinations of ideas.[5]

So, in the search for the beliefs and values of pre-revolutionary Russia, two authors may produce very different findings. Is this because they have set about it in different ways and is one more valid than the other? How has White established his? By and large he derives his attitudes from existing institutions. *Because* of autocratic government, knowledge of and faith in representative government was weak; autocratic government *produced* personalised attachment to authority. He does not, so explicitly, derive the lack of liberal notions of law and individual rights from the existing institutions, rather he fudges the issue: 'In Russia, on the contrary, it was considered entirely proper that the government should assume responsibility for all aspects of a citizen's welfare, moral as well as material, and that it should establish such rules as it saw fit for this purpose' (p. 33). If he is to be consistent he ought to derive this view from the then government practice. But, he might say, the relationship between normative views and government practices is very complicated; we cannot simply assume that the 'is' of practice produces the 'ought'. Fair enough. The relationship *is* complicated and this is precisely why anyone who is concerned to establish what a set of political values or attitudes were in a particular society at a particular time must first spell out for us what their understanding of this relationship is – and justify it. One cannot one minute assume that the type of political authority produces certain attitudes and the next minute argue that the relationship is two-way or some other – *unless* one is prepared to offer a framework which justifies this way of proceeding.

What is rather odd about the method of White and others of establishing the traditional political culture is that they usually like to argue that political culture is *not* derived from the institutional set-up and practices, rather that yesterday's beliefs inform today's beliefs. Now, if today's political culture has its origins in yesterday's political culture, we would expect our authors to seek the source of the traditional political culture – not in yesterday's politics and society – but in the belief system of an even earlier stage of that society. Furthermore authors who claim that today's dominant (that is, most widespread) political culture – as discovered in surveys – is *not* the offspring of existing government practices can in no way suggest that it is appropriate to seek an earlier period's dominant political culture in that period's political practices. They themselves have claimed there may be no relationship between these two things. If they employ certain deductive methods to discover the traditional political culture then surely, on grounds of consistency alone, they should use the same methods to establish the contemporary political culture. We would look to White, for example, to describe the one-party system, the election process (highly organised but not aimed at giving the electorate choice of a government), the lack of government accountability, *nomenklatura*, censorship and state-ownership, and to argue, as he did for the pre-revolutionary period, that these institutional features are responsible for today's political culture. Indeed, one could easily, on this basis, 'identify' the following type of political culture for the Soviet Union: a weak attachment to notions of a two-party system, the strength of patron–client relations, the belief that a good leader is what matters, support for notions of a government responsible for citizen welfare and morality, and so on. But this will not do either. We cannot simply run off attitudes and values from the existing political institutions and practice – but neither does that mean we can ignore them entirely. There does seem to be some connection. The relationship still has to be explored – and we shall come back to it in a moment.

Let us first take note that the identification of the traditional political culture seems to be a major stumbling-block. Apart from Brown and Wightman, who have comparable survey data for the two periods (and Gray who does not have any for either), our subjectivists ask us to treat as comparable their inferences and intuition for one period and survey data for a later period. They fail to show us that they have identified the 'subjective perceptions' of the earlier period and are inconsistent in their method of establishing past and present culture. The result is a non-starter: unless we have identified the traditional political culture we cannot tell how different from or similar it is to today's.[6]

How then should we set about it? The most convincing accounts seem to be those which possess a framework which can explain not only the emergence of a particular belief and its demise but will also allow us to make sense of what came afterwards. Let me give just one example. In his treatment of the Just Tsar myth, Field suggests 'In its simplest and most common expression, popular monarchism took the form of the adage "The Tsar wants it, but the boyars resist". "It", of course, was justice, or tax relief, or a redistribution of land – whatever the *narod* most wanted'.[7] It was rational for peasants to adopt the myth: it enabled them not only to put forward radical demands but also, if unsuccessful, to appeal for leniency on the grounds of having honestly believed that they were acting as the Tsar had wished. But by the turn of the century it was becoming progressively less useful and other ways of achieving demands were opening up; it had collapsed before autocracy went. This is a very crude synopsis of Field's sensitive analysis. For our purposes the important points are the following: it is autocratic rule which provides the basis for the belief, the necessary condition, but it is not a sufficient condition. We need to introduce a notion of the group's interest in holding such a belief, of the rewards it offers, of outside influences (or their absence) and of the autocratic authority's willingness to sustain or foster such a belief. Bearing this in mind, we can 'explain' why the myth dies and – more interesting perhaps – why it resurfaces (of course in different garb) among *certain* sections of the Soviet population at a time when again autocratic power is rampant. It does *not* crop up again among the peasantry but in the camps among the party members – for them it is a rational response and one which authority fosters. But its emergence under Stalin is in no way dependent upon the existence of the earlier peasant myth.[8]

One further point on the finding of the traditional culture. As we have seen, two observers may well produce different descriptions. In part this is because we construct the culture from the 'bountifulness' of data, from our vision of the political system and of *what came after*. To identify, we have to select; we select by some criterion of importance. Important for what? The answer may be 'important in the light of subsequent events'. This is a perfectly valid exercise. We rewrite history, reassess history, from the vantage point of the present. But what this means is that if our contributors to the Brown–Gray volume had sat down in 1950 or in the 1930s or – in the case of Russia – in 1912, they would in all good faith have produced a very different set of political cultures for those pre-revolutionary periods from the ones they have produced for those same periods today. Again, this only *matters* if the claim is being made that our perception of the past is to be used as objective independent data in an exercise to establish whether yesterday's values 'caused' today's. Unfortunately this is what the subjectivists do want to do. Given that they have identified past values precisely *because* of what has come after, they cannot then use them to explain what followed. This is to fall into a trap similar to that of inferring attitudes from behaviour and then using them to explain behaviour: we cannot first infer the past from the present and then use it either to compare two periods or to explain the present.

This is not to say that we should throw our hands up in despair and abandon the whole undertaking. It is to say that we have to think very hard about what we are doing: that we must recognise both that we are selecting and what is the basis of our selectivity. Pye, in an interesting and thoughtful discussion of political attitudes, suggests that, given the 'bountifulness of subjective political attitudes', we have to start with hypotheses about the political system (the macro-model) ' "as if" certain values, sentiments, and orientations were the most critical in giving the collectivity its distinctive character'. If we think of political culture as being those values or perceptions which are the 'critical' ones, the significant ones, in a society, then we cannot just assume they will show up in surveys; they need not be 'the ones that may be the most distinctive among all the attitudes a population may hold'.[9] Pye is here talking specifically of the problem of establishing whether a particular set of perceptions goes with a particular type of political order. We have first to posit what we think such a set might be and then we have to search for evidence of such a set – but we cannot assume that surveys will provide the evidence one way or another. But Pye's point applies more generally too. Given the 'bountifulness of subjective political attitudes', we have to make prior judgements on what we are interested in, on what counts as views, on how to organise the perceptual hotchpotch of a society to give it some form and meaning. And we shall do this differently depending upon our concerns.

Let me give an example. To try to identify the political beliefs in a particular society (be they the most commonly held or the most 'critical' ones) in order to compare them with those in another society (or the same one at a different point in time) is one exercise. If however the aim is 'to identify those features of political belief or behaviour which are historically derivable, specific to a particular national or other sub-group, *and likely to have a continuing influence upon its future political evolution* (my italics)'[10] the exercise is quite different because here the concern is with 'those particular beliefs or aspects of behaviour that have had an influence upon subsequent developments or beliefs'. In this case we should start with present attitudes and ask which aspects could only be understood with reference to past experience; we would simply not be interested in any earlier beliefs (however important they may have been at the time) that did not relate to present beliefs. Similarly our description of today's political culture would be – not 'today's attitudes and beliefs' but 'those aspects of today's attitudes which (I predict) are going to have a formative effect upon the future' and that might well mean ignoring today's most commonly-held or critical views.

Depending then upon what it is we want to investigate, our 'data set' must vary; and, depending upon the nature of the data set, only certain questions can be investigated. The trouble with our subjectivists is that they assume that only one data set exists, regardless of the very different problems they wish to investigate.

CONTINUITY BETWEEN PAST AND PRESENT

The conviction that past experience must be treated as a variable in an explanation of the present (which of course it must but the question is 'how?') produces a rather strange claim that people are the product of their histories rather than, by implication, of something else. White suggests that 'Soviet citizens remain overwhelmingly the product of their distinctive historical experience rather than of Marxist–Leninist ideological training' (p. 49). Brown, seemingly more cautious, argues 'But on the evidence available we are not able to conclude that the social structure conditions political culture to a greater extent than the specific historical experience of a people' (p. 4); similar class and economic formations may be accompanied by 'striking differences of political culture'. Now, of course, as we travel from one country to another we are aware of different sentiments, attitudes, values – as we are of tastes in food, clothes and music. The societies are different; the people are different. As White tells us, immigrants to Israel from the USA and the USSR have very different expectations and values. This seems quite uncontroversial. (My attitude to British politics and retail trade is very different depending upon whether I am returning from a year in the USA or the USSR.) People are the products of different societies, with different histories – and history stops yesterday. The historical experience of the Russians, the Czechs, the British or Americans today includes all aspects of their society and its relationship to others, includes Marxist–Leninist ideological training and changes in social structure (if that has occurred), up until the present. To say 'citizens of country X are a product of their history' or that their perceptions are a consequence of their historical experience is 'true' because there is nothing else of which they or their perceptions could be the consequence – and this remains true whether one then goes on to offer cultural, economic or other explanations.

But this is quibbling, it may be said, what White *means* is that the more distant past has been more important than the previous twenty or fifty years in making the present what it is. Now, if *this* is what is being said, we shall need some very clear criteria by which we can judge whether such a statement is true or false. We must know just which period 'history' refers to – when it begins and ends – and how we can assess the influence of that period compared with the influence of the more immediate past. Unfortunately White does not offer us any criteria by which we could test the validity of such a statement. How should we disentangle the possible influence of the Tsarist past from, let us say, the more recent Stalinist past? Surely this must be attempted if we are to claim that past experience matters? Brown's statement too has to be rewritten as 'there are certain aspects in a society's past that are more important than recent changes in social structure in fashioning today's political perceptions'. Again this is a statement which may be true or false and which only very careful analysis can prove or disprove. We know that industrial society, to take one example of a very general social order, can be accompanied by a variety of political orders and political perceptions; we know that fairly similar political institutions may exist in societies with different perceptual worlds. What we want to know is which factors – the speed of economic change, the type of economic change, the role of the state, the relationship with other states, intellectual movements within and outside the country, historical memories, religion – are the more important in producing the political orders and the perceptions, how the factors interact, whether the interaction is the same in different societies or not and whether we can establish any general rules. Are there, for example, cultural lags which operate differently depending upon the type and length of time a particular social or political order has held sway? Nothing is proved of the relative importance of any of these simply by noting the existence of countries with broadly similar economic and social orders and different political perceptions. We want to know why fascism caught on in Germany and not in Britain; whether Stalinism was a Russian phenomenon, that is, whether distinctive aspects of the Russian political past were responsible and, if so, which.

The political culturalist wants to argue that past culture is a crucial factor in forming today's culture. Fair enough. But then the relationship has to be spelt out. This has to be done by examining and rejecting explanations of today's culture which do *not* include past culture as a variable, and *by tracing the process by which perceptions are transmitted over time.* It is strange that the subjectivists do neither.

From a comparison of survey data of 1946 and 1968, and other survey data of the late 1960s, Brown and Wightman infer the existence of strong beliefs in social-democratic values in Czechoslovakia. They then suggest 'The contrast between the expectations of a majority even of Czech Communists and what actually followed February 1948 was within a few years to strengthen attachment to those values and political beliefs on which the Party leadership and the mass media poured scorn' (p. 173). The argument is as follows: there were beliefs; government practice went against these beliefs; the beliefs emerged more strongly. The authors then quote Mlynář for his argument that 'pre-revolutionary beliefs' came 'to fill a void created when the expectations of the majority of society who had supported the ideology of "the first phase of the revolution" were not met. Disillusionment set in first among the working masses' (p. 173). Now, Mlynář could be arguing one of several things and for someone concerned with the transmission or creation of values it is critical to know which. The suggestion could be that Masarykism 'even in the primitive and ill-thought-out form of a simple belief in the renewal of democratic principles' (p. 173) (which appeared in 1968) was a widely held Czechoslovak belief in the inter-war years; it was jettisoned by many (by the majority?) in favour of socialism after the war; disillusionment followed and people (the same people?) went back to their old beliefs. This is one possibility, although it cannot include all those who were too young to have had beliefs either pre-war or in 1948. Or he could mean that there never was a shift from Masarykism to socialist values (which seems to be Brown and Wightman's assumption) – although his suggestion of a void suggests that old values were dropped. Yet again, Mlynář could mean that before the war some sections of society held Masarykist views, they held on to them, and – as Communist party rule failed to meet the aspirations of the rest (the majority) – they were there as an alternative for the disillusioned who now embraced them for the first time. Or does one not even need the presence of any alternative? Was not perhaps a 'simple belief' in democratic principles the spontaneous response to a repressive anti-democratic regime?

It is tantalising not to know which of these scenarios is the more correct; if only they were explored we should be able to see if and how beliefs are transmitted, which groups play a key role, how the political order affects belief systems. What we cannot assume, from the existence of two similar sets of beliefs at different periods of time, is that they enjoyed an unbroken existence. The 'same' beliefs can sprout, from different roots, at different periods. To think otherwise is to join hands with the crudest economic determinist. Compare 'Masarykism was a petty-bourgeois phenomenon of the inter-war years; its existence today must be explained by the continued existence of petty-bourgeois strata in society' with 'Democratic values existed in 1946; their existence today must be attributed to their never being displaced'. Both of these are *possible* explanations but neither is satisfactory.

If the authors of the volume could show us that there is a significant relationship between democratic perceptions in the different countries today and those countries' past experience of democracy or previous perceptions, then, at least, we would be prepared to entertain the suggestion that there is a *causal* connection between past and present beliefs. But quite apart from the initial problems of defining 'democratic values', estimating how strong they were and how strong today, there is no suggestion from the contributors that such a relationship can be demonstrated. Gray himself suggests that Hungary and Poland

show the same commitment to democratic values as does Czechoslovakia and that there is nothing in their past political culture to
suggest that they should. He finds this surprising but it is only
surprising if one assumes that today's values owe their existence to a
past set, rather than – as he himself mentions – to 'the experience of
Communist government'. Indeed, to play devil's advocate, might it not
be that *no* previous experience of democracy encourages democratic
beliefs? Had the Czechoslovak inter-war republic continued to exist
perhaps the survey results of 1946 and 1968 would have shown far *less*
enthusiasm for democratic principles; perhaps without *any* experience
of democracy between the wars, the Czechoslovaks of 1968 would
have been far more passionately convinced that the answer to society's
ills lay in social-democracy? Perhaps they would have reacted far
sooner and more strongly against party rule had they not experienced
the limitations of parliamentary democracy?

If what we are trying to do is to explain the existence of political
beliefs, then we must choose our words carefully or the language we
use obscures two quite different explanations. 'Traditional beliefs
resurfaced', 'pre-revolutionary beliefs still exist today' – are these
statements saying that people today, finding themselves in a particular
situation, independently produce ideas that *resemble* those of their
counterparts of an earlier period or does their author mean that
today's views owe their existence to an earlier set?

THE SIGNIFICANCE OF SUBJECTIVE PERCEPTIONS

Suppose we do have comparable survey data on attitudes for two
different periods, as do Brown and Wightman for Czechoslovakia. We
first have to ask what we want to hypothesise or investigate on the basis
of such data. Of course it is interesting to read of the responses people
give when asked questions about the past and present or their
assessment of leading politicians in 1968; it is interesting to note the
differences in the responses given by Czechs and Slovaks. But *what*
does it tell us that is interesting? We do not know whether these
responses are politically relevant: whether we should take them into
account in understanding how the political system has come about,
why it operates as it does, and in predicting change. Survey data are
equivalent to other information that is politically neutral until put in a
framework. We can collect a lot of information on the changing
financial situation of MPs, the ages of Central Committee members,

the national composition of the Council of Ministers but in and of themselves the data are dead until we breathe some life into them. So what should we do with the responses people give when asked about their views of past and present?

The founding fathers of political culture made a perfectly proper attempt to give us an answer. These responses, they said, tell us of people's orientations, perceptions and fundamental values and there is a causal relationship between these orientations and the type of political system. Brian Barry has argued out the difficulties inherent in this claim,[11] and the contributors to the Brown–Gray volume would accept that it cannot be upheld. Pye, as we have already mentioned, has noted that there is no reason to believe surveys will reveal the critical values in a polity. So what might be the significance of the views expressed in response to surveys?

We could advance some predictive hypotheses whose testing would enable us to see whether they are a critical set in influencing activities. For example, the existence of a particular set of views at time *A* will lead to a particular pattern of disturbance at time *B* if official policy offends these views. The testing of such a hypothesis would be very complicated – it would have to be done comparatively and this in turn would engender the cross-cultural problem – but it could be set up now, for the future. It obviously could not be asked of the past. The nearest we get to something of this nature is Brown's 'In such a case, a crisis triggered off by other stimuli (frequently but by no means always economic) may produce a more open political situation in which the strength and direction of political change may be strongly influenced by the dominant – and no longer dormant – political culture' (p. 5).[12] He suggests that Czechoslovakia in 1968 should be thought of in these terms: 'part of an adequate *explanation* of particular political conduct is likely to be in political cultural terms, and explanations in terms of institutional power or of interest will simply not be enough' (p. 5). But this is a milk-and-water claim. Who ever would deny that in times of crisis (and not only in times of crisis) people search for new, old, 'better' ways of organising society, based on their beliefs, hopes and assumptions? We draw on our own cultural heritage, we draw on *others'*, we produce new ideas, we discover old ideas, we react against existing institutional injustice, we believe everything is possible or nothing will change. We do not need a new concept of political culture to say this.[13] But apart from this the problem is that the survey data on the views of 1946 in no way at all explain the ferment of intellectual and political ideas, the aspirations, hopes and subsequent actions of the population in 1968 – any more than do the 1968 survey data. As Pye would say, the surveys do not reveal the critical set.

However, as we suggested earlier, the Brown–Gray authors are not really concerned to make claims for casual connections between 'subjective perceptions' and political actions. But, if we are not to make predictions about actions from 'beliefs', then – as Gray himself states – political culture (defined in this way) becomes of much less interest. The desire to make such connections remains strong. We find Gray making the surprising claim that 'the results of political change so far in the Communist countries have been consonant with what we know of their previous political experience and culture' (p. 267). His inclusion of 'experience' (which can cover a multitude of sins) indicates the difficulty of limiting the discussion to subjective perceptions but, even as it stands, his statement is hard to take. Has Czechoslovakia since 1948 been, or is it today, more of a democratic society than Hungary, Yugoslavia or Poland? What in Yugoslavia's history would have led one to expect that unity could have been preserved as harmoniously as it has? What in China's past would have prepared us for the Great Leap Forward, the Cultural Revolution or 'the mass line'? Gray traces 'the mass line' to Mao's awareness of peasant aspirations in the Hunan rebellion of 1926 and he suggests that 'All the seeds of the Great Leap Forward and the Communes were already present in the Indusco movement' (p. 213) but this is not enough. There was nothing in these events in the Chinese past (which had their counterparts in, for example, Russia) which would have led us to expect that they, rather than others, were going to exert an important influence on future political developments; the presence of Mao, even in Gray's account, becomes crucial for their having had any effect at all. Nor is it so certain that the Great Leap would not have happened had there been no co-operative movement. In Russia the co-operative movement was seen as providing a foundation for quite a different political strategy. Of course it is true that political leaders are influenced by events or gain inspiration or ideas from particular social phenomena – and in this sense the past provides guidance – but if this quite uncontroversial claim is all that Gray wishes to maintain, then the political culture approach adds nothing to our understanding of the present.

If we are not interested in subjective perceptions as predictors of future actions why are we interested in them? One answer might be that we can use them as evidence of the degree of legitimacy a regime has in the eyes of the people or as a way of establishing the degree of value consensus within a society. This certainly is an interesting area and one to explore. But it is difficult – what are we to count as evidence of legitimacy, and what are we to make of the patterns of value agreement and disagreement? The kind of survey data we have for the Communist countries cannot get us very far. Our authors do talk of dominant and sub-cultures but I have in mind a more general problem than this: to what extent are people's answers to questions about abstract political values, or the nature of society, or their country's past consistent with their answers to more concrete questions about their everyday lives? If they are not – or if they are in some respects and not in others – then we must ask ourselves why this should be and what the significance or meaning of inconsistent responses is. If the abstract political values conflict with everyday ones, which are we to treat as the more important – either in talking of legitimacy or as evidence of value consensus? Mann has suggested that, in the case of liberal democracy, consistency is greater for the professional and educated groups in society than for the working class.[14] And he asks whether it might be that only those with a share in power 'need develop consistent societal values' (p. 435). He also suggests a possible explanation for working-class inconsistency: the schools and the media present general images of society and values which are absorbed by the working-class but which do not tally with their everyday experience; they are unable to forge new abstract ideas which would enable them to interpret their reality. Several interesting thoughts come to mind with reference to Communist-party states but let us leave the question of explanation to one side for the moment. The point here is that the question of establishing what the sets of values held within society and within groups and classes are and assessing the significance of the responses – if we are to talk of legitimacy or consensus – is a more complex problem than that of dominant and sub-cultures. Are the values consistent for any group, class (and if so which?) in all or only some Communist countries? Surveys in the Soviet Union tend to show widespread support for collectivism, for helping society, for extensive state intervention in social life; more concrete surveys show that in terms of actual participation, there are clear differences between the more and less well-educated and skilled; that the same sample may profess the importance of social organisations but when asked how useful they actually are, give them a pretty poor rating.[15] Do we here see the same kind of general commitment to abstract values but, as Mann suggests for liberal democracy, an inconsistent working-class? Or not? What do we make of the rather *different* abstract political values expressed in the Soviet Union and in Czechoslovakia and the very *similar* group differences in participation rates within the two societies? Do Czech and Polish views on their country's past square with their answers to questions on the kinds of government policy they favour today? Do they square for some groups within society and not others?

If we consider that people's responses are significant as an index of political attitudes within a society, then we need to identify the critical areas in advance, and decide on our criteria for legitimacy, for consensus. As far as I can see, this still needs to be done.

OFFICIAL CULTURE AND THE NEW SOCIALIST MAN

If more needs to be done on the analysis of popular values, the treatment of official values by our subjectivists is cavalier indeed. Their position can be paraphrased as follows: in Communist-party states there are rulers with an 'official ideology' (or 'Marxist–Leninist values') which is taught, broadcast, appears in the press; we would have expected this to have produced a 'new Socialist man' with the appropriate values; instead we find a population, either remarkably ignorant politically,[16] or holding views which conflict with elements of the official ideology. Since, furthermore, we discover that some of the views resemble those held in earlier periods, we must recognise that official ideology has failed to dint previous values.

But, if we look at Schöpflin's variation on this theme, we see the problems it lands us with. 'On the one hand, the official Marxist–Leninist set of values is overtly – or at least ostensibly – committed to producing a revolutionary transformation of society along highly egalitarian lines, whilst on the other the existing government has succeeded in creating a relatively stable, cautious system that bears an uncanny resemblance to the pre-war, neo *k.u.k.* (*königlich und kaiserlich*) order. The paradox may be explained by the failure of the Communists to effect fundamental changes in the dominant political culture of Hungary so that, once the revolutionary breakthrough period came to an end and policies of partial reconciliation were adopted, traditional values resurfaced' (p. 153). But, if the leadership is only 'ostensibly' committed to the transformation, presumably it is 'really' committed to something else and, until we know what this 'something else' is we cannot talk of failure or a clash of values.

What is the ideology of the rulers in Eastern Europe, the USSR or China? We must spell out the message coming through the ideology, trace the changes in it and relate them to the practice of the rulers. And, furthermore, we have to see the rulers themselves as members of the society, sharing a common heritage, but now subject to the pressures and influences of their position as rulers. Gray does draw our attention to this latter problem when he suggests:

> At the risk of oversimplification, one could suggest that there are two Communist Party political cultures. The first is represented by the long-term aspirations and expectations grouped round the idea of 'new socialist man'. The second is the operational code of the hierarchical, self-perpetuating party, enjoying a monopoly of political power (p. 260).

If we accept that there is a 'hierarchical, self-perpetuating party enjoying a monopoly of political power' then – precisely because this for a start is in contradiction with an organisation of society in which socialist man could exist – we have to ask 'how do we interpret official ideology?' Is it that there is a yawning and visible gap between official claims and practices? Should we, if this is the case, discount official words as being incapable of having any impact? Or is it more complicated than that? Is it that the ideology itself comes to reflect 'an operational code of a party in power'? If the latter is true, then the following explanation offered by Gray may be queried. 'Liu Shao-ch'i, for example, leaned in every policy choice he made towards the élitist, the centralist and the bureaucratic. This is not to argue that his choices were wrong, but simply that they are all consistent with the view that he was strongly influenced by the old political culture' (p. 223). Consistent maybe, but equally consistent with the view that in a hierarchical, authoritarian, bureaucratic system, the leadership tends to seek certain types of answer and to produce these kinds of policy responses. Indeed the regularity with which the different Communist party leaderships, or sections of them, in countries with very different earlier political traditions have come up with similar types of answer as to what is needed to run the country or economy more efficiently would suggest that the institutions of power are the crucial factor here.

As examples of such leadership responses, we can mention: reliance on administrative reorganisation as a way of coping with economic failings; campaignology; stress on cadres as the decisive factor, accompanied by the tendency to attribute shortcomings to the failings of individuals; the cult; ambivalent attitudes towards the intelligentsia, a recurrent swing in attitude towards workers and peasants (the backbone of the revolution versus the ignorant masses). We find similar responses in very different cultural settings and little to suggest that some of the major 'differences' (for example, workers' councils in Yugoslavia, the mass line in China, the experimental economics of Hungary or Romania's independent stand) can be attributed to a cultural past. Of course there are differences which can be so attributed, for instance, the position and role of the Church in Poland or Lithuania. On a different level, the East Germans observe a much higher level of legal nicety when it comes to publishing and repealing laws than do their Soviet counterparts. It is tempting to ascribe this to different legal traditions.[17] But, in contrast, the East German women's intellectual community is much more progressive and concerned with feminist issues than their Soviet sisters whom we might have expected, if past history was the crucial factor, to have been in front.[18] There are others which require examination. For example, descriptions of political practices in Azerbaijan suggest that the whole system of office-holding and economic administration is permeated by buying and selling; whether it is party jobs, degrees or factory directorships – all are bought and sold.[19] Now, bribery is certainly not restricted to Azerbaijan and the buying and selling of favours of one kind or another seems fairly widespread throughout the Soviet Union. But let us suppose that it is not nearly so marked in Latvia or East Germany where (for argument's sake) there was little tradition of running government in this way. We could hypothesise that the one-party system with its method of appointment to 'valuable' jobs in conditions of scarcity is going to favour such a phenomenon but that it is where such tendencies already exist that it offers them a framework within which they can 'take-over' the system. And then we would look and see whether or not the evidence supported such a suggestion.

We would be trying to establish which cultural patterns can survive regardless of institutional arrangements (for example, the Church in Poland or law-making), which the new arrangements encourage or allow to persist (for example, bribery in Azerbaijan, the clan system in Albania), and which new ones they actually create (for example, bribery in Latvia, campaignology). As part of this we would have to establish which cultural patterns have died – and why. This whole area is a fascinating one that needs exploring and is not of central concern to the subjectivists. I doubt however whether it makes much sense to try to examine attitudes or beliefs without looking at this at the same time. Furthermore, a study of attitudes is going to have to ask the same kinds of questions concerning the impact of institutional arrangements and not only institutional arrangements but also, for example, the type of revolution it was, the nature of the Communist party and the problems facing the leadership.

But to return to official culture. Hegedus, in describing the leadership's response to the growing white-collar intake into the party, gives us a nice example of leadership perceptions:

> It seemed to us at the beginning of the fifties that this unwelcome development in the party's composition was attributable to subjective errors on the part of the lower ranks of the party leaders . . . there was a case in which we expelled the first secretary of a provincial party council from the party on a charge of excluding manual workers from the party. It literally did not occur to us that the cause of this phenomenon, which was felt throughout the country, might be structural. However, as time passed, it was natural that the recalcitrance of the process which one sought to suppress began to induce doubt in the functionaries themselves. A line of thinking developed which, adopting the ideology of bureaucratic management, came to consider the decreased participation of the direct producer in the composition of party membership and in the activities of the society almost a natural development.[20]

We notice both how the leadership's position influences its reaction to phenomena and how its views change. To what extent then does official ideology remain internationalist? Or, to return to Schöpflin, how much does official ideology stress egalitarian ideals? In the words of Lev Kopelev:

> The actual ideology of the Stalinists, which still lives today, permeating our social existence and our daily 'private' existence, our school books, newspapers and literature, is an ideology of authoritarian bureaucratic party discipline, of superstate chauvinism, of unprincipled pragmatism in the interpretation of history, and economic or ethical questions . . . Authoritarianism, chauvinism, and pragmatism – these are the integrally essential characteristics of the really dominant conservative ideology while all the conventionally sacred (revolutionary, internationalist, democratic, socialist, humanistic and so on) formulae or even lengthy outpourings are in essence simply decorative trinkets, purely external ritual relics, 'vestiges', like the form of address 'comrade' or the motto 'workers of the world unite'. In its true essence the Stalinist ideology is

significantly further both from the old Bolshevism and even more from all varieties of Marxism, old and new, than from certain contemporary conservative nationalist and religious ideologies – among them the 'neo-Old-Belief' which permeates the 'Letter to the Leaders'.[21]

If Kopelev stresses 'authoritarianism, chauvinism and pragmatism' as the hallmarks of official ideology, Bahro argues that the official image of new socialist man is that of a possessor, a consumer, a defender of his own particular interests, not those of humanity.[22] Szelényi suggests:

> If someone were to analyse carefully the ideal type of 'socialist man' – *a test still to be done* (my italics) – he would find striking similarities with the values and tastes of the highbrow upper-middle class of any advanced industrial society. 'Socialist man' should read books, listen to music, be dressed like and behave with his children as doctrinaire left-wing academics do.[23]

Regardless of the differences between them, Hegedus, Kopelev, Bahro and Szelényi – and they are not alone in this – all agree that official political culture is a far-cry from what Marx, Engels or the early Bolsheviks had in mind as Marxist–Leninist values.[24]

It is odd that any one concerned with culture should neglect this crucial question of changing official values and their content. In neither article nor book does White confront it. He argues that, despite some changes, 'the predominantly centralised political culture which the Bolsheviks inherited in 1917 . . . has in many ways persisted up to the present day'; where the Bolsheviks have tried to go 'beyond the traditional culture' they have had very little success.[25] The implication is that the leadership has consistently tried to push something called Marxist–Leninist culture (which remains constant) and that traditional values and behaviour have determined whether it has had any impact or not. But if, for example, we accepted Kopelev's or indeed Bahro's account of official culture, we might well argue that the meritocratic patriots who people the streets of Moscow, Berlin or Warsaw share their rulers' views in basic respects. We could go on to argue – as I suspect Kopelev would – that official culture has been remarkably *successful* in instilling its values in society at large; it would indeed be very odd if we found any 'new *socialist* men' at all. (Bahro suggests that there are a few but that, not surprisingly, they are regarded with dismay by rulers and people alike.) We are reminded of the Tucker thesis which takes the argument one stage further: it is the *leadership* which reverts to traditional values and imposes them upon society, which in turn is receptive towards them. On the face of it this sounds more plausible than a suggestion that the leadership remains unadulterated bearers of a new ideology while the society all around them remains in the grip of the old values. Why should the leaders be exempt?

If we are interested in the relationship between official values and society's values, we must dissect official values. This is not at all easy – the very different descriptions given above are witness to that – but it has to be done. Until we have identified our ideal type of socialist man, we have no way of knowing whether official and popular culture are at variance with one another or in accord. And until we know *that* we cannot possibly start talking of the influence or lack of influence of the one upon the other.

A moment ago we outlined an argument that the reason for today's meritocratic patriots is the success of official culture in stressing such values. This implies a successful socialisation process. But what if Brown and Wightman raise the problem of Czech loyalty to Masaryk or other responses that are hard to square with regime values? A very different interpretation might be in place:

> The empirically identifiable values, aspirations and way of life of the actual physical workers are confronted with the ideals of 'socialist man', who socially and in class terms is a faceless creature devised by Soviet Marxist ideologues . . . (that is 'with values and tastes of the highbrow upper-middle class') . . . If a semi-skilled factory labourer in Prague does not match up to this ideal, then he should be ashamed of himself. State socialist society does not permit self-identification in terms of position in the social structure. One cannot be proud of being a worker or peasant, Jew or Christian – the cultural image is a homogeneous one, conflicting or competing values do not exist . . . I would suggest that the quite extreme nationalism of East European communism is in fact rooted in this social identity crisis. Since class identity is impossible, nationalism becomes the only available socio-psychological tool to support social pride and create social identity.[26]

Now this suggests not that official ideology is creating men in its own image but that it *is* responsible for the values that emerge. It is not that it is simply irrelevant or that it is waging a losing battle against a consistent set of unchanging traditional values (as the political culturalists would have us believe) but that it is one important factor in creating the *new non-socialist* values. To return to Mann for a moment, could it be that it is because the official ideology so badly interprets reality for the intelligentsia and working-class with its notions of a simple class-structure and harmonious class relationships that they both seek another identity, that is, a national identity? Or, to put it even more positively, does the notion of 'socialism in one country' (that is, in a particular historic state) mean that the past can only be interpreted in terms of older national heroes? Or, another suggestion, could it be because the professional and educated in Eastern Europe have had such a little share in power that they (unlike their counterparts in the West) hold an inconsistent set of values, a set which includes certain images of their country's past, individualistic values, nationalist and socialist aspirations? To pursue this line of thought a little further, is it that what we see happening now in Eastern Europe and the Soviet Union is the intelligentsia's attempt to have a share in power and that this is necessarily accompanied by their attempt to fashion values in a way (in *their* way) that allows them a consistent set? Can it be done under a one-party system?

A number of different images both of official culture and of society's culture, and a number of different explanations of the relationship between them, are then possible. This is what makes the question so interesting. What is disappointing is that the subjectivists (and White in his book) do not even discuss them. Because of the assumption that official culture is unchanging and easy to identify they dispense with any analysis of it. Someone should take, for example, the concept of 'equality' or of 'an egalitarian society' and trace what has happened to it in the USSR since 1917 or in China and Eastern Europe since the war. Why do Soviet intellectuals and officials today criticise arguments in favour of reducing differentials and argue that egalitarianism is petty-bourgeois, a phenomenon of a primitive peasant society, whereas their conterparts of the 1920s interpreted the matter quite differently? Kolankiewicz and Taras mention the tension between meritocratic and egalitarian aspirations in Poland.[27] Is this a new or an old feature of Eastern Europe and how do the conflicting aspirations of different groups influence official views? Or, to take a different and important question, what happens to the concept of the party as the vanguard of the working-class, to the concept of 'proletarian' in the different countries and what is the relationship between this and the role the party plays in society? White discusses political participation at length but never analyses for us changes in the official concept of participation. With – and after – the revolution, mass participation in the Soviets was seen as desirable for the following (and not necessarily compatible) reasons: it was a new form of grass-roots democracy which would dispense with officialdom; it was a way of educating the people to become administrators; it provided a counter to bourgeois institutions; it was an indication of support for Bolshevik rule. Only one of these reasons survived into the Stalin period; under Khrushchev official attitudes shifted again – as well as reaffirmations of loyalty to the regime, there was the desire to involve more people in community affairs, to shake up entrenched bureaucratic cliques and improve local amenities. And today?

For a start we could ask whether official culture in all these societies takes on the same tinge, changes in the same ways, or shifts in different directions. Bahro roots the ideology in the continued division of labour but also refers to different cultural pasts playing a part. Could we then distinguish between similar shifts that take place and slight variations which can be attributed to the different past cultures? Or are there important differences in the various leaderships' perceptions of the world which stem from the very different tasks facing, for example, the party leadership in East Germany, China and Cuba? Perhaps this is the more important factor. Or is it the relationship between classes and groups within society and the political structures? This would take us into the analysis of the sets of values and beliefs of the different groups and classes within society – the most difficult area of all given the lack of data but without doubt the most important.

For Bahro, culture in the capitalist West and under actually-existing-socialism is very similar; the Chinese have at times considered Soviet and American ideology to be hardly distinguishable; from an American perspective there is little to choose between Chinese and Soviet communism whereas, for the two involved, there are still crucial differences in assumptions and aims. There is a whole world to chart here, full of perils for the unwary, but one that badly needs charting.

NOTES AND REFERENCES

1. Archie Brown, Introduction, p. 1 in A. Brown and J. Gray (eds) *Political Culture and Political Change in Communist States*, 2nd edn (London and New York, 1979). Unless otherwise noted, all references are to this edition.

2. Robert C. Tucker, 'Culture, Political Culture, and Communist Society', *Political Science Quarterly*, vol. 88, no. 2 (June 1973) p. 182.
3. Brown and Gray, *Political Culture and Political Change*, p. 34.
4. In his subsequent book, *Political Culture and Soviet Politics* (London, 1979) he adopts a wider definition which includes behaviour. The political culture of a group of people becomes 'its political "way of life" as well as its political psychology' (p. 164) but he never clarifies for us which aspects of behaviour are included and which excluded. But, regardless of definitions, his analysis of Tsarist political culture is the same in both his contribution to the Brown–Gray volume and his book. Unless noted otherwise, any future references are to White's chapter in Brown and Gray (eds) *Political Culture and Political Change in Communist States*.
5. Engels in *Perepiska Marksa i Engelsa s russkimi politicheskimi deyatelami* (Moscow, 1951) p. 341, quoted by A. Walicki in G. Ionescu and E. Gellner (eds) *Populism* (London, 1969) p. 88.
6. I leave out the question, although one might expect our subjectivists to discuss it, of language changing its meaning over time: the same statement may *mean* something different twenty years, let alone fifty years, later. Somehow we have got to tackle this problem if we are interested in changing political values, just as we cannot ignore the cross-cultural problem in doing comparative analysis.
7. D. Field, *Rebels in the Name of the Tsar* (Boston, Mass., 1976) p. 14.
8. My argument suggests that to understand and explain Soviet beliefs which may *resemble* earlier beliefs we have to posit sharp breaks, a *discontinuity* in the transmission of ideas, between Tsarist and Soviet periods. Hence I part company with White at a very early stage.
9. Lucian W. Pye, 'Culture and Political Science: Problems in the Evaluation of the Concept of Political Culture', in Louis Schneider and Charles Bonjean (eds) *The Idea of Culture in the Social Sciences* (Cambridge, 1973) p. 73.
10. White, *Political Culture and Soviet Politics*, pp. 15–16.
11. For the founding fathers, see for example Gabriel A. Almond and Sidney Verba, *The Civic Culture* (Princeton, New Jersey, 1963) and Lucian W. Pye and Sidney Verba (eds) *Political Culture and Political Development* (Princeton, New Jersey, 1965). Brian Barry's critique is in his *Sociologists, Economists and Democracy* (London, 1970).
12. The authors of the Brown–Gray volume want to distinguish between official values and those held by the citizens (the majority) of a society where the two do not coincide. The concept 'dominant political culture' seems to mean 'values shared by a majority of the population'. As such, there need not be a dominant political culture and equally it can coexist with minority sub-cultures. See Brown, pp. 7–8.
13. There is a fascinating set of questions here: are there some circumstances which encourage the participants to look in particular directions to find answers? When is past experience seen as important, when are answers sought outside, when are all discarded in search of new? How do the nature of past experience, the type of social order, and present structures affect the social consciousness of different groups in society? We can begin to examine these by, for example, comparing revolutionary

situations in different cultural and political environments, to see whether similar or different political values emerge; do pre-existing ideas persist, how influential are they?

14. Michael Mann, 'The Social Cohesion of Liberal Democracy', in *American Sociological Review*, vol. 35, no. 3, p. 432.

15. White, *Political Culture and Soviet Politics*, ch. 7 presents many data on participation rates; on attitudes towards effectiveness, see M. T. Iovchuk and L. N. Kogan (eds) *Dukhovnyi mir sovetskogo rabochego* (Minsk, 1972) pp. 198, 204.

16. Both Dyker and Schöpflin mention this in their contributions to *Political Culture and Political Change in Communist States*. More recently the *Morning Star*, 18 September 1979, carried a report of a survey carried out in 1976 and 1977 of over 800 Hungarian Communist youth leaders, which discovered that 'some of those interviewed thought Josef Stalin was commander-in-chief of the German Army while others said the former Soviet leader was governor of Hungary during the 1950s . . . 17 per cent knew nothing about Lenin . . . only 13 per cent of those questioned were able to go beyond the fact that he was a "revolutionary and a famous statesman"', etc.

17. Leslie Holmes, *The Policy Process in Communist States: Politics and Industrial Administration* (Beverly Hills and London, 1981) makes this point.

18. Barbara Einhorn provides an interesting account of East German developments in 'Women in the German Democratic Republic: Reality Experienced and Reflected', paper presented to the annual conference of the Political Studies Association of the United Kingdom, April 1980.

19. I. Zemtsov, *Partiya ili Mafiya* (Paris, 1976) although clearly aiming to be sensational and lacking in analysis is worth reading on this.

20. Andras Hegedus, *Socialism & Bureaucracy* (London, 1976) p. 67.

21. Lev Kopelev, 'A Lie is Conquered only by Truth', in Roy Medvedev (ed.) *Samizdat Register I* (London, 1977) p. 237.

22. Rudolf Bahro, *The Alternative in Eastern Europe* (London, 1978) pp. 263–4.

23. I. Szelényi, 'The Position of the Intelligentsia in the Class Structure of State Socialist Societies', in *Critique* (Glasgow), nos 10–11, p. 73.

24. One is reminded of Meyer's 'As it is the image of the culture which Communist élites would like to see emerge from the revolutions is strikingly similar to western images of modernity . . . It envisages the perfection of the functional division of labour for individuals and groups, the participation of all to the limits of their expertise and competence and the bureaucratisation of all areas of day-to-day decision-making . . . Finally it works towards such goals as national independence, strong defensive capabilities and national integration, meaning cultural integration of all component groups and urbanisation of all life', 'Communist Revolutions and Cultural Change', in *Studies in Comparative Communism*, vol. V, no. 4, p. 367.

25. White, *Political Culture and Soviet Politics*, p. 166.

26. Szelénvi, 'The Position of the Intelligentsia . . .', pp. 73–4.

27. Indeed in his subsequent work on equality in Poland, Kolankiewicz

provides many data and an interesting analysis of views on the desirability of equality versus inequality in Poland: 'Socialist Equality: Changing Prospects for Egalitarianism in Contemporary Polish Society', paper presented to the XI National Convention of the AAASS, October 1979. This kind of detailed background study is what we need if we are to get at perceptions and values and to see how and why they arise.

3 Political Culture: Some Perennial Questions Reopened

JOHN MILLER

Mary McAuley's is an important and compelling chapter, one which may well arouse irritation or dismay, but one of genuine radicalism which should give considerable pause to writers using the term political culture in writing on Communist systems. She has convinced this writer, at least, that we need to come to terms with her case before pursuing the political culture 'approach' further. I find myself in broad disagreement with one aspect of her critique, but otherwise accept that the term, as used hitherto, has entailed serious difficulties in practice and in principle. Examination of these prompts some suggestions for a way in which political culture might be redefined and redirected in focus.

Let me begin with the area of disagreement. The overall impact of McAuley's chapter is to suggest, I think, that attempts to provide an *account* – as distinct from *examples* – of the role of cultural continuity in Communist politics have caused more confusion than they have resolved, and it would follow that such accounts may be, so far, better left unattempted. The bulk of the material for her arguments is drawn from the collection edited by Brown and Gray,[1] and this leads me also to concentrate my arguments somewhat on that book as well as on McAuley's chapter.

Let us distinguish between the definition of 'political culture' and its logical status as a term. Brown and Gray use political culture to denote 'the subjective perception of history and politics . . . fundamental beliefs and values . . . foci of identification and loyalty . . . political knowledge and expectations' whilst White argues for a broader usage 'the attitudinal and behavioural matrix within which the political system is located'.[2] They differ as to whether the term embraces political behaviour or not; what they share is the reference to the *subjective perceptions* of people in politics, and its logical status as a *label* for an *area of scholarly emphasis or focus*. As such it has a similar status to such phrases as 'élite', 'interest group', 'policy-making' – or indeed 'agriculture' or 'the military'. The authors who began to apply the term in Communist area studies in Britain in the late 1960s, under the particular influence of Verba's article 'Comparative Political Culture',[3] believed they were redirecting attention to an area of the subject that had been woefully neglected and that this neglect was vitiating a balanced understanding of Communist societies.[4] Redirecting focus to the area they labelled 'political culture', they were not claiming any distinctive research *method*,[5] nor that political culture was a more important field of investigation than others, nor that it was a label for what the authors found to be the essential features of Communist systems.[6] This needs to be spelled out because of the confusion spread in the subject by the use of the word 'approach', and the loose use of the word 'model'.

They also believed, I think – and this theme will be resumed below – that they were labelling something discrete and identifiable by elementary inspection, that is that the labelling process did not involve, *prima facie*, any judgements as to the internal structure of what they were studying or its relationships with other social phenomena. In this McAuley claims they were mistaken.

Their purposes in directing attention to the area labelled political culture were to combat reductionism, particularly the belief that accounts of Marxist–Leninist ideology or of Soviet-type institutions were sufficient in themselves for an understanding of Communist systems and their outputs; to reverse what looked like a frightened retreat from history and geography in English-speaking education;[7] and to correct what they saw as undue preoccupation with the explicit (often public relations) aspects of life in Communist states. Two examples of this may be useful. Students are always fascinated by what appears to them a quite unnatural (as well as non-Marxist) obsession of Communist governments with control and security, and, associated with this, by the contrast between the apparent stability of the USSR, and the quiescence of its population and the restlessness of most of Communist Eastern Europe. Accounts based on ideology or institutions do not give this prominence, let alone significance. Accounts of 'Communist socialisation', stressing the explicit (official education and the official media) invite the conclusion that most people in Communist states are 'convinced' people, usually convinced Communists, occasionally convinced dissidents. I believe this to be an erroneous picture, not only of people in Communist states, but also of the way in which the convictions of the ordinary man everywhere are arrived at and held, and of the relationship between convictions and behaviour.

An important aspect of the emergence of the political culture focus should be pointed out here. The circumstances in which it became needful to combat reductionism and redirect the focus of scholarship were pedagogical, or more broadly, interpretative[8] circumstances, and not research ones; because it is through our teaching, not through our research writing that our ideas gain most currency, and through their currency, may be turned into clichés. The reason why the usefulness, or not, of the label 'political culture' matters, is much more because its use influences public opinion, than because of its impact on research.[9] So although political culture is a label for an area of scholarly, including research, focus, its prime *use* will be in communicating the products of scholarship, that is in interpreting Communist systems to non-specialists. What is entailed in this sort of interpreting?

The obligation to teach as well as to research, to synthesise as well as to analyse, is an obligation to provide an *account*, as coherent and comprehensive as possible, of the present state of knowledge in a subject. This obliges us to draw on the most recent research, but it asks for something going beyond that: the use of good sense, judgement, experience and intuition about the conclusions of other people's research, about topics not covered by close research at all, indeed ones where rigorous research conclusions may seem impracticable or in principle impossible. The rules and methods of synthesis are not the same as those of analysis, but we need facility in both, and synthesis becomes hollow and analysis trivial if their relationship is severed. Because of this, teaching is a difficult balancing act between, on the one hand, the organising and simplifying of material so as to be clear and convincing, and, on the other hand, the struggle against the manufacture, marketing and servicing of clichés.

The tension is particularly acute in Communist area studies. Because of the importance of Communist states in the contemporary world, and the importance of public opinion about them, we cannot be rid of our obligations to give an account which goes beyond the summary of rigorous research findings. On the other hand, because the world's *agitprop* machines and its intellectual fashions have both been particularly preoccupied with Communism we have a particular duty to combat clichés in this field.

Some teachers would dispute the above definition of the teacher's role. Teaching is something simpler, they would say: nothing more than the communication of successfully tested hypotheses, of research methodology in fact. I do not find this satisfactory. In principle there is no relationship between the falsifiability of hypotheses and their importance; the hypotheses we might assemble as the best examples of methodology are likely to be the ones closest to laboratory conditions and furthest from social complexity. And, in practice, our duty is to give training in judgement and argument, not merely in research. And in subjects such as the social sciences, communication of some version or other of the data occurs whether we like it or not; we have a responsibility to contribute to this, however unsatisfactory our current methodology or conceptual frameworks.

These considerations prompt my first comment on McAuley's chapter. It is that it is concerned exclusively with the use and consequences of the term 'political culture' for *research*, in criticism of a book designed, I think, to be a comprehensive *account* of its subject in the sense outlined above. As such, her criticisms, however cogent in the field of research method seem not to be directed at the principal function of the book. Teachers of Soviet history, politics or society usually have to cover a lot of background material in order to place the Soviet period in intelligible context. The evidence on recurrent patterns in Russian and Soviet politics is impressive and McAuley is not denying its essential correctness.[10] How, teachers may validly ask, are they to classify and label this evidence if political culture is a term that takes us one step forward and two steps back?[11]

McAuley would seem to have two options in replying to this. The first – which I would support – would be to the effect that the *term* 'political culture' (not, however, the concern with recurrent patterns in history, nor with subjective perceptions in politics) should be abandoned and replaced by one or several more sophisticated terms, ones which identify distinctions at present being obscured by the label 'political culture'. The second would be to say that attempts at such accounts should indeed be discontinued, to be replaced by a series of case-studies of such hypotheses as can be satisfactorily tested. And this comes close to saying that Russian and Soviet material is not of importance in itself, but only in so far as it is useful for the teaching of social science methodology. I believe she does not do enough in her present chapter to allay suspicion that she may incline towards this latter alternative.

Viewed in this light the dispute between McAuley and those she is criticising contains elements of a perennial dispute between two ways of understanding the study of society: that represented by traditional historiography and area studies, with their emphasis on a coherent account of intrinsically interesting and important subject matter; and that represented by the social *sciences* (in the strict sense of that latter word) with their stress on the advancement of discipline and scientific method and their loyalty to the injunction that 'what we cannot speak about we must consign to silence'.[12] Each perception has its virtues and its vices. The former runs the risk of sliding into conformism or journalism, or of eliciting these in students. To be sure, it has liberated itself from simplistic generalisations about national character, but its central concern is still with synthesis rather than with hypothesis testing. On the other hand, done well, it is capable of crystallising the essence of a culture or a society, in a way that the piecemeal, hypothesis-testing, analytical methods never can. What would constitute a valid critique of such an attempt? In so far as it rests on analysis, criticism of analytical defects is of course needed. But in so far as it is synthesis, can there be any other test of it than the perennial test: does it, with all our judgemental faculties, 'fit experience'?

None of this, of course, exonerates writers from the scrutiny, critique and revision of analytical methods. The doubts being cast by McAuley on the term 'political culture' as a 'tool of analysis' are of two kinds: first, that the term itself was ill-chosen and invites confusion of some important distinctions; and, second, that the term has not been applied with enough rigour or tenacity. It is convenient to pursue the latter line first; in principle it may not be an irremediable matter, but the problems attendant on applying political culture in practice may be near-insurmountable, especially in the case of Communist area studies.

The principal way in which the term has not been used as carefully as it might is the tendency to infer traditional culture from aspects of current behaviour. In the case of poorly documented and inarticulate societies it may seem there is little else we *can* do. But it carries with it dangers of, first, selectivity towards one's evidence, past and present, and, second – in so far as the intention is to *explain* current behaviour – of circularity.[13] There is simply no alternative to the following procedure: first, define what it is in contemporary behaviour that requires explanation; second, *without resort to contemporary behaviour*, establish what, on the balance of probability, was the pattern of traditional political culture concerning analogous behaviour; and, third, test the former against the latter. But the investigation of traditional political culture and the explanation of present politics can not be conducted at the same stage of inquiry.

As was stated above, there was an impatience among the contributors to the Brown and Gray collection with a tendency to take official, textbook Marxism–Leninism and 'Communist socialisation' too much at face value; hence the redirection of attention towards the 'dominant' (that is, mass) political culture. The impatience, I think, was of two kinds; first, with the ascription of a simply exaggerated role to Marxism–Leninism; and, second, with a simplistic image of socialisation and of conviction, almost of a 'one-to-one correlation' between what people are taught and what they believe, or between what they believe and what they do. It is in this latter area that writing hitherto on political culture in Communist states has not been searching enough and interesting and important questions remain to be delineated and tackled. Almost certainly this will require drawing on the work of philosophers and social psychologists for a more careful understanding of what we mean by the acquisition, 'holding' and application of beliefs.[14]

Let me give an example of this. Educationists use the label 'hidden curriculum' for the messages successfully conveyed during education, as distinct from what education purports to teach. This may mean, narrowly, what we really acquire at school, as distinct from what a teacher thinks he or she is conveying, or, more broadly, what we learn from our circumstances rather than from school.[15] Would it not be enormously fruitful to make the common sense assumption that Marxist–Leninist educational curricula, and indeed life in general in Communist-ruled societies transmit implicit normative messages that may be utterly at variance with official ideology?[16] Might we not discover an 'operational code' here, not just for the Kremlin, but for officials and citizens alike?

In this way, it might be possible to reconcile what are, *prima facie*, two mutually inconsistent themes in accounts of Soviet society. The one highlights the strong pressure towards discipline and reward-dependent co-operative behaviour in Soviet upbringing with its expected political consequences of conformism and governability.[17] The other takes for granted that success, even survival, in the world of Soviet politics (perhaps increasingly in society generally) depends on individualistic and anti-social skills of calculation and manipulation, in fact on competitiveness and *kto kogo*.[18] If political culture is to throw light on the world of policy-making it needs to tell us which of these two images is closer to the truth, or how they might be integrated.

A recent writer on the 'Machiavellian' personality, A. F. Davies, has suggested a connection between it and unintentional rewards in child-rearing; 'perhaps the "open" parent is reliably the cool operator's first "con"?'.[19] To pursue this line of thinking, might not the origins of Machiavellian behaviour in Soviet society lie in the perceived *contrast* between indulgent child-rearing and discipline in schools?[20]

What of the charge that the term 'political culture' was *in principle* poorly chosen, and invites confusion? The choice of a label for an area of research is not as simple a matter as it might seem. A label is not an heuristic device; it raises no questions, it generates no hypotheses (only human classificatory activity can do that!). But two characteristics must be present for an object to earn a label: it must be sufficiently distinct from other things to warrant distinct treatment; and its internal heterogeneity must be trivial (from the point of view of the research exercise in question) by comparison with what distinguishes it from other objects. If these criteria are not satisfied, then the application of a label may serve, indeed, to 'paper over' distinctions that need to be probed; and hence to block off avenues of inquiry, or to pre-empt research answers. So the net effect of a poor choice of labels may be the fostering of clichés. It is McAuley's contention that the criterion of relative internal homogeneity of the object labelled was not satisfied and that hence the term 'political culture' may serve as an impediment to research progress. If one concedes this, it would be necessary to abandon the term 'political culture' as not representing anything sufficiently homogeneous as to deserve a distinct label, and to replace it with several sub-terms. This would be to treat it in the way the term 'totalitarianism' has been treated.

The definitions of political culture given in the collection edited by Brown and Gray make two things clear: first, that it is a label for subjective *perceptions* of politics; and, second, that it is a claim as to how these came to be as they are. 'Perceptions' is a difficult word, covering a broad spectrum of things which should perhaps better be kept separate. McAuley, following Barry,[21] distinguishes between such things as values, attitudes and beliefs on the one hand, and rational calculation of *interest* on the other. The two behave in different ways; in particular, for our present purposes, the notion of interest focuses on individuals operating independently of each other, whilst the notions of value and belief draw attention to social continuity and the interdependence of people in society.[22] To be useful, our new terms will have to observe the distinction between values and interests.

The term 'political culture' also contains a judgement on social processes. It 'is the product of the specific historical experience of nations and groups'; it is 'historically conditioned', 'traditional' and an 'inheritance'.[23] On this basis the studies criticised by McAuley provide a wealth of illustrations of the way in which post-revolutionary Communist politics can be extraordinarily similar to the pre-revolutionary politics of the same place and of the way in which official Communist policies may be thwarted or influenced by conservative or restorationist attitudes among the population.[24] They often take for granted, however, that these extraordinary similarities are cases of *continuity*.

Now McAuley does not dispute at all that similarities between pre- and post-revolutionary politics occur, nor that official policies come under pressure from people holding attitudes similar to those of the past; nor does she dispute that transmission of attitudes will play a part in this. Her point is simply, and crucially, that one cannot assume that all cases of seeming continuity are cases of *transmission*, and that it makes a big difference to one's findings if one discards that assumption. In fact there would seem to be three broad ways in which people today might arrive at perceptions that are like those of the past:

1. tradition or inheritance (henceforward 'private transmission') from one generation to the next by way of family, friends, peer-group and a child's observation of how adults behave towards each other;
2. 'official' or 'secondary' socialisation under the influence of state-controlled education and communications media. In most societies primary and secondary socialisation,[25] though logically distinct, may be difficult to distinguish in practice. In the case of the Communist states the *explicit* message of secondary socialisation is relatively clear, uniform and distinct from that of primary socialisation and this makes investigation of the Communist states (for once) a bit easier. It should not be forgotten, however, that there may be strong implicit messages in official socialisation and that both the explicit and implicit messages may overlap with those of 'private transmission';[26]
3. calculation by individuals of their *interests* that resembles the way these calculations have been made in the past, because objective circumstances are similar and elicit similar interests.

Now the important point about (2) and (3) is that they are mechanisms for the 'separate creation' of perceptions in each individual and generation; the existence of particular perceptions does not depend on their being *handed on* by persons who already hold them. Hence, if these two mechanisms are at all significant, similar behaviour might be identifiable before and after major social upheavals in which lines of private transmission had been broken; and behaviour might be seen to change when official socialisation policies or objective circumstances changed. In neither case need conclusions about traditional culture, whether of continuity or collapse, be drawn.

Now scholars may differ as to the relative weight to be assigned to beliefs and values, or, alternatively, to rational calculation. In particular one may be sceptical of the image of the individual reckoning his interests in isolation; beliefs, values and interests alike are *shared* things, acquired and expressed in, and only in, societies, and thus not so sharply distinguishable. Brown and McAuley would seem to be at odds on this, and it would seem to be the second perennial question reopened by the current debate. But whatever one's personal position, McAuley is surely right in asking that the precise mechanisms whereby history repeats itself (private transmission, personal or group rediscovery?) be argued out in general terms and in more detail.[27]

If this is not done, it is easy to build two kinds of insensitivity into one's findings. First, one may attribute to tradition and conservatism defensive strategies that people could have devised out of their best interests, whether they had an inheritance to draw on or not, and merge with these the (possibly much more interesting) cases of genuine conservative intransigence that go against strategy and interest. To identify private transmission with some certainty, and to distinguish the traditional (the cultural in a strict sense?) from the strategic, one needs to identify cases where contemporary perceptions *cannot* be accounted for except with reference to the past. An attempt at this will be made below.

A second insensitivity promoted by the stress on private transmission is an insensitivity to social discontinuities and upheavals, and, in particular, a neglect of the problems of Stalinism, one of this century's greatest social upheavals. White, for instance, gives an impressive account of the ways in which Soviet politics since Stalin resemble pre-revolutionary Russian politics, and it is an account I would not dispute. But he devotes very little space to the Stalinist period and it is thus easier for him to label the resemblances as 'continuity' rather than, say, 'replication'. Now the period from the beginning of collectivisation to the end of the Second World War must have been one of very serious interruption to private transmission of values and beliefs. Longer here than anywhere else in twentieth century Europe, more children were not brought up by their relatives and more adults were guarded in their own behaviour, even before children. Clearly private transmission of values was not totally severed, but if one wants to assume the *substantial* maintenance of a tradition against such an onslaught, this needs to be argued out and a possible conclusion drawn. For instance, might one not be dealing with a more invulnerable and intransigent tradition than others in Europe – than the German tradition, for instance, which would seem to have been considerably altered by its twentieth-century vicissitudes? This would be something worth stressing if it could be cogently demonstrated. But what would one *mean* by showing that some traditions are more 'intransigent' than others? Intransigent by virtue of the content of their values or beliefs, or because of the way in which these values or beliefs are 'held'?

Alternatively, if one accepts that private transmission of the Russian tradition was substantially *interrupted* in the Stalin period, one might argue for instance in the following ways about Stalin and the years since 1953:

1. After a period of great tribulation the Soviet people have responded particularly positively to the conservative, disciplinarian, conformist, welfarist government of recent times (rejecting for example, Khrushchev's experimentation), and in this they have resembled the German people under both Adenauer and Ulbricht. The values summed up in the slogan '*keine Experimente*' (no experiments) were a defensive posture adopted in all three societies in response to similar traumata. If the Soviet version of this defence posture is more reminiscent of the Russian past than the German ones are of theirs, it is because such situations have been more frequent in Russian history. This would be an example of the argument that similar circumstances elicit similar perceptions of interest.

2. Although private transmission of values was impaired, *public* transmission of very similar values through officially controlled education and media continued under Stalin. That is, *Stalinism* was very close to the traditional political culture. This would have important implications for our understanding of how Stalin came to power in the first place, and how he maintained his position – something that should have a central place in any account of the

Soviet Union and something which it is crucial for the political culture focus to illuminate, if it is to maintain its credentials.

Thus far this chapter – with an opening caveat – has argued, in broad agreement with McAuley, that failure to distinguish between values and interests, or between transmitted and separately generated perceptions, has been a serious shortcoming in accounts of political culture in Communist states. For remedy McAuley recommends some concrete steps: first, establish independently the most probable pattern of traditional values: second, test the null hypothesis that a piece of today's political behaviour can be explained wholly in terms of today's circumstances, without reference to the past. If this hypothesis has to be rejected, that is, if our problem is inexplicable except by invoking the past, then we should examine the proposition that traditional values were of the sort which, if transmitted, would prompt today's behaviour. If they were, our proof will still be considerably strengthened if a mechanism of transmission can be pointed to.

How would such a remedy work in practice? Not usually (most readers will suspect) so neatly as in the case of the myth of the Just Tsar.[28] Usually – especially in the case of unstudied or inarticulate societies – we would lack firm evidence about traditional values, as the writers in the Brown and Gray collection made perfectly clear, and it is not easy to construct specific hypotheses about social matters without their becoming either so limited in applicability as to be trivial or so broad that it is difficult to know what does or does not constitute relevant evidence.

Let us work through an example. Few would deny that the 'party saturation' (proportion of people in the Communist party) is a datum of importance for gauging the effectiveness, perhaps also legitimacy,[29] of Communist systems. Variations in party saturation, particularly in a large and polyglot state such as the Soviet Union, are therefore an important object of investigation. For the USSR as a whole, it has long been recognised that the best social correlates of party saturation are socio-economic indices of developed infrastructure, such things as the number of people in white-collar occupations, the number of people with education beyond the legal minimum or the retail turnover per head.[30] Moreover this correlation transcends to a quite considerable extent the cultural differences associated with different ethnic affiliation; Georgians and Armenians are highly educated and economically developed and have had higher party-saturation levels than Russians, whilst Uzbeks, Turkmen or Tadzhiks are less developed economically, have fewer qualified personnel and their party membership is correspondingly lower. However some of the non-Russian ethnic groups and areas of the USSR do not adhere to this relationship. They show low party-saturation where we should expect it to be high on socio-economic grounds, and vice versa. Most conspicuous of the major groups in their deviation from this relationship are, in the one direction, Latvians and Estonians, and, in the other, Kazakhs.[31] Table 3.1 gives the relevant party saturations, and compares them with the proportion of the population with tertiary or secondary specialist education, usually a good correlate.[32]

TABLE 3.1   *Party membership and specialist education, 1970*

	Adults in Party (as percentage)	*Those with Specialist Education (as percentage)*
USSR	9.4	12.3
Russians, Union-wide	10.1	13.9
Estonia: Estonians	5.6	13.4
Non-Estonians	11.3	16.3
Latvia: Latvians	5.2	13.7
Non-Latvians	10.0	17.0
Kazakhstan: Kazakhs	10.5	8.0
Russians	7.0	14.0

It will be seen that Kazakhs have a rate of party saturation among adults higher than the average for the USSR as a whole and considerably higher than that of the Russian population of Kazakhstan. In Estonia and Latvia the situation is the reverse: very low party membership among the titular populations and rates twice as high among non-titulars, principally Russians. For none of the three titular populations are education levels a pointer to party membership; they *are* in the case of non-titulars in Latvia and Estonia, though not of Russians in Kazakhstan.

The hypothesis that contemporary socio-economic indices are a sufficient 'explanation' of levels of party membership is falsified, at least in the case of Balts and Kazakhs, and this prompts us to look beyond them for some other relationship; this means almost inevitably looking back in time, whether into the recent or the more remote past. Let us next survey knowledge about the past of these three ethnic groups.

ESTONIANS AND LATVIANS[33]

These have both been Lutheran Protestant cultures since the Reformation, and had comparatively high levels of urbanisation, industrial development and literacy (including rural literacy) at the end of the nineteenth century. Farming was (much more than elsewhere in the Tsar's realm) cash-crop rather than subsistence farming and trading relationships, internal and external, pre-dated industrialisation. For centuries there had been extensive links – not just economic, but also administrative, religious and cultural – with North Germany and Scandinavia.

Both Latvia and Estonia were independent states between 1918 and 1940 and were then incorporated into the USSR. The subsequent Sovietisation of their politics and economics involved the sacking, if not deportation, of a considerable proportion of the élite, especially in the 1944–9 period. Without doubt the fact that substantial recruitment into the CPSU did not begin until 1944 will still be a major factor in their low party-saturation levels; compared with most other Soviet republics, these two have simply had much less time in which to achieve such targets as might have been set. It should also be noted that, although Russians were quite numerous in Latvia and Estonia before 1918, their proportion increased considerably by immigration after 1944.

KAZAKHS[34]

The Kazakhs are by tradition Sunni Muslims but it has been an Islam very much of the outer periphery, retaining pagan elements in ritual and theology, in a manner reminiscent of parts of sub-Saharan Africa today. They retained a nomadic pastoral economy and considerable elements of tribal organisation into the twentieth century and Russian government did not penetrate deeply before the Revolution. Literacy in 1926 was 7 per cent.[35] Beyond this we can say very little to refine these rather broad characterisations or that is specific to the Kazakhs.

In 1916 there was a large-scale revolt of Kazakhs, along with other

Central Asians, against conscription, which was put down with considerable losses on both sides. This conflict was followed in the early 1930s by collectivisation, which in Kazakhstan amounted to 'denomadisation' and their conversion, by force if necessary, into sedentary farmers or unskilled workers. Clearly a demographic catastrophe, on the way to genocide, occurred, with the loss, by 1939, of something like a third of the Kazakh population by death or emigration.[36] From this time Kazakhs have been a minority in their republic, a situation reinforced by European immigration, especially in the 1940s and late 1950s.

Awareness of events before 1941 should prompt reconsideration of the conclusion that party membership among Latvians and Estonians is low simply because they have had less time in which to be recruited. It undoubtedly contains some truth, but its impact is softened by the facts, first, that Kazakhs have not been entering the CPSU on a large scale for very much longer than have Balts,[37] and, second, that in both cases, the period of real absorption into the Soviet system was accompanied by hostility and violence, not only between non-Russians and Russians, but between non-Russians and Soviet Communists. It is not unreasonable to assume that many Balts and Kazakhs merged their hostility to Russians and to Communists – came to perceive the CPSU, in effect, as a predominantly Russian organisation for the furtherance of a Russian set of ideas.

It is also apposite to point out how *similar* political conditions have been in the Baltic States and Kazakhstan since 1944. In addition to the legacy of hostility to the ruling group and the influx of Russian settlers, these similarities would include such familiar features of Soviet government as standardised institutions, standardised external control of the media and of educational curricula and strict privacy of policy-making, with restriction on local access to the latter. The major way in which the two regions *differ* is in absolute levels of prosperity, skill or productivity; and this only serves to pose the question more acutely; how to account for high party-membership among Kazakhs and low among Balts, in defiance of usually reliable socio-economic correlates, and with secondary socialisation held largely constant?

At this point the adherents of an 'unreformed' notion of political culture – in the sense that McAuley is attacking – might well feel in their element. If radically different behaviour results out of substantially similar circumstances, they might say, then seek the explanation in traditional values. It would be extraordinarily tempting to point, on the one hand, to the Protestant and individualistic culture of the Balts, and, on the other, to the tribal and nomadic background of the Kazakhs, and to suggest that the values of each would be likely to foster a different response to external pressure; from the latter an accommodatory strategy of 'if you can't beat them, join them', and from the former an intransigent strategy of 'count me out'.[38]

Now this *might* be correct. But suppose the pattern of party membership had been the other way round, low for Kazakhs and high for Balts. Would it not also have been tempting to point to the political quietism and convention of 'rendering unto Caesar' that has often been alleged against German and Scandinavian Protestantism, and, on the other hand, to the tradition of the *Jehad* and of smiting the enemies of God on earth that has often surfaced in Islam?[39] If this were done, the 'bountifulness of subjective ... attitudes' (even where the evidence is as tenuous as it is with the Kazakhs) and our failure to settle in advance which should count as relevant, would have led us into the kind of circularity against which McAuley warns. To repeat: either conclusion might be correct, but the logical step is dubious.

It is time to reappraise the bland claim that 'conditions' – in particular, secondary socialisation – have been substantially similar in Kazakhstan and the Baltic States since 1944. What of the third major influence on perceptions noted above, namely interests as opposed to values? Data bearing on interest diversity in Soviet society are notoriously scarce, but two things can be pointed out. First, Latvians and Estonians are a majority in their titular republics, whereas Kazakhs, since the 1930s, are a minority in theirs. Second, in certain important areas of education, levels are approximately equal for Latvians, Estonians and Russians in the Baltic, whereas there is great *in*equality between Kazakhs and Russians in Kazakhstan. This difference is especially true of the qualifications called 'secondary specialist' in the USSR.[40] These – essentially, completed secondary school with a supplement of vocational training – are the qualifications held by about 13 per cent of the workforce (as at 1970) and are likely to be (second only to tertiary degrees) the qualifications sought after by ambitious and upwardly-mobile teenagers. In towns in Kazakhstan there are three times as many Russians as Kazakhs; in urban technical employment there are probably five times as many Russians as Kazakhs, and maybe more.[41] In the Baltic states, on the other hand, urban technical employment is distributed among the nationalities roughly corresponding to their share of the urban population. Graduate employment presents still another picture; in most republics it is distributed reasonably according to ethnic configuration in the towns, and, in many, the titular population has an advantage over local Russians.[42]

I should like to suggest that the distribution of sought-after professions among ethnic groups can be seen not just as a datum, but as an *index of perceived opportunity*. Though a young urban Kazakh will hardly be familiar with the statistics, he is likely to have an amorphous awareness of the message behind them: that his entry into a good job will be difficult, and that, in the case of jobs requiring secondary specialist qualifications, it will be in the face of very stiff competition, if not what he perceives as discrimination. A young Latvian or Estonian is much less likely to perceive the matter like this.

Are there any weapons or resources the young Kazakh could acquire to make this competition less unequal? Yes, indeed. He might very well see admission into the party as just such a resource, as the item in his *kharakteristika* which could make the difference between failure and success. And if in this manner an unusual number of such Kazakhs gained entry into the party, it would be explicable in terms of interest rather than of values. Further, the argument that competition for unequally distributed goods encourages people to cast round for additional resources – like party membership – seems much less likely to apply in Latvia and Estonia. Ordinary Balts need not see themselves at any particular disadvantage regarding entry into desirable jobs.[43] Like Kazakhs, they may well have no great sympathy for the CPSU; unlike Kazakhs, they may also have no great *interest* in party membership, because it cannot procure for them much that they might otherwise lack.

An argument can thus be mounted to the effect that the differences in party saturation between Balts and Kazakhs can be accounted for in terms of perceptions of individual self-interest, irrespective of any pro- or anti-Communist values, or of obstinate or complaisant attitudes in the traditional political cultures. It is an argument that would chime in with the theme in the literature on ethnicity which associates heightened ethnic tension with unequal competition for the goods of economic development.[44]

But objections to the argument will be apparent, two in particular. First, why does it seem to be applicable only to secondary specialist employment, and not to graduate employment – surely the object of greatest ambition? Is it because entry into graduate employment, though fiercely competitive, is not (substantially) an *unequal* competition? More importantly, the argument cannot be generalised to other republics. Uzbekistan, for example (whose party saturation, it will be remembered, behaved according to 'predictions'), shows much more severe differentials between the Uzbek share in the population and their share in graduate or specialist employment.[45] If these are the conditions which promote competition, and the drawing of party membership into the competitive arena, in Kazakhstan, why are there no signs of such competition in Uzbekistan? This difficulty is all the more telling because the Uzbeks would seem to be a very cohesive, self-aware and self-reliant nationality. There is only one obvious way in which the Uzbeks' situation differs from that of the Kazakhs. They are a clear majority in 'their own' republic, whereas the Kazakhs (accompanied only by the Kirghiz) are a minority in theirs, and have become it during the Soviet period. Could one extend the argument as follows? Among Kazakhs, competitiveness is generated, not just by individual self-interest, but by awareness of the ethnic configuration, by the knowledge of being a minority and the wish to restore an old ascendancy, whereas Uzbeks feel relatively relaxed about their position in Uzbekistan and feel less need to compete for their place in it.

This sounds appealing, if speculative; but it has forsaken the concept of individual self-interest. To speak of Uzbek 'cohesiveness' or 'relaxedness' sounds suspiciously like speaking about features of a *culture*. And to act out of 'awareness of the ethnic configuration' is to act out of *group* interest (conceivably, even when this conflicts with individual interest); and surely one of the early things an interest group does is to articulate its fellowship in the form of values and culture?

Have we not come full circle? Not quite. Whereas we began with an understanding of political culture in terms of 'beliefs and values . . . knowledge and expectations', our focus is now on features of society ('cohesiveness', for example) which help or hinder the maintenance or implementation of beliefs and values. It is a focus on structure and patterns of organisation.[46]

What I think is the vital difference between the political cultures of the Balts and of the Kazakhs now comes into view. The cultures of Latvians and Estonians are more firmly rooted and cohesive and have greater capacity for survival, both because of their internal structure and their international (western) contacts. Deportation or dislodgement of the élite was not a body-blow to their culture, because the élite were not the sole *Kulturträger*. Widespread literacy, cash-crop farming and trade had given ordinary people the means and the incentive to be clear and independent about their values.

Contrast the Kazakhs, largely nomads and with 7 per cent literacy.

To destroy their élite was literally to decapitate society,[47] to cut *everyone* off from their culture, which was known only to the few and communicated orally and by authority; it was to destroy the cohesiveness and self-awareness of Kazakhs as a society.[48] The survivors, in evolving new authority patterns, will have been ideal candidates for assimilation into someone else's culture. Nor, I suspect, did a sense of being part of the world-wide Islamic culture come to their aid. There is very little sign of interaction, or would-be interaction with the more solidly Muslim lands to the south, in the way that there has always been strong contact, say, between Uzbekistan and Persia.[49]

In simple terms, the Latvians and Estonians were better equipped to hold their values (any values!) against external encroachment than were the Kazakhs.[50] What I think stands the test in the political culture approach is not the concern with the *content* of beliefs, values or tradition, but the concern with their *form*: their cohesiveness and mechanisms for their maintenance, survival or adaptation. And this serves to remind us that the defining characteristic of a culture is, after all, not the presence of particular values or ideas, but the imposition of sense and order on the mental world.

At this point I feel that I have reached a clearing. It would be splendid if it led on to the High Plains.

NOTES AND REFERENCES

1. Archie Brown and Jack Gray (eds) *Political Culture and Political Change in Communist States* (London and New York, 1977). One contributor to this volume, Stephen White, later amplified and modified his treatment of the theme in *Political Culture and Soviet Politics* (London and New York, 1979).
2. Brown and Gray, *Political Culture and Political Change*, p. 1; White, *Political Culture and Soviet Politics*, p. 1.
3. Lucian W. Pye and Sidney Verba, *Political Culture and Political Development* (Princeton, New Jersey, 1965) ch. 12.
4. The present author was at Glasgow University in the late 1960s with six of the contributors to the collection edited by Brown and Gray, and thinks it may be useful to recall what the enterprise looked like to participants at the time.
5. Thus a 'political culture' 'approach' is not an analogous activity to a 'kremlinological' (better, cryptological) approach.
6. Brown makes this clear, *Political Culture and Political Change*, pp. 2, 4, 13; also White, *Political Culture and Soviet Politics*, p. 15. It follows that such things as the 'bureaucratic', 'developmental' or 'industrial society' approaches are also not logically analogous.

7. On these two points I am in agreement with White's comments in Chapter 4 of this volume.

8. Meaning by this that in one's capacity as a teacher one communicates not only with pupils but with colleagues in other disciplines and with laymen.

9. I think it is fair to say that the word 'totalitarianism' has been widely rejected in universities because it creates more confusion than it solves in teaching, not because it lacks utility as a label for something highly specific at a research level.

10. Despite her doubts about White's summary of the principal themes of Russian nineteenth century history (Chapter 2) McAuley does accept recurrent patterns – for instance, the Myth of the Just Tsar.

11. I detect elements of just such a complaint in White's contribution to the present volume (Chapter 4).

12. L. Wittgenstein, *Tractatus Logico-Philosophicus* (London, 1922) p. 7.

13. McAuley (Chapter 2 of this volume), is particularly thorough on these points and there is no need for me to amplify them. I suspect here the influence of Brian M. Barry, and in particular his *Sociologists, Economists and Democracy* (London, 1970) pp. 89–96. Incidentally, McAuley directs her critique on this point against those who define political culture more narrowly, restricting it to subjective *perceptions*; but it would seem that the problem could occur also with the broader concept of political culture, that which embraces both perceptions *and* behaviour. This is because the relationships between perceptions and behaviour have to be tackled, whether they are part of the internal structure of political culture, or the link between it and the rest of life.

14. To speak of a person 'holding' a belief seems calculated to obscure the fact that the package of a person's perceptions is internally contradictory, different beliefs being invoked in different circumstances. Would we ask the same questions about the relation between beliefs and behaviour if we pictured the former as 'elicited' rather than 'held'? This seems to me the best answer to the question McAuley poses concerning the re-emergence of democratic views in Czechoslovakia (Chapter 2). It is surely doubtful whether many Czechoslovaks – whatever their age or political affiliation – were *unaware* of what democratic views were like.

15. For a summary of the term 'hidden curriculum', with further references, see D. H. Hargreaves, 'Deschoolers and New Romantics' in Michael Flude and John Ahier (eds) *Educability, Schools and Ideology* (London, 1974) esp. pp. 189 and 209, note 4.

16. We already make a rather similar assumption when we ascribe to Soviet readers sensitivity to *podteksty* ('things read between the lines').

17. The *locus classicus* is Urie Bronfenbrenner, *Two Worlds of Childhood* (London, 1971) especially chapters 1–3. To be fair, Bronfenbrenner qualifies his claim 'that collective upbringing does achieve some of its intended effects', by adding immediately, 'at least at the school age level' (p. 80). Like many other visitors to the USSR, I have been impressed by observations of Soviet *vospitanie* (upbringing) that coincide with those of Bronfenbrenner; and at the same time have been nagged by the question, 'can this be the environment that moulds successful Soviet *politicians*?'.

18. It is less easy to document authors who are explicit about these

assumptions, because the exponents of the theme are interested in political output not in psychology, still less in upbringing; but the assumptions would be implicit in most 'kremlinological' writing. P. B. Reddaway in *Soviet Studies*, vol. XVII, no. 4 (April 1966) pp. 473–7 provides a rare example of reflection on the psychological basis of official behaviour. The writings of George Feifer would seem to me increasingly to portray Machiavellian behaviour as a feature of Soviet society.

19. A. F. Davies, *Skills, Outlooks and Passions: a Psychoanalytic Contribution to the Study of Politics* (Cambridge, 1980) p. 65–7. It is noticeable how in colloquial Russian the word *durak* (fool) is frequently applied to people who might seem to be model products of 'collective upbringing'.

20. Bronfenbrenner, *Two Worlds of Childhood*, pp. 9–14, thinks that the 'nurturant' aspect of Soviet child-rearing should not be mistaken for 'permissiveness or indulgence'. But it is noticeable that his evidence at this stage is taken from child-care manuals.

21. Barry, *Sociologists, Economists and Democracy*, *passim*.

22. Their distant origins are thus, respectively, liberal and conservative; see Barry, *Sociologists, Economists and Democracy*, pp. 7–11.

23. Brown and Gray, *Political Culture and Political Change*, pp. 1, 16, 18, 25.

24. 'Restorationist', in order to make it clear that these attitudes are not necessarily to the 'right' of official Communist ones, as those of the Czech reform movement in 1968 were not.

25. For this distinction, see P. L. Berger and T. Luckmann, *The Social Construction of Reality* (New York, 1967) pp. 129–47.

26. Dyker in Brown and Gray, *Political Culture and Political Change*, ch. 3, esp. p. 78, would, I think, agree that 'self-management' socialism in Yugoslavia is a case of this.

27. Thus the general treatment of this issue in Brown and Gray, *Political Culture and Political Change*, pp. 4–6 and White, *Political Culture and Soviet Politics*, p. 18, is, in my opinion, not very satisfactory. Brown's specific account of the Czechoslovak case is a more complex one; see, for example, *Political Culture and Political Change*, p. 167.

28. McAuley, Chapter 2.

29. Caution about the implications for legitimacy is in order because it is not clear how much party saturation levels reflect social preferences rather than party planning. On this question, see McAuley's article cited in note 31.

30. For this conclusion in general terms see T. H. Rigby, *Communist Party Membership in the USSR* (Princeton, New Jersey, 1968) esp. pp. 501, 510–12; and B. Harasymiw, 'Les déterminantes sociales du recrutement et de l'appartenance au parti communiste de l'Union Soviétique', *Revue d'Etudes Comparatives Est–Ouest*, IX (1978) pp. 43–87. Statistical treatment began, so far as I know, with D. P. Hammer, 'The Determinants of Communist Party Membership in the USSR', paper presented to the annual meeting of AAASS, Denver, Colorado, March 1971; this was followed more comprehensively by J. A. Dellenbrant, *Regional Differences in the Soviet Union* (Uppsala University, Research Center for Soviet and East European Studies, August 1977).

31. For an independent study of this question, see another article by Mary

McAuley, 'Party Recruitment and the Nationalities in the USSR', in *British Journal of Political Science*, vol. 10, part 4 (October 1980), 461–87. It will be seen that she is using the same data but I have arrived at somewhat different conclusions. I am indebted to her for helpful discussions on the subject.

32. Sources for Table 3.1: for party data, *Kompartiya Kazakhstana za 50 let* Alma-Ata, 1972) p. 324, and, with interpolation, *Partiynaya zhizn'*, No. 19, 1967, pp. 14–15; No. 14, 1973, p. 18; the assumption was made that the party saturation of Latvians and Estonians Union-wide and inside their titular republics is the same; though unlikely to be correct, this would not distort the pattern in Table 3.1 appreciably. For data on adults (defined as those aged 20 or more) *Itogi vsesoyuznoy perepisi naseleniya 1970 goda* (Moscow, 1972–3) vol. II, pp. 13, 53, 73; vol. IV, pp. 360, 365, 378, 381–2. The age distribution of Russians in Kazakhstan was assumed to be the same as that of all Russians outside the RSFSR. For data on specialist education, see ibid, vol. III, pp. 20–1, 28–9, 206; vol. IV, pp. 393, 490–1, 518, 545.

33. For background, see in particular W. Kolarz, *Russia and Her Colonies* (London, 1953) pp. 104–16. On literacy rates, see *Naselenie SSSR (chislennost', sostav i dvizhenie naseleniya) 1973* (Moscow, 1975) p. 44.

34. See Kolarz, *Russia and her Colonies*, pp. 262–71 and S. V. Utechin, *Everyman's Concise Encyclopedia of Russia* (London, 1961) pp. 260–3.

35. See Frank Lorimer, *The Population of the Soviet Union* (Geneva: 1946) p. 58.

36. The crucial evidence was assembled by Lorimer, *Population of the Soviet Union*, p. 140. A certain amount of anecdotal confirmation can be found in J. D. Littlepage and D. Bess, *In Search of Soviet Gold* (London, 1939) pp. 130–1, 175–81; in Godfrey Lias, *Kazak Exodus* (London, 1956) pp. 61–2; and in N. I. Zhurin, *Trudnye i schastlivye gody: zapiski partiynogo rabotnika* (Moscow, 1982) pp. 34–5. Littlepage would seem to have coined the word 'denomadisation', but he may have been translating *otkochevka*, a term used by Zhurin.

37. There were 6 647 Kazakhs in the Kazakhstan party in 1925, 11 634 in 1926 and 55 451 in 1942; see *Kompartiya Kazakhstana . . .*, pp. 63, 172. Recruitment of Kazakhs into the party will have been further complicated by repeated purges, particularly of natives, for which see Kolarz, *Russia and her Colonies*, pp. 264–6.

38. Let me emphasise that this example is of my own devising. However, I do not think it is unfair to many accounts of political culture, and indeed, I know of people who accept it as the preferable explanation.

39. An attempt was actually made to treat the 1916 revolt as a *Jehad*, according to Utechin, *Everyman's Concise Encyclopaedia*, p. 365.

40. See *Itogi . . . 1970 . . .*, vol. IV, Tables 62, 67 and 72. For the purposes of this argument it is preferable to use data on employed rather than total population, and to look particularly at urban figures, those more likely to be affected by pressures for social mobility.

41. This claim depends on the percentages cited in the previous note and a rather hazardous attempt to estimate the distribution of employed population by nationality and between town and country.

42. It tends to be overlooked that, although Russians reserve for themselves a minority of key political positions in the non-Russian republics, titular non-Russian nationalities usually get their fair share of managerial or administrative grade jobs, and sometimes they have a definite advantage. The stability of the non-Russian republics could owe a lot to these 'titular' élites.

43. It must be clear that here we are discussing occupations where party membership is not obligatory and hence where social preferences for or against membership have had a chance of becoming explicit. Some tentative calculations suggest that low party membership among Latvians is particularly the case among Latvians in technical employment. If this is correct, it is reminiscent of one of the occupational backgrounds from which Solidarity in Poland drew support.

44. See, for example, D. L. Horowitz, 'Multiracial Politics in the New States' in R. J. Jackson and M. B. Stein (eds) *Issues In Comparative Politics* (London, 1971) pp. 164–80, esp. p. 172; Mary Fainsod Katzenstein, *Ethnicity and Equality: the Shiv Sena Party and Preferential Policies in Bombay* (Ithaca, 1979) esp. pp. 197–200.

45. See *Itogi . . . 1970 . . .*, vol. IV, Table 61.

46. I sought to make a similar case about the understanding of Leninism on pp. 1–3 of Archie Brown and Michael Kaser (eds) *Soviet Policy for the 1980s* (London, 1982, and Bloomington, Indiana, 1983).

47. Kolarz, *Russia and her Colonies*, p. 264 and Littlepage, *In Search of Soviet Gold*, pp. 130–1 mention that clan chiefs and mullahs were particular targets.

48. An analogy might be Tibet without its lamas and its monasteries.

49. Kazakhs looked more north-west towards Tatary and Kazan', whose assimilation into Russian culture had been under way for centuries. And for an even more complex account of the situation, which further reinforces my point, see A. Bennigsen and C. Lemercier-Quelquejay, *Islam in the Soviet Union* (London, 1967) pp. 14–15, 24, 26, 29.

50. My colleague Dr R. B. Jeffrey reminds me that this conclusion resembles his own in *The Decline of Nayar Dominance: Society and Politics in Travancore, 1847–1908* (London, 1976). External pressures, chiefly economic, eroded the power of the matrilineal Nayar caste; their initial impact was on Nayar familial and authority structures, which was then followed by a reappraisal of Nayar values.

   In general the Indian state of Kerala would seem to be a splendid testing ground for hypotheses about political culture. It has many of the attributes of a developed society, for instance better educational and welfare indices and a lower birthrate than elsewhere in India; yet its GNP per capita (the expected correlate?) is well below the Indian average.

4 Soviet Political Culture Reassessed

STEPHEN WHITE

It may seem rather soon to reassess a subject of which one has recently completed a book-length study.[1] Nor, indeed, do I feel that there are more than a few substantial points on which I would as yet wish to undertake a major revision of the general treatment of Soviet political culture presented in my *Political Culture and Soviet Politics*. Given the breadth of a subject of this kind, however, particularly when (as in the definition I prefer to use) patterns of political behaviour as well as political beliefs and values are subsumed within the concept of political culture, there are inevitably aspects of the subject on which new evidence now exists, points that may have been neglected in the earlier discussion, and issues in the analysis of Soviet political culture that require fuller consideration and perhaps some adjustment of emphasis. In this chapter I propose to focus on two such issues, both of which are central to my own work on Soviet political culture as well as to that of most other scholars who have written on this theme. These are the distinctiveness of the pre-revolutionary Russian political culture, and the extent to which its chronological successor – the political culture of the contemporary USSR – may usefully be regarded as a continuation of that earlier political culture rather than as a radical break with it.[2]

In the light of some of the other contributions to this volume it may be helpful to distinguish at the outset between what may be called the concept of political culture and the political culture approach. The *concept of political culture* may be regarded as a term in the political science vocabulary similar to terms such as 'regime' or 'political system'. Like these, it serves as a convenient shorthand label for certain aspects of the politics of a nation or a social group, whether these be defined as collective orientations to politics or, more broadly, as the political 'way of life' of the nation or social group in question. Despite the risk that political culture used in this sense may simply become, as Lucian Pye has warned, 'a pretentious way of referring to political behaviour',[3] there is now, I think, a substantial scholarly consensus that the concept of political culture does provide a useful means of referring to aspects of politics that extend beyond formal institutional boundaries, without necessarily assuming that it has any substantial explanatory utility. This, as I understand it, is the position taken by Robert Tucker in his paper on 'Culture, Political Culture and Communist Society': 'the concept of political culture' he writes, 'may be of value in assisting the scholar to take his bearings in the study of the political life of a country, to focus on what is happening or not happening and to raise questions for further thought and research – without itself explaining anything'.[4] The task at this level is essentially one of 'thick description', to use Clifford Geertz's terms, or of the 'political ethnography' of the society or group in question; no prior assumptions are made, or need to be made, of a causal or explanatory character.[5]

Going beyond this is what may be called the *political culture approach*, which considers the political culture of a nation or social group in historical or diachronic perspective. This is the way in which I myself made use of the term 'political culture' in my study of Soviet political culture, it is the approach adopted by the contributors to the Brown–Gray volume on political culture and political change in Communist states,[6] and it is the approach adopted by the contributors to Pye and Verba's classic study, *Political Culture and Political Development*.[7] As I understand it, the adoption of a perspective of this kind need not necessarily imply the view that the present is wholly to be explained in terms of the past (although some authors do come close to holding this view). The issues of continuity or change should rather be considered an empirical one, with the relationship between past and present being seen as a matter relevant for examination from such a perspective rather than one to be resolved in advance by definitional fiat. A number of studies of Communist political culture have in fact emphasised change rather than continuity in the political cultures they have considered – the work of Fagen and Zeitlin on Cuba comes particularly to mind in this connection[8] – and clearly any adequate application of the political culture approach will include elements of both.

It should be pointed out, finally, that a political culture approach does not provide – and so far as I know, has never been presented as providing – a satisfactory explanation for all aspects of the politics of a nation or social group. Like all models or approaches in the social sciences it may be capable of providing certain insights that are not otherwise available, but inevitably at the cost of neglecting other and, from a different point of view, more important insights. The political behaviour of a Brezhnev or a Liu Shao-chi, for instance, may indeed owe something to the larger political culture within which they have been socialised and within whose constraints they must work; but it may owe something also – indeed, in some cases, it may owe everything – to the situation in which they find themselves as leaders of large bureaucratic organisations. The political culture approach is generally applied to nations or social groups, not to individuals, but even in respect of nations or social groups, so far as I know, it has never been suggested that it provides a total explanation for all forms of political belief and behaviour. Most recent studies of political culture, on the contrary, have taken care to point out that a political culture approach should be seen as complementary to, not as a substitute for, other models and approaches to the study of political penomena.[9]

The result may seem to be what Mary McAuley calls a truism: that the political culture of a nation or other group may to some extent be the product of – although not wholly determined by – its previous political experience. But truisms, after all, are still true, and obvious though such a proposition may seem today, it was not always so regarded when (for instance) structural–functional explanations were at the height of their influence, nor when reductionist forms of Marxism were in vogue which regarded the political superstructure of a society – including its political beliefs and behaviour patterns – as wholly determined by its economic base. Indeed, the adequacy of even straightforwardly institutional analyses of Communist politics has come to look increasingly doubtful, at least in recent years, as their patterns of political behaviour and (so far as we can tell) belief diverge ever more widely from each other despite what is still largely a common institutional framework. A political culture approach, emphasising the nationally specific as well as the systemically universal in such states, has come to seem increasingly helpful in this context to political scientists in the West as well as, perhaps more surprisingly, in Eastern Europe;[10] it is my view also, and I believe that the contributions to this volume will largely vindicate it.

THE PRE-REVOLUTIONARY RUSSIAN POLITICAL CULTURE: HOW DISTINCTIVE WAS IT?

Any attempt to characterise the political culture of a nation – indeed virtually any attempt to generalise in history or political science – involves a degree of over-simplification. The dangers are compounded when dealing retrospectively with the political culture in question – there is always the possibility that one will select, consciously or unconsciously, only these aspects of a previous political culture which support one's hypotheses about the present – and when dealing with many centuries of previous history and with a wide variety of ethnic groups and local variations. In the case of the pre-revolutionary Russian political culture, for instance, it is important to bear in mind that the writ of the central government, however impressive, did not in practice extend beyond the urban areas and major administrative centres, and that many parts of the country – Poland, Finland, the Cossack lands, the Baltic and parts of Central Asia – enjoyed a considerable degree of formal as well as informal autonomy over all or part of the pre-revolutionary period. The reforms that followed the October Manifesto of 1905, such as the establishment of an elected *Duma*, the reform of the press laws and the legislation of trade unions, must also be given due weight; these were considerable changes, and to some, at least, they presaged the transformation of what was still an autocratic regime into a constitutional monarchy on the Western model.[11] And at the same time popular trust in the Tsar, always ambiguous, was steadily diminishing and in the end did not protect him from his overthrow by popular demonstrations in 1917 and indeed before that from the most widespread peasant revolts in Europe.[12]

Nor was there anything inevitable or pre-ordained about the course of Russian political development up to that point, as I also argued in *Political Culture and Soviet Politics* and in my contribution to *Political Culture and Political Change in Communist States*.[13] Early medieval Russia saw the emergence of forms of communal self-government, the *veche*, which were similar to those that existed at the same time in Western European states such as Italy, and these forms of government continued to develop in Novgorod, Pskov and elsewhere until their conquest by the expanding Muscovite principality, where such institutions had not developed, in the late fifteenth and early sixteenth centuries. (Moscow saved Russia from the Mongols, as Herzen put it, but 'having suppressed all that was free in the life of Russia'.)[14] As late as 1917, when the Russian 'constitutional experiment' came to an end, alternative paths of development were arguably still open; the municipal elections of that year, for instance, found the electoral machinery working 'reasonably well' and the electorate 'politically aware', and as many as fifty political parties had come into being to contend for the support of the public. In the elections to the Constituent Assembly, somewhat later in the year, the electorate, in the view of most scholars, had again a fairly clear understanding of the issues at stake.[15] Judgements on such matters may reasonably vary, but it seems clear at least that Russians were not in some biological sense incapable of sustaining a less despotic political order than that which they have experienced for most of their history, or that their history held out no other potential.

Notwithstanding all these qualifications, whatever the alternative possibilities might have been, it seems to me a matter of historical fact that the pre-revolutionary Russian political culture was on the whole more centralist, more interventionist and more collectivist than its major European or North American counterparts, and that we are justified, on the record, in describing it as a 'distinctive and deeply-rooted set of orientations to government'.[16] I can find nothing 'extraordinary' about such a characterisation; on the contrary, it seems if anything to reflect too faithfully the mainstream of scholarly consensus. The point, however, is a contentious one, and given its implications for a political cultural analysis of Soviet politics it should perhaps be given more extended consideration than was possible in *Political Culture and Soviet Politics* or in my contribution to the Brown–Gray volume. In the first part of this chapter I propose to look more closely at the central issue involved in this interpretation: how distinctive was the pre-revolutionary Russian political culture in a European or more broadly comparative perspective?

There have been several attacks upon Russian 'exceptionalism' in this context, some of them of a polemical character.[17] A more serious case has recently been made by an academic historian of Russia, Paul Dukes. Russia, Dukes points out, established reasonably close relations with the rest of Europe at least as early as the sixteenth century, and was an important if indirect participant in the 'general crisis' of the seventeenth century. Her social structure at this time was in many respects comparable with that of Spain and France, and there were more specific parallels in (for instance) the formation of religious sects and the rise of modern science.[18] In the eighteenth century, Dukes goes on to argue, Russia was by no means so backward economically and even politically as is usually supposed. Although constitutionally more absolutist than states such as France, the government of Russia was, like them, subject to social checks, and there were close intellectual contacts with what was happening elsewhere in Europe. Some form of absolutist government was in fact the norm, at least on the continent of Europe, for most of the nineteenth century, and the Russian form of absolutism, in Dukes' view, was in fact quite similar to the Prussian form of absolutism on which it was often explicitly modelled. The conclusion follows logically that Russian history is 'not an exception to the general course of world history, even though it does possess certain distinctive features'.[19]

The argument that developments in Russia should be seen as of a part with developments elsewhere in continental Europe, with the English-speaking rather than the Slavic world as the exception that requires explanation, is certainly one that needs to be taken seriously. The legal systems of pre-revolutionary Russia and of Eastern Europe also, for instance, were generally similar to and often directly modelled on the Romano-Germanic legal systems that prevailed elsewhere in continental Europe at this time.[20] In the countries with this tradition law tended to be conceived of as a body of general and comprehensive rules of conduct, not as a series of individual decisions made by judges, and the divisions of law and legal terminology were very largely the product of the legal science constructed on the basis of Roman law by the European universities. Legal rules in all these countries were generally codified, the Russian codes of the nineteenth century being inspired by those of Prussia and Napoleonic France, and court procedure generally followed a similar pattern, with an inquisitorial rather than a presiding judge and with the jury occupying a much less prominent place than in the common law countries.[21] Administrative justice was also dispensed in pre-revolutionary Russia, as in the continental European countries, by a system of administrative courts (the Russian Procuracy, set up by Peter the Great, was remodelled in 1864 along the lines of the French *Conseil d'Etat*) rather than, as in the common law countries, by a variety of boards, commissions and tribunals.[22]

These parallels may be pressed further. In administrative structure, for instance, there were considerable similarities between the French prefectorial system and the Russian gubernatorial system of the nineteenth century and earlier; foreign organisational principles such as *collegia* were frequently adopted for the work of bodies such as ministries, and indeed in many cases foreigners, particularly Germans and Dutch, themselves occupied the leading positions.[23] The notion of a 'service nobility' also took much of its inspiration from Branden-burg–Prussia, part of what has been called an 'Eastern European type of absolutism' with features common to Prussia, Russia and some of their neighbours, and the Russian Table of Ranks of 1722, which systemised the relationship between noble rank and service to the state, was in fact directly based upon Prussian as well as Swedish and Danish examplars,[24] The educational system also drew heavily upon Central European experience, the elementary school system upon the system that prevailed in Austria, while at the other extreme the Academy of Sciences, founded in 1725, was modelled to a large extent upon the Prussian Academy of Sciences, founded in 1700, and for many years it was 'dominated, if not actually run, by German and German-trained scientists and scholars'.[25] The active intervention of the state in economic development was also as characteristic of Prussia and later the German Empire as it was of Russia, with Witte and Stolypin playing the role of 'Russian Bismarcks' in this connection.[26] Again it is the Anglo-Saxon experience, not the Russian, that appears to be anomalous.

Cross-national comparisons of political behaviour, though not without their difficulties, also reinforce the point that contrasts between Russian and particularly Central European experience may be drawn too sharply. The establishment of a constitutional regime certainly came rather later in Russia than in her major European neighbours, including Germany and Austria (Table 4.1). Great Britain led the way in this respect, establishing a constitutional regime as early as the seventeenth century, followed by the USA, where a regime of this kind was established about a century later. On the continent of Europe the establishment of a constitutional regime was generally a development of the French revolutionary era, or of the period of the revolutions of 1848; Russia, where a quasi-constitutional regime came into existence as late as 1905, is certainly a laggard in this respect. The establishment of a parliamentary regime, however, occurred not long afterwards, in 1917 (on a reasonable definition), and here Russia is more in line with the experience of other European states, where the establishment of a regime of this kind was generally a matter of the later nineteenth or early twentieth century. Russia is comparable in this respect with a number of the Scandinavian countries, and is in fact a year in advance of its Central European neighbours Germany and Austria (see Table 4.1).

The extension of the franchise, considered on a comparative basis, is also less conclusive evidence of the political backwardness of Russia

TABLE 4.1   *The establishment of constitutional and parliamentary regimes*

Country	First constitutional regime	First parliamentary regime	Current parliamentary regime
Great Britain	1689	1741	1741
USA	1787	1789	1789
France	1789	1792	1870
Netherlands	1796	1848	1868
Sweden	1809	1866	1866
Spain	1812	1863	1978
Norway	1814	1884	1884
Belgium	1815	1831	1831
Luxembourg	1815	1830	1868
Portugal	1822	1862	1974
Denmark	1848	1901	1901
Italy	1848	1876	1944
Austria	1848	1918	1945
Germany	1848	1918	1949
Finland	1869	1917	1917
Iceland	1874	1920	1920
Turkey	1876	1908	1921
Russia	1905	1917	1917

SOURCES: Peter Gerlich, 'The Institutionalisation of European Parliaments', in Allan Kornberg (ed.) *Legislatures in Comparative Perspective* (New York, 1973) p. 100; Arthur H. Banks (ed.) *Cross-Policy Time Series Data* (Cambridge, Mass., 1972) various pages.

than perhaps I suggested in *Political Culture and Soviet Politics*. Russia, admittedly, was rather slower to make an initial extension of its parliamentary franchise than all the other European and North American countries for which data are available (see Table 4.2). The extension of this first limited franchise to one that embraced the whole adult population, however, took a century or more in some cases, and Russia was not in fact very different from the majority of its European neighbours in granting universal male suffrage in the First World War period. So far as the vote for women is concerned Russia (and later the Soviet Union) was actually some years in advance of the majority of its

Soviet Political Culture Reassessed

TABLE 4.2   *Extension of the franchise in selected countries*

Country	First extension of suffrage	Universal male suffrage	Universal female suffrage
France	1789	1848	1946
Netherlands	1796	1917	1919
Sweden	1809	1921	1921
Norway	1814	1897	1913
Spain	1820	1869/1907	1869/1907
Germany	1824	1869/71	1919
Luxembourg	1830	1919	1919
Belgium	1830	1893/1919	1948
Great Britain	1832	1918	1928
Portugal	1833	1911	1974
Denmark	1848	1920	1920
Austria	1848	1907	1918
Italy	1848	1912	1946
Finland	1869	1906	1906
Turkey	1876	1921	1934
Iceland	1877	1915	1915
Russia	1905	1917	1917

SOURCES: Peter Gerlich, 'The Institutionalisation of European Parliaments', in Allan Kornberg (ed.) *Legislatures in Comparative Perspective* (New York, 1973) p. 106; Dieter Nohlen, *Wahlsysteme der Welt* (Munich, 1978) p. 37; Arthur H. Banks (ed.) *Cross-Policy Time Series Data* (Cambridge, Mass., 1972) various pages.

European and North American counterparts; a fully equal adult suffrage was introduced in Russia by the Provisional Government in 1917, but in Britain, for instance, a franchise of comparable inclusiveness was not introduced until 1928, and in two European countries (Switzerland and Portugal) a fully universal adult suffrage was not achieved until the 1970s.[27]

Finally, I made a good deal of electoral participation in *Political Culture and Soviet Politics*, contrasting the low proportion of Russian citizens admitted to the franchise as late as 1910 with the much larger proportions of the population who took part in parliamentary elections in the United Kingdom, France, Germany, Italy and the USA at the same time. Here again, however, a broader geographical focus and a more extended time scale shows that these differences were less sharp than may have been originally suggested (Table 4.3). Clearly, as the last major European country to establish an elected legislative body, the expansion of electoral participation in Russia was bound to lag some years behind its European and North American counterparts. Viewed from a broader perspective, however, what is perhaps more striking is how slowly electoral participation expanded in all countries, not only Russia, at least until the First World War years. Before this time only a few countries had electoral participation rates which exceeded 10 per cent of their respective populations, and in only two countries, France and Belgium, did the rate exceed 20 per cent.[28] The formation of a mass electorate, in fact, is a development of relatively recent years; Russia lagged behind to begin with, but by the First World War, if not earlier, it had a rate of electoral participation greater than that of many other European countries as well as contemporary liberal democracies such as Japan. In all these matters the differences between Russia and its European and North American counterparts appear to be differences of degree, rather than of kind.

This having been said, it seems to me important not to go to the other extreme and minimise the differences – often, as we have seen, considerable ones – that emerge from such comparisons. As late as the First World War, Frederick Barghoorn notes, Russia was still 'a despotic country', with a tradition of autocracy which made it (in Leonard Schapiro's words) 'a society apart in the European community'.[29] It was, for instance, the only country apart from Turkey that required a visa from a European or North American visitor; its treatment of religious minorities, such as the Jews and schismatics, was unusually severe by the admittedly unenlightened standards of the time; and the rule of law had made little headway with either government or citizens. Restrictions upon political activity were also unusually strict. Several European states had legislation on their statute books for dealing with crimes against the state; but none attached so much importance to them, or defined them as widely and loosely, as did Russia. Since 1845, as Richard Pipes points out, with but a short interlude between 1905 and 1917, 'it has been a crime in Russia to seek changes in the existing system of government or administration, or even to raise questions about such issues'. And no other country in the world at this time had two kinds of police, one of them, the Department of Police (successor to the infamous Third Section) to protect the state against its citizens, the other to perform

TABLE 4.3 The development of electoral participation in selected countries (1850–1975) (largest percentage of population taking part in national elections in each decade)

	1850–9	1860–9	1870–9	1880–9	1890–9	1900–9	1910–19	1920–9	1930–9	1940–9	1950–9	1960–9	1970–5
Britain	2	3	5	7	9	10	13	32	46	53	55	52	51
USA	13	14	15	18	19	17	17	26	33	35	37	37	37
Belgium	1	2	2	2	13	21	22	26	28	34	58	56	56
Sweden	0	0	0	1	1	3	10	29	43	48	54	57	62
Netherlands	1	1	2	3	5	9	12	38	45	50	52	53	54
France	10	9	19	20	20	22	21	22	23	48	42	33	46
Norway	1	1	1	3	7	11	22	34	46	50	53	53	55
Denmark	2	2	3	4	5	9	15	38	43	49	50	56	60
Italy	–	1	1	4	4	4	12	18	21	22	58	60	61
Austria	0	0	0	0	1	4	12	51	28	50	62	62	61
Germany	–	–	6	6	7	8	11	36	16	8	55	58	59
Portugal	2	2	2	2	2	2	5	4	5	7	8	6	0
Spain	0	1	5	2	6	8	6	2	14	0	0	0	0
Turkey	0	0	0	0	0	0	0	0	1	15	38	29	27
Russia	0	0	0	0	0	2	26	34	55	56	64	63	63

SOURCES: Tatu Vanhanen, 'Global Trends in Electoral Participation, 1850–1975' (paper presented to the ECPR Florence Workshops, March 1980); Soviet electoral statistics.

ordinary police duties, both of which were under largely nominal administrative, rather than judicial, supervision.[30]

So far as the freedom of the press was concerned, also, Russia lagged seriously behind. By 1890, it has been suggested, the Russian press had reached a stage of development that the French press had reached as early as 1830 and the German and Austrian press had reached by 1848, and most European countries had adopted laws guaranteeing the freedom of the press by the 1860s or 1870s, a generation earlier than the comparable Russian legislation of 1906 after which the press was still treated, in Seton-Watson's words, in a manner that 'would have been considered insufferable in a Western country'.[31] Restrictions upon elections and the activities of political parties were also 'unique in Russia', according to the most careful comparative examination of such matters. The Russian franchise was the most limited of any that existed in a European country; and the electoral law of 1907, which reduced still further the limited franchise granted in 1905, 'lacked a precedent in any country'.[32] The Russian legislation of 1906, which for the first time permitted the formation of associations such as trade unions, was similarly more restrictive than that which existed in any other European country apart from Austria.[33] Despite pressures from the gentry, Western ideas and so forth, as Donald Treadgold has put it, 'the centralised state and the decisive power of the autocrat lasted until a few days before abdication in 1917', and the state remained the arbiter of thought and culture 'in a manner not true of the West'. [34]

These, admittedly, are largely institutional differences, rather than the differences in political belief and behaviour with which, in my view, the student of political culture should be primarily concerned. The distinction, however, may be drawn unduly sharply. Laws, after all, define the areas within which political activity can legitimately take place; a restrictive franchise and limitations on the activities of political parties and the press are bound to limit the diffusion of political experience; and a relatively impotent parliament is not likely to encourage a population to conceive of political change in terms of the formation of political parties, the winning of electoral majorities and so forth. The complex relationship between objective possibilities, political beliefs and behaviour patterns is indeed a central issue in political cultural analysis. Mary McAuley rightly notes the diversity and frequently ambiguous character of popular political values, as I did myself in *Political Culture and Soviet Politics*. The 'naive monarchism' of the peasants, for instance, precluded the possibility of a conflict of interests between the tsar and his people; but if the peasants felt their immediate material aspirations were being frustrated it followed that the tsar's real wishes were not being implemented and that government instructions need not necessarily be obeyed.[35] The legend of the 'Just Tsar' also contained a good deal of retrospective idealisation, and the tsars themselves do not appear to have been above a bit of discreet encouragement to popular perceptions of this kind by demagogic appeals and in other ways.[36]

Popular political beliefs were also, to an extent, the product of the objective situation within which peasants and others happened to find themselves. Peasants' lack of interest in the Duma and its proceedings, for instance, appears to have been at least in part no more than the result of their disillusionment with the decisions that it took on matters that most concerned them. The creation of the Duma in October 1905 seems in fact to have been greeted enthusiastically by the peasants, who assumed that it would lead to the redistribution of the estates. Both the First and Second Dumas, however, failed to agree upon a radical solution to the land question in line with peasants' wishes, and when the revised electoral law of 1907 was introduced, severely restricting the electoral rights they had previous enjoyed, the peasants' response appears to have been to lose all interest in an assembly from which they were unlikely to gain anything of value. As a group of peasants from the Tver province put it, when asked in the autumn of 1908 if the Duma should be retained in its present form, reformed, or abolished, '[We] see no reason . . . [to reform the Duma], for . . . no matter what kind of Duma there is, [we] still won't get the land for nothing.'[37] As Brian Barry pointed out in his critique of Almond and Verba's *The Civic Culture*, a pattern of political beliefs may be the product of the manner in which a political system in fact operates, not necessarily the reason that it operates the way it does.[38]

However, this is a major problem only for those who take a narrow or psychological definition of political culture; for those, like the present author, who prefer a broader or more anthropological definition, the relationship between political opportunities, political beliefs and political behaviour is simply (if one may put it so) an empirical matter to be resolved in the light of the evidence available, with no prior assumptions about causality necessary or even desirable. It must be sufficient for present purposes to note that patterns of political belief in pre-revolutionary Russia do not appear, at least, to have been exclusively the result of the objective opportunities that presented themselves. In the case of the attitudes of peasants towards the State Duma, for instance, their relative indifference and limited opportunities to exercise influence are both well established; but it is not clear that the former was simply the logical consequence of the latter. As Leopold Haimson has argued, it is important not only to consider the political conditions under which peasants took part in elections to the Duma but also 'more enduring features of peasant attitudes and political culture' such as their attitudes to the political process, to the party system and to the concept of representation itself. There were considerable variations in peasant political behaviour between one part of the country and another, for instance, which seem to relate more closely to factors such as religion and nationality than to structural variables such as patterns of land-holding or differences in political opportunities. And more generally, Haimson argues, a good deal of explanatory weight should be attached to the peasants' 'stubborn political particularism' and their limited identification with political parties, even those that they had favoured with their votes.[39]

It is obviously no easy matter to establish the *mentalités collectives* of the past. I am not persuaded by the evidence presented by Mary McAuley, however, that my characterisation of the pre-revolutionary political culture is seriously at fault – although obviously any general characterisation must fail to do justice to a hundred individual nuances and variations. There may, for instance, have been indiscipline and irreligion in the Russian Army during the First World War; but according to the best modern scholarship the level of desertion has been greatly exaggerated, Russian soldiers remained 'overwhelmingly patriotic', and it is a 'complete fabrication to suggest that the army had dissolved [by] 1917'.[40] Nor does it appear that the demands presented to bodies such as the Congresses of Soviets in the last years of the old regime bear 'no traces' of the pattern of political orientations I presented in *Political Culture and Soviet Politics*. Workers' attitudes towards the Duma, for instance, appear to have been by no means free of 'tsarist illusions'.[41] And according to Marc Ferro, who is the only Western historian to have examined the relevant archives, of a hundred petitions which industrial employees submitted to various central authorities in March 1917, scarcely any mentioned socialism; indeed political matters such as the formation of a democratic republic and the early meeting of the Constituent Assembly generally attracted much less attention than a reduction in working hours, an increase in pay and the improvement of sanitary conditions in the workplace. As Ferro suggests, on the whole 'the workers sought to ameliorate their condition, not to transform it'.[42]

Similarly, in the countryside, Ferro found that the peasants were primarily concerned about the land, but that they wanted it to be distributed more equitably rather than converted into public property, and there was a greater bias than there would have been in the West towards the regulation of such matters by the village community as a whole.[43] The peasantry, it appears, still tended to look upwards for guidance and direction, and had a largely local and traditional political horizon. In the words of an instructor from the provincial section of the Moscow Soviet Workers' Deputies, 'The peasantry say frankly that they are waiting for people, like the spring sun, who would explain to them what to do, how to act.' Levels of political sophistication remained low; there appears to have been little ability to think or conceptualise in general terms, and peasant delegates who were sent to the city to discover the true state of affairs, exposed to the political rhetoric of the time, frequently returned home more uncertain and confused than when they had departed.[44] The legend of the 'Just Tsar' appears also to have persisted.[45] Engels may have found this admittedly complex pattern of orientations incredible and bizarre; those who had a closer first-hand acquaintance with it, such as Lenin and Trotsky, did not hesitate to describe it as 'absolutist' and 'semi-Asiatic', and Marx himself could scarcely have been more categorical in his references to the 'bloody mire of Mongolian slavery' that still characterised the Russia of his day.[46]

In the end the evidence probably does not permit a definitive resolution of matters of this kind, which have long been the subject of differing interpretations by scholars and will probably continue to be so for the foreseeable future. Clearly, pre-revolutionary Russian political culture shares a number of similarities with the political cultures of other European states, particularly (and perhaps more than I was willing to recognise in *Political Culture and Soviet Politics*) with the absolutist states of central and Eastern Europe. At the same time, however, on virtually all the variables we have chosen for consideration, Russia was the state farthest towards the authoritarian or collectivist end of the continuum, followed by Turkey, the Iberian states and by Prussia and Austria, while the United Kingdom and the United States, followed by Scandinavia and Western Europe, were consistently farthest towards the other, liberal or individualist, end of the continuum. It seems to me an open question whether cultural values, such as religion or political beliefs, or structural variables, such as social systems or the performances of government, were more responsible for this situation. Of Russia's relative position in these respects there seems, however, to be little doubt, nor do I regard it as entirely a coincidence that it was the states towards the authoritarian or collectivist end of the continuum, Russia included, which largely failed to survive the First World War with their political systems intact and in which a democratic political order was subsequently to prove most vulnerable when challenged by the Nazis or by Communist revolutionaries.

SOVIET POLITICAL CULTURE: HOW MUCH CONTINUITY?

With the issue of continuity and change, as with the issue of the distinctiveness of the pre-revolutionary political culture, an extreme view in either direction has little to recommend it; the only serious question for discussion is whether the emphasis should be placed towards one end or the other of the continuum between these polar opposites. Again, as I understand it, the political culture approach takes an entirely open and empirical attitude towards the connection between past and present, as it does towards the question of the distinctiveness of the pre-revolutionary political culture. It may, for instance, be the case that central features of the pre-revolutionary political culture appear to have persisted into the post-revolutionary period; but equally, it may not. Some studies of the political culture of other Communist states, as I have already noted, have in fact inclined towards the view that change is more important than continuity. Richard Fagen argues that in Cuba, for instance, there has been a largely successful attempt at the 'transformation of Cuban man into revolutionary man', and in some other communist countries, such as China, a number of studies have similarly inclined towards the view that a radical change in political beliefs and behaviour has occurred since the establishment of a Communist regime and particularly since the Great Proletarian Cultural Revolution.[47] As in the Soviet case, these seem to me entirely matters for discussion and empirical examination, not for prior assumptions or pre-determined conclusions.

There is also a danger, related to the kinds of issues discussed in the previous section of this chapter, of examining matters of this kind in a purely retrospective manner, thereby attributing an excessive degree of predictability to what may at the time have been a highly contingent and multifaceted series of events. As we have already noted, there were several points at which developments in pre-revolutionary Russia might have taken a course other than the one they did, and, as Jerry Hough has reminded us, it would be as wrong to regard every aspect of contemporary Soviet politics as wholly determined by the revolution of 1917. Conceivably, for instance, the more pluralistic political system of the 1920s might have become institutionalised, a possibility emphasised by those who stress the democratic features of Lenin's thought and the viability of the alternative presented by figures such as Bukharin;[48] or alternatively a military dictatorship might have come into being, as in so many other Eastern European states in the inter-war period, and we might then be inclined to trace it back to relations between the state and the armed forces in the late tsarist period.[49] Events, as we know, took a different course; but that does not mean that they could have taken no other.

The view that the contemporary political system of the USSR is essentially a product of communist party policies, owing little or nothing to pre-revolutionary antecedents, is found in its most extreme form in the writings of some Soviet émigrés. Vladimir Maximov, for instance, has argued that to see a direct connection between the Soviet and pre-revolutionary periods is to imply that the Russian people are in some sense 'born to be slaves, or, at any rate, born without the guts to oppose repression'. The view that autocracy and repression are 'good enough for the Russians because they know no better' is, he quite rightly points out, 'historically and intellectually untenable'. A large section of the Soviet population, admittedly, lack any experience of democracy – a 'matter of education and historical background, not of any inborn imperfection'. At the same time, he points out, the Russian people 'have protest in their blood – protest at the injustices of human institutions and the inadequacies of the human condition. Men like Solzhenitsyn, Sakharov, Bukovsky and all the other known and unknown representatives of the feelings of our people could not have arisen had it not been for the tensions generated by the Russian people's innate and perennial protest'. Sakharov and Solzhenitsyn, from rather different perspectives, have also taken issue with this view – what might be called the 'Russians know no better' attitude.[50]

As I have already emphasised, any unduly deterministic, still less biological interpretation of Soviet political culture would be histori-cally unfounded as well as insulting, and writers in this school are right to point out that many important features of the contemporary political culture are undoubtly of post-revolutionary origin. The massive political repression that occurred in the Stalin era, for instance, and which has lasted in attenuated form up to the present day, has been on a qualitatively different scale than the repression which occurred at even the worse periods of tsarist reaction.[51] The tsarist censorship, similarly, although undoubtedly among the most severe in the Europe of its time, was far more lenient than the detailed and comprehensive system of censorship that has come into existence under the auspices of *Glavlit*. The range of socialist literature that was permitted by the tsarist censors was very considerable, particularly after the liberalisation of 1905–6; but even before this period they had permitted the publication of works such as the Russian translation of the three volumes of Marx's *Capital*.[52] Travel between Russia and the West was also much less difficult than it has become since the revolution, and, although there were controls upon postal communications, they were nonetheless sufficiently flexible to permit Marx and Engels a series of exchanges with their Russian correspondents that fills a large volume in the standard Soviet edition.[53] In these and other respects it is important to note the changes in the political culture introduced by Soviet rule and particularly by Stalinism, as I noted in *Political Culture and Soviet Politics*.[54] Of what pre-revolutionary period could it have been said, for instance, as Babel' is reported to have done in 1938, 'Today a man talks frankly only with his wife – at night, with the blanket pulled over his head'?[55]

It is possible to take issue with the thesis of continuity from another perspective as well, one which emphasises the changes that have occurred in Soviet political culture since the revolution towards a political culture more in keeping with Marxist–Leninist prescriptions. Soviet scholars, perhaps predictably, have normally taken this view. William Smirnov, for instance, has criticised the tendency of Western scholars to see too great a degree of continuity between Soviet political culture and the political culture of pre-revolutionary Russia, and has suggested the following as the dominant features of the contemporary political culture: increasing homogeneity; the identity of political knowledge and political behaviour; a recognition that the main aim of society is the construction of communism, and that the leading role in that process belongs to the CPSU; a conviction of the superiority of the socio-political system of socialism; internationalism; a predisposition to resolve socio-political tasks in a collective manner; and a high level of psychological and behavioural involvement in politics.[56] David Lane and Felicity O'Dell, among Western scholars, have also been inclined to emphasise the changes that have occurred in Soviet political culture since the revolution, in popular values as well as in those aspects of political behaviour that can be regulated by the authorities, and they have suggested that the Soviet working class – if not all members of the intelligentsia – now represents an 'incorporated' class.[57]

The extent to which popular values have been altered by the efforts of the authorities is a matter on which opinions can legitimately differ.[58] Two important agencies by which the authorities have been attempting to effect changes of this kind, apparently not entirely without effect, should however have received more attention than I was inclined to accord them in *Political Culture and Soviet Politics*. The first of these is new Soviet ritual, or *obryadnost'*, which came into existence soon after the revolution and which appears to have received a renewed degree of emphasis since the 1960s.[59] As present constituted, the system embraces a variety of forms – calendar rituals, life-cycle ceremonies, and festivals of various kinds – with particular forms being developed for particular nationalities, occupational and other groups. The original aim of the system appears to have been to displace religious ceremonies such as baptisms and weddings and to replace them with ceremonies imbued with Communist and secular values, although new ceremonies of this kind now extend to the workplace, induction into the armed forces and other occasions in daily and working life. The evidence so far available on the impact of these ceremonies is limited; it appears, however, that they have secured a widespread degree of acceptance, in part because the individuals concerned have simply taken over and adapted the ceremonies for their own purposes with little regard for the socialising purposes intended by the authorities, and that they have become relatively firmly established in virtually all parts of the USSR with the possible exception of the Central Asian republics.[60]

A more considerable impact upon political values may be produced by service in the armed forces. The Soviet army, as Brezhnev has observed, is a 'special kind of army in that it is a school that fosters feelings of brotherhood, solidarity and mutual respect among all Soviet nations and nationalities'.[61] It is intended by the party to function as the 'school of the nation', welding together a variety of nationalities, social groups and occupations into a unitary force dedicated to Soviet patriotism and the aims of the party at home and abroad, and towards this end an extensive programme of political indoctrination takes place throughout the two years of compulsory military service.[62] Military units are also ethnically mixed so as to guard against the formation of localist political attitudes, the boundaries of military units do not coincide with the boundaries of national–territorial areas, and since Russians predominate within most units their language is naturally the working and social *lingua franca* of the armed forces. National military formations, the (then) Soviet constitution notwithstanding, were abolished in 1938.[63] The impact of these pressures upon the 'functional integration' of servicemen appears to be quite considerable, particularly in the case of Slavs and those from more remote areas, and their influence is reinforced by pre-induction training, by civil defence work and by the activities of auxiliary bodies such as DOSAAF (the All-Union Voluntary Society for Assistance to the Army, Air Force and Navy).[64]

Elements of change in the Soviet political culture, accordingly, are undeniably important. For many scholars, however, they have normally been outweighed by elements of continuity. Poles, for understandable historical reasons, have been among the most eager to demonstrate that the dividing line between civilised Europe and barbaric Asia runs along their eastern rather than their western frontiers. Edward Lipinski, for instance, in an open letter to First Secretary Gierek in 1976, argued that the Soviet road to socialism was not an appropriate one for Poland, conditioned as it was by the 'traditions of Russian state despotism'.[65] Western scholars of Polish origin have been even more forthright. For Richard Pipes, a statist or patrimonial system has existed in Russia, 'whatever the regime and its formal ideology', since at least early medieval times. He sees the origins of contemporary communist behaviour in that country 'primarily in Russian historical experience'; for although Marxism has authoritarian implications, the shape that regimes based upon it assume depends largely upon their indigenous political traditions, which in Europe were mainly liberal but in Russia were largely totalitarian.[66] Zbigniew Brzezinski similarly believe that Soviet politics 'cannot be separated from Russian history', whose dominant feature over the centuries has been its 'predominantly autocratic character'. Brzezinski, indeed, goes so far as to see the October revolution as an act of 'revitalised Restoration', restoring the more vigorously autocratic practices of earlier tsars in place of the feeble indecision of the later Romanovs.[67]

Soviet scholars themselves have not been unimpressed by such arguments. Roy Medvedev, for instance, has pointed out that 'many of the distinctive characteristics of Leninism resulted from the peculiarities of the Russian environment in which the socialist movement began and developed', and that Stalinism, later on, was 'affected by many circumstances and preconditions that were part of

Russian life even before the Revolution'.[68] Boris Shragin, more categorically, has argued that 'despite the phraseology, present-day Russia is no more different from the imperial regime than, let us say, Petrine Russia was from the old Muscovy'. There is, for instance, a 'direct line of oppression from the Tsarist to the Soviet regime', and under both regimes there has been more support for a 'firm authoritarian government which firmly grips everything and everyone' than for basic features of liberal democracy such as civil liberties and a plurality of parties.[69] Established Soviet scholars obviously find it more difficult to argue a thesis of continuity of this kind, or even one of 'national specificity'. Some, however, such as Professor Igor Kon, have publicly accepted that a relatively autocratic historical background, such as Russia's, may place certain constraints upon the development of socialist democracy in the post-revolutionary era,[70] and a number of writers and scholars of neo-nationalist temper have gone still further, arguing, for instance, that Russians' patriotism and devotion to the state has been a constant factor over the centuries, and that particular institutions such as the Red Army have drawn directly upon the traditions as well as structures of their imperial predecessors.[71]

What Zoshchenko has called the 'cast-iron shadow of the past' has also been accorded a good deal of importance in the work of Western scholars, not all of whom are necessarily in sympathy with the political cultural approach.[72] John Armstrong, for example, has written that the outside observer is 'immediately struck by the similarities as well as the differences between the Soviet system and the Czarist regime that prevailed in much the same territory for centuries prior to the establishment of the USSR'.[73] There are striking parallels, he points out, in matters such as the unusually centralised and unrestricted powers of government, the existence of accepted inequalities of rank and status and strong national pride, or even messianism. It is 'generally conceded' that a degree of linkage is involved, Armstrong writes, although it is difficult to establish precisely the manner in which it takes place.[74] Frederick Barghoorn, while similarly aware of contradictory elements and alternative possibilities, has also emphasised that the Soviet system is 'deeply rooted in the Russian and Byzantine past';[75] and many other scholars have taken roughly the same view.[76] Perhaps more surprisingly, a number of Western Marxists or Eurocommunists have also emphasised the extent to which contemporary Soviet politics derives from the Russian historical tradition rather than from communist principles as such, although this may owe something to electoral convenience as well as to dispassion-ate scholarly inquiry.[77]

It has, then, become uncontroversial, even conventional, to stress the continuing importance of Russia's relatively autocratic inheritance upon the evolution of Soviet politics since 1917 – an inheritance by which the Bolsheviks themselves, incidentally, were by no means unaffected. How is this inheritance perpetuated, Mary McAuley wants to know; what are the mechanisms of transmission? Not very different, it seems to me, from the mechanisms by which national identity is transmitted across the generations in a country such as Scotland, where major social institutions such as the church, the legal system and the educational system, as well as a complex of social practices and norms, have combined to preserve a high level of national self-identity despite almost three hundred years' membership of the United Kingdom.[78] In the Soviet case these mechanisms of transmission embrace, first of all, the family, which has retained a degree of autonomy despite several attempts to politicise it; literature, particularly the nineteenth century classics, which preserve a direct link with the values and behaviour patterns of the past; religion; oral tradition and social custom; and art, music and folk culture, of the liveliness of interest in which, primarily as a means of access to the pre-revolutionary past, there is no shortage of recent evidence. Cultural associations such as the All-Union Voluntary Society for the Preservation of Monuments of History and Culture, which has a present membership of more than 12 million, serve to assist and legitimise this interest.[79]

There is a considerable degree of direct institutional continuity, moreover, which must serve, to some extent, as in other countries to structure patterns of political behaviour and to influence popular attitudes and expectations. There are direct continuities in the legal system, for instance, between the peasant courts of the 1860s and the comrades' courts of the Soviet period,[80] between the Russian and the Soviet criminal codes,[81] between tsarist and Soviet anti-parasite laws,[82] as well as in other areas.[83] Similarly, structures of government show a considerable degree of continuity between the pre- and post-revolutionary periods. Practices such as the presentation of mandates (*nakazy*) to elected representatives and the recall of deputies who have lost the confidence of their electors, as well as many of the working procedures of the Supreme Soviet itself, are of pre-revolutionary origin;[84] and in the structure and workings of central government there are striking continuities in such matters as the organisation of ministries, the essentially technical role of ministers and the limited authority of the government as a whole. This was the apparatus which, as Lenin remarked in his *Testament*, we 'took over from tsarism and slightly anointed with Soviet oil'.[85] These continuities – which could be paralleled in other fields[86] – often extended not simply to the institutions themselves but to the personnel employed within them.

Apart from institutional continuities of this kind, as E. H. Carr has pointed out, there are long-term continuities of other kinds which typically tend to re-emerge in the aftermath of great revolutions such as the French and Russian revolutions. Broadly speaking, Carr has argued, 'the greater the distance in time from the initial impact of the revolution, the more decisively does the principle of continuity reassert itself against the principle of change'.[87] There are three main reasons for this. First, environmental influences remain constant: the size and material endowment of the country, the security of its frontiers and so forth. Second, a number of changes are unavoidably associated with the assumption of governmental power by a formerly oppositional political movement, whether this be the early Christians, the French revolutionaries or the Russian Bolsheviks: 'the mere act of transforming revolutionary theory and practice into the theory and practice of government involves a compromise which inevitably breaks old links with the revolutionary past and creates new links with a national tradition of governmental authority'. And third, the assumption of governmental power places upon any group, whatever its political complexion, the necessity of establishing a *modus vivendi* with the states with which it is, at least for the time being, obliged to coexist, leading ultimately to the re-entry of the country concerned into the international community. The parallels between the Russian and the French revolutions in this respect, writes Carr, are 'particularly close'.[88]

As Carr points out, the process of post-revolutionary adjustment in Russia had a dual aspect. In the first place, as in France, it involved the re-emergence of longer-standing institutional structures and practices after a period in which they had been under revolutionary challenge. And in the second case, unlike France, it involved an attempt by the indigenous political tradition to reassert itself against a political doctrine, Marxism, which was of external, Western origin.[89] Seen in this perspective the revolution, particularly after Lenin's death, represented a reversion to a pattern of state-led economic development in order to catch up with the West which had been instituted at least as early as Peter the Great. From that time forward, writes Carr, 'the development of state power in Russia proceeded at a forced pace under the watchword of military necessity'. This pattern of development had three important consequences. In the first place, it produced a 'chronically ambivalent attitude to western Europe which ran through all subsequent Russian thought and policy': the West was a model to be emulated and admired, but at the same time a threat to be feared and held if possible at arm's length. The form that this pattern of development assumed, secondly, was one of 'revolution from above': reforms took place, not through the pressures of social groups or autonomous institutions, but through the exercise of government authority, often precipitated by external crisis. And third, the pattern of development imposed by these conditions was one, 'not of orderly progress, but of spasmodic advance by fits and starts – a pattern not of evolution but of intermittent revolution'. This pattern has continued to mark the course of subsequent Russian history.[90]

The applicability of this description to post-revolutionary Russia should scarcely require emphasis. The stated purpose of the new government, admittedly, was different: the construction of socialism, whether internationally or 'in a single country'. Functionally, however, Stalin represented a return to the tradition of a 'revolution from above', building up the might of the state in a manner not very different from that of the reforming autocrats of the past, and the objective he proclaimed of 'catching up with and overtaking the West' had obvious pre-revolutionary precedents at least as far back as Peter the Great.[91] (The parallel was one that Stalin himself appears to have favoured.)[92] It drew, also, upon the same ambivalent attitude towards the West: a 'combination of intellectual inadequacy and emotional superiority', as Isaiah Berlin has described it, 'a sense of the West as enviably self-restrained, clever, efficient and successful; but also as being cramped, cold, mean, calculating, and fenced in, without capacity for large views or generous emotions, for feeling which must, at times, rise too high and overflow its banks, for heedless self-abandonment in response to some unique historical challenge, and consequently never to know the rich flowering of life'; a combination, on the one hand, of 'intellectual respect, envy, admiration, desire to emulate and excel', and on the other, 'emotional hostility, suspicion, and contempt, a feeling of being clumsy, *de trop*, of being foreigners'.[93]

It is surely not too much to see in these terms, as many have done, the differences between the westernising Mensheviks, inclined to take an orthodox social democratic view of Russia's historical destiny, and the more Slavophil Bolsheviks;[94] or between the cosmopolitan Trotsky and the more prosaic Stalin, less familiar with western Europe but more closely attuned, it appears, to the views of the unsophisticated cadres who were rising through the ranks of the Bolshevik party at this time;[95] or between dissidents such as Sakharov and Solzhenitsyn, the latter much less inclined than the former to place his faith in Western liberal institutions such as a free press and a multi-party system.[96] Nor is it unreasonable to see neo-Slavophil continuities in the reluctance of the contemporary political leadership, no doubt with considerable popular support, to yield to Western pressure over such matters as Afghanistan or the Olympic Games. Pressures of this kind were particularly intense during the Cold War period, as Brezhnev has recalled in his memoirs, and the American government proposed then as now to restrict the export of a number of commodities to the USSR:

> This was not the first and, unfortunately, not the last occasion on which the capitalist powers, setting their hopes on our difficulties, tried to dictate their will to us, to interfere in our internal affairs. The calculation was simple: it will make no difference, they said, the Soviet Union will ask for these machines, this steel plate, the Communists have nowhere to turn to, they will come cap in hand, they will get down on their knees. . . . And what, did we perish? Retreat? Stop our movement? No! The foreign wise men miscalculated in their policy, and it is useful to recall this today inasmuch as it is both instructive and topical.

An attitude of this kind towards foreign pressure, it has rightly been remarked, 'undoubtedly represents a very powerful element in the Soviet political tradition'.[97]

The popular appeal of such attitudes is not easy to determine precisely. In part, at least, they appear to reflect a deeply-held and long-standing popular attitude towards outside influence, as I have just suggested; but in part also they may be the result of an attempt by the political authorities to manipulate political attitudes in order to mobilise the population behind the party's policies of the moment, a point to which I shall return. There is, however, no doubt that, whatever its origins, the establishment of a strong and powerful state, occupying a central place in world politics as well as in sport, science and other fields, is an objective that commands a great deal of popular sympathy, and that many Soviet citizens take a pride in the Soviet system and its achievements whatever their attitude towards Marxism–Leninism as such. Many years ago it was attitudes such as these that encouraged the *smenovekhovtsy* or Change of Landmarks group to reconcile themselves to the Soviet system, though not necessarily to its formal ideology, and to return home to play a part in its further development;[98] and even today, it appears, old White Russian émigrés now living in the West still take some pride in the recently-acquired might of the Soviet Union and the respect it commands at home and abroad. 'It is a wicked system, but it has muscle and [it] is *ours*', as this attitude has been summarised.[99] Even an imprisoned general, in Maximov's *Seven Days of Creation*, is at peace because at least he is in his own country:

> A full general . . . in a lunatic asylum . . . Just look at him – he is contented. Yes, contented! This awful Russian nostalgia! He doesn't mind what he is – slave, or beggar, or homeless dog – as long as it's in his homeland. 'The homeland', as he calls it! The fact that this very same homeland has first disowned him, then made him run the gauntlet of its prison camps from Kolyma to Pot'ma, and finally, as a special favour, graciously permitted him to draw rations in a madhouse until his grave is dug – none of that counts.[100]

The encouragement of hostile attitudes towards real or imaginary foreign enemies has, of course, traditionally been the way in which unpopular autocracies have attempted to retain their power, and there is some evidence that at least a section of the political establishment in the USSR may be prepared to give covert or even open support to more or less Russian nationalist opinion for what may well be the same purpose.[101] Nationalist or more traditional attitudes of this kind, however, do not need to be conjured up by the party authorities; they have a well-established independent existence of their own. It is revealing that Lenin, for instance, despite his firm opposition to anything savouring of a cult of personality, was unable to prevent a process of deification taking place during his lifetime which must clearly have owed something to the personalisation of political authority that existed in the tsarist period;[102] and his preservation in mummified form after his death, a form of obsequies that had obviously little to do with Marxism, has been described as the 'first major accommodation of the ruling ideology to national feeling and tradition'.[103] Nor can the political leadership have sought to promote the legend of Lenin as a 'good tsar' who had been let down by his subordinates and who was still alive, according to persistent rumours, despite the reports of his death, and who would shortly return to deliver the people from their new oppressors.[104]

Examples of this kind make it easier to tease out the authentic and spontaneous from the coerced and prescribed in Soviet political culture, though the exercise (as in other countries which present fewer obstacles to empirical inquiry) is obviously a difficult and probably cannot be a conclusive one. As the collective farm chairman drunkenly ruminates in the latest instalment of Voinovich's Chonkin saga, the two are so closely interconnected as to be virtually indistinguishable:

> Who is responsible for it – the people or the system? Come what may, he cannot get to the truth; on the one hand people seem to mould the system, but on the other the system seems actually to consist of them.[105]

If particular forms of belief or behaviour assert themselves, however, despite the proclaimed and apparently the real objectives of the political authorities at the time (such as the Lenin cult, or religion); or if émigrés and others who have no reason or incentive to see any merit in the Soviet system nonetheless declare themselves in favour of a number of its more important characteristics, then it would seem not unreasonable to conclude that we are dealing for the most part with genuine popular values and aspirations, not simply with opinions that have been prescribed by the political authorities of the day. The same is true if distinctively Soviet patterns of political belief and behaviour continue to manifest themselves at a time when the population concerned has a chance of doing otherwise, such as when they are removed temporarily from Soviet governmental control by circumstances such as foreign occupation. Imperfect though they are, it is perhaps by taking test cases such as these that the political scientist can approach most closely the test tube and laboratory of his natural scientific colleague.

The Second World War (1941–5) is perhaps the most obvious example of a test case for the USSR of the kind I have described above. There is no doubt that nationalist symbols were indeed exploited at this time by Stalin in an attempt to gain popular support, as he had attempted to do earlier in the 1930s. The slogan 'Fatherland War', for instance, was revived in 1941, the same slogan that had been used by Russian nationalists and conservatives to describe the war against Napoleon; Stalin's celebrated speech of 3 July 1941 was addressed to 'brothers and sisters' rather than to fellow proletarians; and he did not scruple to identify the Soviet cause with heroic figures from the Russian past such as Alexander Nevsky, Suvorov and Kutuzov, many of whom had been revered by patriots and conservatives in the pre-revolutionary period.[106] 'We will never rouse the people to war with Marxism–Leninism alone', as Stalin is reported to have remarked at the time.[107] And yet, independent of this fairly transparent attempt to manipulate symbols, there is no doubt, from literature, the observations of contemporaries, diplomatic despatches and other sources, that Hitler's invasion provoked a wave of genuine popular opposition and that feats of heroism were performed which are inexplicable other than in terms of a commitment to maintain the independence and territorial integrity of the state and of the Soviet system. Stalin 'did not rely on terror alone but also on the support of the majority of the people' at this time, as Roy Medvedev has noted; the battle cry '*Za rodinu, za Stalina*' (For the motherland, for Stalin) seems to have become universal more or less spontaneously and quite apart from any efforts by the authorities themselves to promote it.[108]

This, admittedly, appears to have been a response more typical of the Russian than of the non-Russian and particularly the non-Slavic population of the USSR;[109] and it might also be objected that, given Hitler's objectives and the likely fate of any who fell into his hands, there was little real alternative but to resist. The same does not apply, however, to the Russians who defected to the German side and fought against the Soviet government, and it is remarkable that even when in a position and presumably under some incentive to repudiate as much as possible of the Soviet system, defectors still retained an attachment to many of its most distinctive features. George Fischer, for instance, has pointed out that the most extended statement of objectives put out by the Soviet pro-German forces under General Vlasov – the Prague Manifesto – did not in fact disavow the October revolution, although it was bitterly critical of 'Bolsheviks' and the 'Stalin clique'.[110] The Manifesto supported the February revolution, which had established political liberty, but it went on to point out that the Provisional Government had been ineffectual and indecisive in promoting the social and economic reforms that were clearly necessary. The Manifesto called for the overthrow of Stalin's tyranny and for the conclusion of an 'honourable peace' with Germany; it promised national self-determination, the abolition of the collective farms, the release of political prisoners, freedom of conscience, assembly and the press, and the equality of all before the law. Free education, medical care, holidays and old-age security were likewise to be guaranteed by the state to all (as indeed they had been under the Soviet regime).

The rights of private property, however, were to be inviolable only when 'earned by work'; the free choice of land-use granted to the peasants covered co-operative farming as well as individual home-steads; workers were to be guaranteed 'social justice and protection . . . against any kind of exploitation'; and intellectuals were to be provided with the opportunity to create freely, but only if this was 'for the well-being of their people'. There was a strong emphasis upon state planning, and, as Fischer notes, the Manifesto revealed a deep distrust of the Western capitalist democracies, the 'plutocrats of Britain and the USA, whose powers are based on the suppression of other countries and peoples', as well as of any form of socialism, which would 'inevitably' lead to similarities with Stalinism.[111] The Manifesto called instead for the establishment of a 'free people's political system without Bolsheviks and exploiters'; its central article of faith was nationalism, the glorious common destiny of the peoples of Russia when left free to follow their own traditions and aspirations. Although the circumstances were ones in which the movement's differences from Soviet socialism might be expected to have been exaggerated as far as possible, the Manifesto could in fact well serve as a description of central tenets of the Soviet political culture as we have derived them from other sources: collectivist, with a strong emphasis upon national-ism and a powerful state whose extensive powers should be used to promote the welfare of all citizens, hostile to the abuses of power characteristic of Stalinism but also anti-capitalist, and favourable to state control and at least partial ownership of the economy in the interests of the community as a whole.[112]

CONCLUSIONS

The task of the political culturalist, as I understand it, is a relatively modest one. In the case of a Communist state, it should be his task, first of all, to identify the main features of the pre-revolutionary political culture, bearing in mind the biases inherent in the evidence available for such a purpose and also the dangers of reading retrospectively into the past the features one wishes to 'explain' in the present. The treatment of the pre-revolutionary Russian political culture I presented in *Political Culture and Soviet Politics* is, I hope, largely free of this tendency, although I have tried to suggest in this chapter that the distinction between democratic West and autocratic East may perhaps have been drawn unduly sharply, particularly when the central European states are brought more fully into consideration. The second task, as I understand it, is to identify the main features of the contemporary political culture, a task which is again not without its difficulties in a Communist state (as indeed elsewhere) but which may be tackled in a not entirely unsatisfactory way by the employment of the wide variety of sources that can be drawn upon for this purpose. These two tasks, as I see them, are largely if not entirely descriptive in character, and no assumptions need or should be made of a causal or explanatory character at this stage of the analysis.

The third and more difficult task is to compare the pre-revolutionary and contemporary political cultures to see to what extent, if at all, the former appears to have made a continuing contribution to the latter. This contribution may appear to be substantial; or, as some have argued in respect of China and Cuba, it may appear to be relatively unimportant. My own conclusion, in respect of the USSR, is that the element of continuity is very important, perhaps, as I have tried to indicate in this paper, even more considerable in some respects than I originally suggested in *Political Culture and Soviet Politics*; but there is, of course, no one-to-one relationship between past and present and elements of discontinuity, such as political repression and the treatment of organised religion, can by no means be neglected. This conclusion is, I believe, largely supported by what I have described in this chapter as test cases: occasions, that is to say, when beliefs or behaviour patterns have conformed to longer-standing cultural traditions despite the efforts of the authorities to change them, or when émigrés, with no reason to identify with any aspect of the Soviet system, nonetheless continue to support a number of its most distinctive features, or when an explicitly anti-Soviet military movement, with every opportunity and incentive to denounce the very basis of the Soviet system, nonetheless proposes to replace it with a system which would be fairly similar in all but its removal of the 'Stalin clique' and arbitrary repression. The fourth task, not considered in this paper, is to examine the extent to which the political culture, however defined, is likely to influence future patterns of political development and change.

It is difficult to see how one might 'prove' the importance of continuity in this connection without the ability to conduct laboratory experiments in the manner of the natural scientist. John Armstrong, who is generally persuaded of the merits of a political culture approach, believes it is simply 'impossible' to establish linkages of this kind empirically;[113] and it has to be said that no very great success has yet been achieved in attempting to resolve such matters at a more general level – to establish the causal primacy of 'determinacy' or 'choice', as Gabriel Almond has put it.[114] Historians, in much the same way, have been little more successful in resolving the issue of the relationship between religion and the rise of capitalism originally posited by Weber.[115] It may, however, be possible to move at least part of the way towards an explanation, as I have tried to suggest in this chapter, by considering situations in which a particular variable, such as Soviet governmental control, is removed from the situation, or in which a particular variable, such as a political system of the Communist type, is held constant, allowing differences between one Communist state and another or between one Soviet republic and another to be attributed to factors such as their respective political cultures which differentiate them.[116] Problems of this kind are not unique to the study of the Communist states, but this has not prevented comparativists in other areas from according causal primacy to cultural factors in explaining matters such as the existence of democracy, differences in the policy process between one country and another and comparative levels of economic performance.[117] Just like political scientists in other areas, I believe, students of Communist politics need to 'take the historical cure' and be prepared to accord a degree of causal weight to factors, such as political culture, which relate to the distinctive attributes of the states they study as well as to the institutional and other features they share in common.

NOTES AND REFERENCES

1. Stephen White, *Political Culture and Soviet Politics* (London and New York, 1979).
2. I have not attempted in this chapter to deal directly with all the points raised by Mary McAuley in her contribution to this book, partly because, as in her remarks on the 'official' political culture, they fall outside the scope of the discussions of political culture both in my book and in the volume edited by Brown and Gray (eds) *Political Culture and Political Change in Communist States*, which were explicitly concerned with political culture at the mass rather than élite level; partly because – as for instance on the differentiation of political values by social group – we do not, in my view, have sufficient evidence to proceed very much farther than the discussions presented in those volumes; and partly also because her paper is considered separately by John Miller in Chapter 3. Where her arguments are directly relevant to the issues treated in this chapter, however, I have tried to give them due consideration.
3. Lucian Pye, 'Culture and Political Science: Problems in the Revaluation of the Concept of Political Culture', in Louis Schneider and Charles M.

Bonjean (eds) *The Idea of Culture in the Social Sciences* (Cambridge, 1973) p. 68.

4. Robert C. Tucker, 'Culture, Political Culture, and Communist Society', *Political Science Quarterly*, vol. 88, no. 2 (June 1973) pp. 173–90 (Tucker argues more generally, however, for a 'cultural approach to politics': ibid, p. 181).

5. Clifford Geertz, *The Interpretation of Culture* (London, 1975). A distinction similar to that proposed here is suggested in David J. Elkins and Richard E. B. Simeon, 'A cause in search of its effect, or what does political culture explain?', *Comparative Politics*, vol. 11 no. 2 (January 1979) pp. 127-45, esp. p. 131.

6. Archie Brown and Jack Gray (eds) *Political Culture and Political Change in Communist States* (London, 1977; 2nd edn, 1979 [subsequent references are to this edition]).

7. Lucian W. Pye and Sidney Verba (eds) *Political Culture and Political Development* (Princeton, New Jersey, 1965).

8. Richard R. Fagen, *The Transformation of Political Culture in Cuba* (Stanford, 1969); Maurice Zeitlin, *Revolutionary Politics and the Cuban Working Class,* rev. edn (New York, 1970).

9. Brown and Gray, *Political Culture and Political Change*, pp. xii–xiv and elsewhere; White, *Political Culture,* pp. x–xi.

10. Some recent references are noted by Archie Brown in *Problems of Communism*, vol. 28, nos. 5–6 (September–December 1979) pp. 106–7, note 16; see also L. N. Kogan, 'Politicheskaya kul'tura sotsializma', *Nauchnyy kommunizm*, 1979, no. 5, pp. 56–63; Yu. Tikhomirov, 'Politicheskaya kul'tura v obshchestve zrelogo sotsializma', *Politicheskoe samoobrazovanie*, 1978, no. 7, pp. 28–36; the references in note 56 below; and a Soviet application of the concept to China, L. A. Bereznyi, 'Teoriya "politicheskoy kul'tury" i nekotorye voprosy izucheniya Kitaya', *Narody Afriki i Azii*, 1978, no. 4, pp. 59–72. Earlier usages are noted in White, *Political Culture*, p. 192, note 3.

11. Marc Szeftel, *The Russian Constitution of April 23, 1906. Political Institutions of the Duma Monarchy* (Brussels, 1976) chs. 5 and 6, examines this issue thoroughly.

12. White, *Political Culture*, p. 34 and chs. 2 and 3, *passim*.

13. Ibid, pp. 22–4; and White, 'The USSR: Patterns of Autocracy and Industrialism' in Brown and Gray (eds) *Political Culture and Political Change*, p. 25.

14. A. I. Gertsen, *Sobranie sochinenii v tridtsati tomakh*, vol. 7 (Moscow, 1956) p. 161; similarly vol. 12 (Moscow, 1957) p. 171. The extent to which the political development of Lithuania presented an alternative model is considered in Richard Pipes, *Russia under the Old Regime* (Harmondsworth, 1977) pp. 38–40.

15. William G. Rosenberg, 'The Russian Municipal Duma Elections of 1917: A Preliminary Computation of Returns', *Soviet Studies*, vol. 21, no. 2 (October 1969) pp. 131–63, at p. 163; John L. H. Keep, *The Russian Revolution. A Study in Mass Mobilization* (London, 1976) p. 324.

16 .White, *Political Culture*, p. 64.

17. For instance Alexander I. Solzhenitsyn, *The Mortal Danger* (London 1980) chs 2–4.

18. Paul Dukes, *October and the World: Perspectives on the Russian Revolution* (London, 1979) pp. 6–12. I am grateful to Paul Dukes for some helpful bibliographical advice on this section of the paper.

19. Ibid, pp. 28–30, 54–5, 74; and chs 1–3 *passim*.

20. Rene David and John E. C. Brierley, *Major Legal Systems in the World Today*, 2nd edn (London, 1978) p. 25 and more generally pp. 21–9.

21. Ibid, pp. 93 and 151.

22. Ibid, pp. 143–4 and 200; Henry W. Ehrmann, *Comparative Legal Cultures* (Englewood Cliffs, New Jersey, 1976) pp. 126–30.

23. John A. Armstrong, *The European Administrative Elite* (Princeton, New Jersey 1973) ch. 1 and p. 276.

24. Dukes, *October and the World*, pp. 50–2. The Table of Ranks is reprinted, with introductory comments, in Paul Dukes (ed.) *Russia under Catherine the Great, vol. 1: Select Documents on Government and Society* (Newtonville, Mass., 1978) pp. 4–14.

25. Marc Raeff, 'The Enlightenment in Russia and Russian Thought in the Enlightenment', in J. G. Garrard (ed.) *The Eighteenth Century in Russia* (Oxford, 1973) p. 31.

26. Dukes, *October and the World*, pp. 58–9. Theodore von Laue, *Sergei Witte and the Industrialization of Russia* (New York, 1963) notes Witte's debt to Bismarck (p. 62 and elsewhere).

27. Dieter Nohlen, *Wahlsysteme der Welt* (Munich, 1978) p. 37. There is a helpful general discussion of these matters in F. H. Hinsley (ed.) *The New Cambridge Modern History, vol. XI: Material Progress and World-Wide Problems 1870–1898* (Cambridge, 1962) pp. 25–32 and 254–62.

28 Of all the other countries in the world, only in Australia, New Zealand and Canada were comparable levels of electoral participation recorded. Tatu Vanhanen, 'Global Trends in Electoral Participation, 1850–1975' (paper presented to the ECPR Florence Joint Workshops, 1980) pp. 6–10.

29. Frederick C. Barghoorn, *Soviet Russian Nationalism* (New York, 1956) pp. 160–1; Leonard Schapiro, *Rationalism and Nationalism in Russian Nineteenth-Century Political Thought* (New Haven and London, 1967) pp. 8–9.

30. Pipes, *Russia under the Old Regime,* pp. 293–4 and 300–2.

31. Eugene N. and Pauline R. Anderson, *Political Institutions and Social Change in Continental Europe in the Nineteenth Century* (Berkeley and Los Angeles, 1967) pp. 251 and 269–70; Hugh Seton-Watson, *The Russian Empire 1801—1917* (Oxford, 1967) p. 629.

32. Anderson, *Political Institutions and Social Change*, pp. 304, 319 and 335.

33. Ibid, pp. 382 and 280.

34. Donald W. Treadgold, *The West in Russia and China. vol. 1: Russia, 1472–1917* (Cambridge, 1973) p. 250.

35 .White, *Political Culture*, p. 61. The peasants' economic individualism

and other aspects of their 'implicitly conflicting beliefs' are considered at pp. 60–1 and elsewhere.

36. Maureen Perrie, 'The Popular Image of Ivan the Terrible', *Slavonic and East European Review*, vol. 56, no. 3 (April 1978) pp. 275–86.

37. Leopold H. Haimson (ed.) *The Politics of Rural Russia 1905–1914* (Bloomington and London, 1979) pp. 225–7; the quotation is at p. 227.

38. Brian Barry, *Sociologists, Economists and Democracy* (London 1970) pp. 48–52.

39. Haimson, *Politics of Rural Russia*, pp. 280–6 and 288–91.

40. Marc Ferro, *October 1917* (London, 1980) p. 84; Allan K. Wildman, *The End of the Russian Imperial Army* (Princeton, New Jersey 1980) p. 364; Norman Stone, *The Eastern Front 1914–1917* (London, 1975) p. 300 (from which the quotations are derived).

41. P. E. Lyubarov and A. S. Rud', 'Proletariat i Gosudarstvennaya Duma', in L. M. Ivanov (ot. red.) *Rossiyskiy proletariat: oblik, bor'ba, gegemoniya* (Moscow, 1970) pp. 186–7, 192–3 and 202.

42. Marc Ferro, *The Russian Revolution of February 1917* (London, 1972) pp. 115 and 121.

43. Ferro, *The Russian Revolution of February 1917*, pp. 123, 125 and 129.

44. Graeme J. Gill, *Peasants and Government in the Russian Revolution* (London, 1979) pp. 30–1; the quotation is at p. 31.

45. A. I. Nil've, 'Prigovory i nakazy krest'yan vo II Gosudarstvennuyu Duma', *Istoriya SSSR*, 1975, no. 5, pp. 99–110, esp. pp. 99–100 and 108–10.

46. Lenin's remarks are quoted in Robert C. Tucker, *Stalin as Revolutionary, 1879–1929* (New York, 1973) p. 22; Marx's description is quoted in G. R. Urban (ed.) *Communist Reformation* (London, 1979) p. 324.

47. Fagen, *Transformation*, p. 2 and elsewhere; on China, see for example M. A. Macchiocchi, *Daily Life in Revolutionary China* (London, 1972) and Jean Daubier, *A History of the Chinese Cultural Revolution* (New York, 1974).

48. See, for instance, Moshe Lewin, *Lenin's Last Struggle* (London, 1969) and Stephen F. Cohen, *Bukharin and the Bolshevik Revolution* (rev. ed.) (Oxford 1980).

49. Jerry F. Hough and Merle Fainsod, *How the Soviet Union is Governed* (Cambridge, Mass., 1979) pp. 4–5.

50. Quoted from his interview with G. R. Urban in *Communist Reformation*, pp. 253–5. On Sakharov, see his *My Country and the World* (London, 1975) pp. 90–1; on Solzhenitsyn, see note 17.

51. Alexander I. Solzhenitsyn, *The Gulag Archipelago*, vol. 1 (London, 1974) chs. 8, 11 and 12.

52. S. G. Pushkarev, 'Russia and the West: Ideology and Personal Contacts before 1917', *Russian Review*, vol. 24, no. 2 (April 1965), pp. 138–64, at pp. 153–4.

53. Ibid, pp. 156–9; *K. Marks, F. Engel's i revolyutsionnaya Rossiya* (Moscow, 1967).

54. White, *Political Culture*, pp. 108–11 and elsewhere.

55. Ilya Ehrenburg, *Eve of War 1933–1941* (London, 1963) p. 195.

56. V. V. Smirnov, ' "Kruglyy stol" po problemam politicheskoy kul'tury', in D. A. Kerimov (ed.) *Politicheskie otnosheniya: prognozirovanie i planirovanie* (Moscow, 1979) pp. 125–33; similarly William Smirnov, 'Political Culture as a Factor of Progress', in V. Semenov *et al.* (eds) *Political Theory and Political Practice* (Moscow, 1979) pp. 199–206.

57. David Lane and Felicity O'Dell, *The Soviet Industrial Worker* (Oxford, 1978).

58. I have attempted to give this issue more detailed consideration in Stephen White, 'The Effectiveness of Political Propaganda in the USSR', *Soviet Studies*, vol. 32, no. 3 (July 1980) pp. 323–48.

59. In what follows I have relied mainly on Christopher A. P. Binns, 'The Changing Face of Power: Revolution and Accommodation in the Development of the Soviet Ceremonial System', *Man*, vol. 14 (December 1979) pp. 585–606, and vol. 15 (March 1980) pp. 170–87; and also Christel Lane, 'Ritual and Ceremony in Contemporary Soviet Society', *Sociological Review*, vol. 27, no. 2 (May 1979) pp. 253–78.

60. Binns, 'Changing Face', pp. 183–4; Lane, 'Ritual and Ceremony', p. 270.

61. Quoted in Teresa Rakowska-Harmstone, 'The Soviet Army as the Instrument of National Integration', in John Erickson and E. J. Feuchtwanger (eds) *Soviet Military Power and Performance* (London, 1979) pp. 129–54, at p. 136.

62. Herbert Goldhammer, *The Soviet Soldier* (London and New York, 1975) ch. 7; and *Sovetskaya Armiya — shkola ideyno-nravstvennogo vospitaniya molodezhi* (Moscow, 1979) pp. 19–20, 31–42 and 73.

63. Rakowska-Harmstone, 'The Soviet Army', p. 134.

64. Ibid, pp. 148–9; Goldhagen, *The Soviet Soldier*, pp. 39–88.

65. Quoted in Rudolf L. Tökés (ed) *Opposition in Eastern Europe* (London, 1979) p. 97.

66. *Russian Review*, vol. 38, no. 2 (April 1979) pp. 184, 192 and 195.

67. Zbigniew K. Brzezinski, 'Soviet Politics: From the Future to the Past?', in Paul Cocks *et al* (eds) *The Dynamics of Soviet Politics* (Cambridge Mass., and London, 1976) pp. 337–51, at pp. 337 and 340.

68. Roy A. Medvedev, *On Stalin and Stalinism* (Oxford, 1979) pp. 184–5.

69. Boris Shragin, *The Challenge of the Spirit* (New York, 1978) pp. 132, 70 and 110.

70. Igor Kon, *Sotsiologiya lichnosti* (Moscow, 1967) pp. 322–3.

71. F. Nesterov, *Svyaz' vremen. Opyt istoricheskoy publitsistiki* (Moscow, 1980) as quoted in the *Current Digest of the Soviet Press*, vol. 33, no. 14 (6 May 1981) pp. 5–6.

72. Mikhail M. Zoshchenko, *Nervous People and Other Satires* (London, 1963) p. 368.

73. John A. Armstrong, *Ideology, Politics and Government in the Soviet Union,* 4th edn (New York, 1978) p. 6 (Armstrong is in fact generally favourable to a political culture approach: see p. vi).

74. Ibid, pp. 6–10 and ch. 1 more generally.

75. Frederick C. Barghoorn, *Politics in the USSR*, 2nd edn (Boston, 1972) p. 18.

76. For instance Hugh Seton-Watson in Urban (ed.) *Communist Reformation*, pp. 322 and 326; Tibor Szamuely, *The Russian Tradition* (London, 1975); Robert Conquest, *Them and Us* (London, 1980).

77. See for instance Santiago Carrillo, '*Eurocommunism' and the State* (London, 1977) p. 163; Jean Ellenstein in G. R. Urban (ed.) *Eurocommunism* (London, 1978) pp. 77–8 and 81.

78. James G. Kellas, *The Scottish Political System*, 2nd edn (Cambridge, 1975) p. 2 and ch. 7.

79. Jack V. Haney, 'The Revival of Interest in the Russian Past in the Soviet Union', *Slavic Review*, vol. 32, no. 1 (March 1973) pp. 1–16, provides a useful survey. On related developments in literature, particularly the *derevenshchiki*, see Geoffrey Hosking, *Beyond Socialist Realism* (London, 1980) esp. ch. 3.

80. Peter H. Juviler, *Revolutionary Law and Order* (New York, 1976) p. 7.

81. N. S. Timasheff, 'The Impact of the Penal Law of Imperial Russia on Soviet Penal Law', *American Slavic and East European Review*, vol. 12, no. 4 (December 1953) pp. 441–63.

82. R. Beerman, 'Soviet and Russian Anti-parasite Laws', *Soviet Studies*, vol. 15, no. 4 (April 1964) pp. 420–9.

83. For a good general survey, see Harold J. Berman, *Justice in the USSR*, revised edn (Cambridge, Mass., 1963) chs. 5–9.

84. Theodore H. Friedgut, *Political Participation in the USSR* (Princeton, New Jersey, 1979) pp. 103 and 132.

85. G. P. van den Berg, 'Elements of Continuity in Soviet Constitutional Law', in William E. Butler (ed.) *Russian Law: Historial and Political Perspectives* (Leyden, 1977) pp. 215–34. See also T. H. Rigby, *Lenin's Government* (Cambridge, 1979) ch. 15; 'Some historical reflections', in Walter McK. Pintner and Don Karl Rowney (eds) *Russian Officialdom* (London, 1980) which emphasises the 'fundamental continuity' of official institutions (p. 16 and elsewhere).

86. Some continuities in agrarian institutions, for instance, are noted in R. W. Davies, *The Socialist Offensive* (London, 1980) p. 341, and in the same author's *The Soviet Collective Farm, 1929–1930* (London, 1980) ch. 4.

87. E. H. Carr, 'The Legacy of History', in *Socialism in One Country 1924–1926*, vol. 1 (London, 1964) ch. 1, at p. 4. This masterly chapter defies adequate summarisation.

88. Ibid, pp. 5–6.

89. Ibid, p. 8.

90. Ibid, pp. 7–11.

91. Ibid, p. 20.

92. Tucker, *Stalin as Revolutionary*, p. 312 (his close interest in Eisenstein's film 'Ivan the Terrible' is also well known).

93. Isaiah Berlin, *Russian Thinkers* (Harmondsworth, 1979) p. 181.

94. Carr, 'The Legacy of History', pp. 16–22.

95. See for instance Medvedev, *On Stalin and Stalinism*, pp. 46–53 and 167; Hough and Fainsod, *How the Soviet Union is Governed*, p. 114; Svetlana Alliluyeva, *Only One Year* (London, 1969) pp. 355–6 and 369. On the

'Brezhnev generation' more generally, see Sheila Fitzpatrick, *Education and Social Mobility in the Soviet Union 1921–1934* (Cambridge, 1979).

96. Alexander I. Solzhenitsyn *et al*., *From Under the Rubble* (London, 1976) pp. 19–23; 'Solzhenitsyn and Russian Nationalism. An Interview with Andrei Sinyavsky', *New York Review of Books*, vol. 26 no. 18 (22 November 1979) pp. 3–6.

97. David Holloway, 'Decision-making in Soviet Defence Policies', in Christopher Bertram (ed.) *The Prospects of Soviet Power in the 1980s* (London, 1980) p. 90. (the quotation is from Brezhnev's *Vozrozhdenie* in his *Leninskim kursom*, vol. 7 (Moscow, 1979) p. 62).

98. Max Hayward and Leopold Labedz (eds) *Literature and Revolution in Soviet Russia 1917–62* (London, 1963) pp. 23–4.

99. Urban, *Communist Reformation*, p. 265.

100. Quoted in ibid, pp. 254–5.

101. Dmitry Pospielovsky, 'A Comparative Inquiry into Neo-Slavophilism and its Antecedents in the Russian History of Ideas', *Soviet Studies*, vol. 31, no. 3 (July 1979) pp. 319–42, at pp. 300–1.

102. Tucker, *Stalin as Revolutionary*, pp. 279–88; Binns, 'Changing Face', pp. 598–9.

103. Binns, 'Changing Face', p. 600.

104. Paul Avrich, *Russian Rebels* (London, 1973) pp. 272–3.

105. Quoted in *Irish Slavonic Studies*, no. 1 (1980) p. 122.

106. Barghoorn, *Soviet Russian Nationalism*, pp. 13 and 39–40.

107. Medvedev, *On Stalin and Stalinism*, p. 124.

108. Ibid, p. 161; Alexander Werth, *Russia at War* (London, 1964) pp. 132, 144–5, 149, 591 and elsewhere.

109. Werth, *Russia at War*, pp. 200, 203 and 573–81.

110. George Fischer, *Soviet Opposition to Stalin. A Case Study in World War II* (Cambridge, Mass., 1952) p. 88.

111. Ibid, pp. 89 and 197; the Manifesto is reprinted in full in ibid, pp. 194–200.

112. Ibid, pp. 194–200. For what it is worth, a study of the only remotely comparable crisis in recent Soviet history, the death of Stalin in 1953, reveals no tendency to reject basic features of the system but rather a fear of the disorder that the absence of a strong authority might entail (see for instance Yevgeny Yevtushenko, *A Precocious Autobiography* (London, 1963) pp. 89–92; Hedrick Smith, *The Russians* (London, 1977) p. 305; Nadezhda Mandelstam, *Hope against Hope* (London, 1971) p. 313).

113. Armstrong, *Ideology, Politics and Government in the Soviet Union*, p. 6.

114. Gabriel A. Almond *et al*., *Crisis, Choice and Change. Historical Studies of Political Development* (Boston, 1973) ch. 1.

115. See, for a recent discussion, Gordon Marshall, *In Search of the Spirit of Capitalism. Max Weber and the Protestant Ethic Thesis* (London, 1981).

116. This point is argued by Archie Brown in Brown and Gray, *Political Culture and Political Change*, pp. 13–14.

117. See respectively Deane A. Neubauer, 'Some Conditions of Democracy', *American Political Science Review*, vol. 61, no. 4 (December 1967) pp. 1002–9; Anthony King, 'Ideas, Institutions and the Policies of Govern-

ments: A Comparative Analysis', *British Journal of Political Science*, vol. 3, nos. 3 and 4 (July and October 1973) pp. 291–313 and 409–23; and Stanislaw Gomulka in Wilfred Beckerman (ed) *Slow Growth in Britain* (London, 1979).

5 Soviet Political Culture through Soviet Eyes

ARCHIE BROWN

My main, though not sole, purpose in this chapter is to show how the concept of political culture has been embraced in writing on Soviet politics within the USSR itself and to discuss briefly the content of that body of work. Though some Soviet writers more than others emphasise the importance of the Soviet Union's historical inheritance from Tsarist Russia, the main stress in their publications is on the newness of Soviet political culture and on the creation of Socialist Man.

Much of this writing is concerned with the conscious official political socialisation effort undertaken by the Soviet authorities in the attempt to create a new Soviet person, but people's fundamental political beliefs and values, political expectations and political knowledge, and hopes and fears are a product of personal experience which cannot be wholly controlled, foreseen or planned by political leaderships. Some experiences make a much more profound impact on popular consciousness than others – the 'salient crises' which, in Sidney Verba's words, 'are most likely to form a people's political memory'.[1] Verba stresses, as does Stephen White in the previous chapter of this book, the importance of looking beyond the direct political experience of the individual and considering 'the political memories passed from generation to generation'.[2]

To accept this is not, however, to disagree with Mary McAuley when (in Chapter 2) she rightly implies that there would be something very odd about any suggestion that the history through which people live will have a less profound effect on their consciousness than will the legacy of the more distant past. In the Soviet case there are *prima facie* grounds for assuming that the Stalin era and the Second World War have made an especially powerful imprint on the popular consciousness.[3] The paradox, whereby Stalin is held in high esteem by millions of Soviet citizens today – even though he was, directly or indirectly, responsible for the deaths of as many of his fellow-countrymen as was Hitler – is not one which can be resolved in a few sentences.[4] But part of the explanation is to be found in the association still present in many people's minds between Stalin and victory over the Nazi invader during the Second World War.

Though opinion in the Soviet Union remains divided on Stalin, and though there is considerable ignorance concerning the realities of the Stalin period among young people, of the fact that Stalin still enjoys substantial popularity there is no doubt. As the former Soviet sociologist, Victor Zaslavsky, has noted:

> a very large number of Soviet workers have a very positive opinion of Stalin and his record. This is not only common knowledge but is also confirmed by the enormous success of pro-Stalin literary and cinematographic works, as well as by some unpublished surveys by Soviet sociologists.[5]

Even among the most recent wave of Soviet emigrants (the majority of them Jewish) Stalin's contribution to the Soviet Union was more highly rated than that of either Khrushchev or Brezhnev. In a survey of 1161 emigrants, conducted by Zvi Gitelman while Brezhnev was still alive, the respondents were asked: 'Which of the following do you think did the most for the Soviet state? Brezhnev, Khrushchev, Stalin, Lenin.' Though an unusually large proportion of respondents (33.9 per cent) offered no answer to this particular question (perhaps because of an unwillingness to say a good word for any of them), Stalin (with 17.8 per cent) came second only to Lenin (22.7 per cent) in the scale of positive evaluation. (Khrushchev received 14.6 per cent support and Brezhnev 11 per cent.)[6]

If more than one in six of a group of disenchanted former Soviet citizens can evaluate Stalin more positively than either of his two successors, we should not be surprised if Stalin is held in high esteem by an actual majority of those still living in the Soviet Union today – certainly a majority of Georgians, probably a majority of Russians. It is notoriously difficult to determine the appropriate weight to be attached to those elements of Stalin's rule which strengthened and reinforced traditional Russian attitudes to holders of supreme power and those elements which were new. Though the scale of the repression far exceeded anything to be found in late Imperial Russia, that fact alone did not lead all those who lived through the Stalin era to condemn it. It is not only that one family's tragedy meant another family's opportunity, but also that upward social mobility did not, of course, depend upon dead men's shoes alone. It rested upon the spread of literacy, the rapidity of industrialisation and the enormous growth in the number of non-manual and supervisory jobs.

Notwithstanding the beginnings made to an exposure of Stalinism during Khrushchev's years in power, we are left with the fact that, as Zaslavsky puts it, 'many workers and peasants have an image of Stalin as a disciplined yet kind leader who sought, sometimes with cruel means, to create an egalitarian and just society, even though his will may have often been distorted by his collaborators'. Zaslavsky adds: 'It is not difficult to recognise in this attitude a residue of the faith in the "good tsar" – the cornerstone of the Russian peasant's traditional political culture'.[7] Yet, while not discounting this factor, Zaslavsky wishes to attach greater weight to the social changes for which Stalin is perceived as having been responsible. He quotes a striking passage from Aleksandr Zinoviev (now best known for his political satire, but formerly a Professor of Logic in Moscow University) who writes:

Why did my mother keep Stalin's portrait? She was a simple peasant woman. Before collectivization our family lived fairly well, but at what price! Back-breaking work from dawn to dusk. And what was the future of the children (there were eleven in the family)? To become peasants or, at best, tradesmen. Then collectivization came; villages were ruined, plundered, and many escaped to town. And what happened as a result? In my family one son became a university professor; another a manager of a factory; yet another a colonel; and three others became engineers. Something like this happened to millions of families. I do not want to pass value judgments, to claim that it was good or bad. I only want to say that at the time, an advancement unparalleled in human history took place in the country, an advancement which promoted many millions from the lowest of social classes to the status of industrial worker, engineer, teacher, doctor, artist, officer, writer, scientist, etc. Perhaps it could have happened without Stalinism, but that is irrelevant. The protagonists of the process knew that it did happen under Stalin and, so it seemed, because of him.[8]

Of all the cataclysmic events of the Stalin era, it is virtually certain that nothing left as deep an imprint on the consciousness of Soviet citizens as the Second World War. The issue of Stalin and Stalinism is a divisive one, and that is one among many reasons why it has not been squarely faced by the Soviet authorities (especially since the fall of Khrushchev). The appalling human and material cost of the Second World War is another matter. The sufferings of Soviet people at the hands of a ruthless external enemy – suffering which embraced all social groups much more evenly than did Stalin's purges which disproportionately affected the intelligentsia, officialdom and the peasantry, as compared with manual workers – and pride in the eventual victory (at a cost of twenty million Soviet dead) are perhaps the 'political memories' which are the most important of all in the USSR today in terms both of the depth of the feeling behind them and of the extent to which they unite party and non-party members, masses and élite, and the various social groups. There is a constant reinforcement of such feelings in the 'official political culture'. It is not surprising that party leaders and propagandists lay such constant stress on the 'Great Patriotic War' in their conscious political socialisation efforts, since there is no other shared experience with which they can so instantly achieve a rapport with their listeners or readers.[9]

Quite deliberate use is made of 'tradition' and ritual in the effort to attain a unified political culture. There are constant demands from Soviet authors professionally concerned with 'the invention of tradition'[10] for still greater use to be made of the Second World War as a source of ritual and ceremonies.[11] The genuinely deep feelings evoked by the war are used, as Christel Lane has put it, to blur 'distinctions between various kinds of loyalties'.[12] An effort is made to link love of the motherland with loyalty to the particular power structure represented by the Soviet system.

The Soviet sources for a detailed study of political culture are numerous and include sociological, social psychological and ethnographic studies published in the USSR, writing on the creation of the New Man and on the effectiveness of propaganda, as well as the insights which may be obtained from creative literature. Some of these sources have been extensively used by Stephen White, but no more than passing attention has been paid hitherto in the West to the Soviet literature which explicitly makes use of the concept of political culture. It must be observed that a substantial part of this writing contains little in the way of new empirical research, but the extent to which the term, 'political culture', has caught on and the use which is made of the concept are themselves matters of interest to the Western student of Communist political cultures.

It is worth noting that the Russian language and Soviet convention have long made greater play with the notion of 'culture' than is common in English-speaking countries. References to people as 'cultured' or 'uncultured' (and criticism of ill-mannered or mildly deviant behaviour as 'uncultured') crop up frequently in the conversation of Russians. It is, therefore, not altogether surprising that once the term 'political culture' had been introduced by Soviet social scientists, it should spread relatively quickly and be taken up also by Soviet politicians and propagandists. There is nothing alien about the sound of the concept and, indeed, as noted in Chapter 1, Soviet authors can (and frequently do) justify its use by recalling that the term 'political culture' was used by Lenin.[13]

One of the earliest uses of the concept of political culture in Soviet academic literature would appear to be by Valeriy Kalensky in his well-informed critique of American political science published in 1969.[14] In a more influential book published in 1970, *Lenin, gosudarstvo, politika*, Fedor Burlatsky writes of the concept 'political culture' gaining 'an increasing recognition in our literature'[15] and his own advocacy of the usefulness of the notion helped to bring it to the attention of broader circles than that of Soviet scholars familiar with the works of Western political science.[16]

Before further attention is paid to the use of the concept by Soviet scholars, it is worth noting how quickly the term 'political culture' entered official Soviet political discourse. As early as June 1974, Leonid Brezhnev used it and naturally the example of the top party leader was soon followed by party propagandists. In that speech to the electors of the Bauman district of Moscow, Brezhnev said:

> The broadening of participation of working people in the running of soviets and in factory management, and the growth of activity of the trade unions, the Komsomol and other social organisations makes especially topical the raising of the political culture of the workers and of extending the degree of openness of the work of party, soviet and economic organs. Already quite a bit has been done in that respect. But we need to go still further along that path,[17]

The notion of political culture was also introduced into the official report of the General Secretary at the Twenty-Sixth Party Congress of the CPSU in which Brezhnev described 'Soviet Man' as 'a person of high political culture',[18] though he went on to observe that by no means all the problems connected with the formation of the 'new person' had been solved, and noted the persistence in Soviet society of problems of egoism, philistinism, avarice and heavy drinking.[19]

Brezhnev's successor in the party leadership, Yuriy Andropov, also made use of the term 'political culture'. In his Lenin anniversary speech earlier in the same year in which he became General Secretary, Andropov quoted Lenin on how socialism could not be created 'by decree from above' since 'a living creative socialism' had to be the work of 'the popular masses themselves'. 'That is why' Andropov continued 'our party considers its very first priority to be a constant concern with raising the level of awareness and of the political culture of the working people'.[20] Andropov returned to the theme of political culture in his article commemorating the centenary of the death of Karl Marx published in *Kommunist* in February 1983. After stressing (to an extent more reminiscent of Khrushchev than of Brezhnev) the 'enormous significance' of the qualitative change represented by the transition from the 'dictatorship of the proletariat' to a 'state of the whole people', Andropov suggested that the 1977 Soviet Constitution had created 'the legislative base for a deepening of socialist democracy'. He continued:

> We do not idealise what has been done and is being done in our country in this area. Soviet democracy has had, has, and, it must be supposed, will have difficulties of growth, conditioned by the material possibilities of society, and by the level of consciousness of the masses and their political culture, as well as by the fact that our society does not develop either in hothouse conditions or in isolation from a world hostile to us, but in the face of the cold winds of 'psychological war' unleashed by imperialism. The perfecting of our democracy demands the removal of bureaucratic 'over-organisation' and formalism – of everything which stifles and undermines the initiative of the masses and which fetters the creative thought and living deed of the working people. We have battled against such phenomena and will battle against them with still greater energy and persistence.[21]

While great practical significance does not necessarily attach to the use of the term, 'political culture', by Soviet leaders and while the suspicion arises that a 'high political culture' would be deemed to have been achieved when everyone thought along the lines of *Pravda* editorials, it is of interest that both Brezhnev and Andropov speak in terms of the need to 'raise' the political culture of Soviet citizens and associate this with their greater participation in politics. Andropov, in particular, appears to see the incompatibility in principle between, on the one hand, a society in which bureaucrats 'over-organise' the mass of the people and, on the other, the creation of 'socialist man'.

Not surprisingly, neither Brezhnev nor Andropov troubled to define exactly what they meant by the term, 'political culture'. Numerous definitions have, however, been offered by Soviet scholars, though in political terms the most authoritative delineation of the concept should perhaps be regarded as the entry contained in the *Concise Political Dictionary* published in an edition of 500 000 copies in 1980.[22] It is of some interest that it was so recently that the concept received that particular mark of official approval; the previous edition of the same dictionary published in 1978 had no entry on political culture. This may in part be connected with the higher degree of recognition of political science as an academic discipline achieved by 1980 than two years earlier. The holding of the world congress of the International Political Science Association in Moscow in 1979 was used by Soviet advocates of a discipline of political science as a way of advancing their subject in the eyes of the Soviet authorities and, indeed, the 1980 *Concise Political Dictionary* was also the first edition of that *Politizdat* publication to include an entry on political science itself (rendered as *politicheskaya nauka* with the alternative term, *politologiya*, given in brackets).[23]

Political culture is defined in that reference book as 'the level and character of political knowledge, evaluations and actions of citizens, and also the content and quality of social values, traditions and norms regulating political relations'.[24] In bourgeois society, the *Concise Political Dictionary* goes on, there is a struggle between the political culture of the exploiting class and that of the exploited, whereas 'in the conditions of socialism a united political culture has been formed which is based on the community of political interests and needs and on the correspondence of the relations of different groups and strata of the population to the existing mechanism of political power'.[25] The 'political culture of socialism' is said to have 'a number of important social functions' – educational (*vospitatel'naya*), regulative and defensive (the last involving 'the protection of the political values of socialism') – which are briefly described in the article.

The Soviet dictionary definition of political culture cited above embraces actions (behaviour) within the concept. Though there are almost as many different definitions of political culture in the Soviet as in the Western literature, a majority of those who use the notion include behaviour within its scope. There are, however, variations on this theme. Vil'yam Smirnov, who is one of the more important Soviet writers on political culture, is careful to stress that political culture, as he defines it, takes in 'patterns of political behaviour, but not behaviour itself'.[26] More generally, Smirnov delineates political culture in the following way:

> In its philosophical aspect political culture is part of the spiritual life of a society, one of the forms of manifestation of its political consciousness. From a political and social psychological point of view a political culture portrays the dynamic unity of political values, orientations, evaluations, patterns of political behaviour, and also the ways and means of its transmission (political socialisation), distinctive to a given society and exercising influence on the nature of the functioning and the direction of the development of its political system.[27]

Georgiy Shakhnazarov and Fedor Burlatsky, in a significant article on the development of Soviet political science published in 1980, single out 'political culture' as one of the 'key categories and concepts' which has been but 'weakly elaborated' in the Soviet literature hitherto.[28] In their own definition, which follows quite closely Burlatsky's of ten years earlier,[29] they emphasise cognition and subjective orientation rather more than behaviour (or patterns of behaviour). As they put it:

> Political culture signifies the level of knowledge and conceptions of different classes, social strata, nations and individuals concerning power and politics, and also the political orientation and political activity shaped by it.[30]

A number of Soviet writers place strong emphasis on the historical dimension of political culture. Thus, for example, Kalensky writes of a political regime depending, *inter alia*, on 'such firm components of the life of a society as the ideology of the ruling class, the political traditions, and the basic value orientations to be found in the mass public consciousness – that is, upon the political culture in the broad sense of the term, understood as the entire historical experience of state development of one or another country'.[31] For Smirnov 'the content of political culture is the product of the protracted historical development of each society'.[32] He notes how political traditions which precede socialism can be transmitted in the process of political socialisation from one generation to another, and for recent negative examples of the consequences of this from a Soviet standpoint, he draws on the experience of China and Poland.[33] Smirnov argues that the creation of a new political culture in socialist society 'clearly reveals the inverse dependence of political culture upon political institutions (the party, other social organisations) and the state as a whole, upon its politico-educational activity'.[34] He recognises, however, that there can at the very least be a time-lag between the creation of new political institutions and the creation of a new political culture.

In the case of the USSR, Smirnov acknowledges an element of 'cultural continuity' between pre-revolutionary Russia and Soviet society, some of which he sees as positive and some negative. As examples of the latter he cites 'such features of Tsarist Russia as the distrust of the masses for everything to do with the state, their alienation from politics, authoritarianism, bureaucratism, etc.'[35] He cites Lenin on how 'very difficult a task' it will be to overcome this, one demanding 'a prolonged period of time and enormous persistence'.[36] The party had had, therefore, to undertake educational work on a gigantic scale in 'the struggle against survivals of the past in the political consciousness of the masses'.[37] At the same time, Smirnov observes, 'the assimilation and perfecting of the political culture of socialism takes place to a significant degree in the process of active participation of the masses in politics, in the administration of the affairs of the society and the state'.[38] Thus, he suggests, 'the political culture of Muscovites' is demonstrated by a sociological survey conducted in the Soviet capital which found that 'only 19.7 per cent of respondents are not carrying out any kind of social work'.[39]

The early 1980s have seen the publication in the Soviet Union of a number of books entirely devoted to the topic of political culture – with titles such as *Political Culture and Youth*,[40] *The Political Culture of Socialist Society*,[41] *The Political Culture of Soviet Man*,[42] and *Political and Legal Culture: Methodological Problems*.[43] The most substantial of these works are the first and the last. The authors of *Political Culture and Youth* base their work partly on the results of a sample survey of over 10 000 young people up to the age of thirty.[44] One of the questions put to the respondents was: 'What would you include in the concept, "political culture of the young person"?' Hardly surprisingly, the survey organisers were told by many of their respondents that out of the several tens of questions in the questionnaire, this one caused them the greatest difficulties.[45] However, a majority of the characterisations of political culture offered by the respondents emphasised 'the necessity of a class approach to the evaluation of contemporary social processes'.[46] The respondents, who (as noted above) later admitted their puzzlement over the political culture question, may well have calculated that, when in doubt, the 'class approach' is as safe a standby as any.

Though Soviet scholars may argue amongst themselves on the scope and significance of many concepts, at the level of more popular education the idea of the 'one right answer', rather than of a variety of legitimate interpretations, holds sway, as is clear when the authors turn to consider some of the shortcomings in the political knowledge of Soviet youth. They write:

> Experience shows that knowledge of the most widespread political concepts at times becomes mechanistic. The young person not infrequently does not go carefully into their content and sometimes even has a mistaken conception of them.[47]

The Soviet investigators of the political culture of young people were somewhat troubled by the answers they received to the question: 'To whom do you prefer to turn for an explanation of questions which are not clear to you?' 39 per cent answered that they turned to their friends; 33 per cent 'to authoritative people (party, Komsomol, trade union or other such workers)'; 10.6 per cent to the means of mass communication; 10.6 per cent to their relatives; and 6.8 per cent to no-one.[48] This does not matter so much, the authors suggest, when the opinions sought are on matters of taste – fashion, music, etc. – although 'even in such an instance the individual appraisal is not always correct and at times the advice of competent people would be not superfluous'. But it is 'more complicated to make judgements about the truth and correctness of one or another appraisal of political phenomena, arising out of a complicated interweaving of a large number of causes, not always "lying on the surface" '.[49]

N. M. Keyzerov, in the longer and more recent of his two books on political culture, displays a wide knowledge of Western social science literature. But while he accepts that there can be different approaches to the study of political culture, drawing upon the experience and insights of different disciplines – for example, philosophy, sociology, political science, law or social psychology – he takes pains to 'underline that the principled positions of the Marxist–Leninist methodology of scientific analysis' have a universal character and applicability in the study of political culture.[50] In common with most Soviet writers, he holds that there are not simply different political cultures but different 'levels' of political culture and he is concerned to contrast the high level of Soviet political culture with the levels to be found in Western countries. He uses political activism as one of the indicators of this. Much of the political activity referred to, it must be said, is of a rather formal kind, such as the observation (to be found also in a number of other recent Soviet writings on political culture)[51] that over four-fifths of the adult population of the USSR took part in the 'discussion' of the draft Constitution which was ratified in 1977. That the enactment of the Constitution as the Soviet Union's fundamental law was preceded by discussion is not in doubt. Those who took part in the discussion of it in a meaningful way may even be numbered in thousands rather than hundreds, but hardly in millions unless mere attendance at a meeting makes one a discussant.

Both the level of political activism,[52] and the level of political knowledge[53] greatly preoccupy Soviet writers concerned with the political culture of the USSR. So far as the issue of political knowledge is concerned, it is of interest that when the rules of the Soviet Association of Political Sciences were rewritten in 1978 a new injunction to members (in Article 2) was that of 'participation in measures to develop the political culture of the country and the popularisation and propaganda of political knowledge'.[54]

At the propagandistic level, as well as on a more scholarly plane, the concept of political culture has assumed an increasing importance in the Soviet Union. This is illustrated in a report of a conference held in Sverdlovsk in 1980 which was attended by 1100 people (including party, trade union and Komsomol officials, scholars, representatives of the mass media and professional propagandists). The conference theme was 'The political culture of developed socialism: the ways and means of its formation' and the event was jointly organised by the Sverdlovsk regional party committee, the Academy of Social Sciences attached to the Central Committee of the Party and the journal, *Politicheskoe samoobrazovanie*.[55] The emphasis was on the system of values common to 'developed socialism' (rather than on distinctive national political cultures or sub-cultures) and on enhancing the role of the mass media and the political education system in the effort to promote 'the growth of the political culture of the population'.[56]

As all this suggests, there is in the current Soviet preoccupation with the concept of political culture some pouring of new wine into old bottles, new terms into old and somewhat leaky conceptual containers. The Soviet literature on political culture exists, however, on various levels, some of them scholarly and some propagandistic.[57] Not infrequently, within the same work there is interesting analysis and discussion and also claims which have more to do with propaganda than with serious scholarship. At its best, however, Soviet writing on political culture enables its authors to attach weight to political factors (including the subjective) in the Soviet Union and other countries which were comparatively little studied in the USSR in the past. At least some of the questions concerning the scope and significance of the concept of political culture which are matters of controversy in Western scholarship are debated also in the Soviet academic literature. Though some common vocabulary and common intellectual interests should not obscure fundamental differences between the possibilities open to Soviet scholars in analysing and investigating their own society as compared with their counterparts in most Western societies, the Soviet literature explicitly devoted to political culture should certainly not be ignored in Western studies of Communist political cultures. That professional students of politics in the East and the West are no longer, as they were twenty years ago, talking past one another in a state of mutual incomprehension may even be regarded as progress of a modest sort.

NOTES AND REFERENCES

1. Sidney Verba, 'Comparative Political Culture', pp. 512–60 of Lucian W. Pye and Sidney Verba (eds) *Political Culture and Political Development* (Princeton, New Jersey, 1965) p. 555.
2. Ibid, p. 554.
3. Though Stephen White's book, *Political Culture and Soviet Politics* (which, in general, I value highly) has some pertinent comments on Stalin and the Stalin period (see especially pp. 108–11), I am still of the opinion expressed in my review of it ('Soviet Man and Soviet Men', *Times Literary Supplement*, 7 March 1980, p. 273) that it accords less attention than they are due to the last twenty or more years of Stalin's life and, in particular, to the great purges and the Second World War.
4. A useful contribution to analysis of this phenomenon is made by Victor Zaslavsky in the chapter on 'The Rebirth of the Stalin Cult in the USSR' of his book, *The Neo-Stalinist State: Class, Ethnicity and Consensus in Soviet Society* (Brighton, 1982) pp. 1–21. See also the reasons given for the adulation of Mao Zedong (which may be read as applying equally to Stalin) by Fedor Burlatsky, 'Mezhdutsarstvie, ili khronika vremen Den Syaopina', *Noviy mir*, no. 4, 1982, pp. 205–28, at p. 210.

112   *Soviet Culture through Soviet Eyes*

5. Zaslavsky, *The Neo-Stalinist State*, p. 10.
6. I am grateful to Professor Gitelman for making available to me these data and for his permission to cite them.
7. Zaslavsky, 'The Rebirth of the Stalin Cult', p. 11.
8. Ibid, pp. 11–12.
9. Examples are legion. For some particularly authoritative ones, see the selections from party documents, Brezhnev's speeches, etc. contained in *KPSS o formirovanii novogo cheloveka: Sbornik dokumentov i materialov (1965–1981)* (Moscow, 1982, 2nd edn).
10. To use the title of a recent collection of studies of this phenomenon in non-Communist contexts. See Eric Hobsbawm and Terence Ranger (eds) *The Invention of Tradition* (Cambridge, 1983).
11. See, for example, N. V. Solntsev, *Rol' progressivnykh traditsiy v kommunisticheskom vospitanii* (Novosibirsk, 1977) pp. 110–11.
12. Christel Lane, *The Rites of Rulers: Ritual in Industrial Society – The Soviet Case* (Cambridge, 1981) p. 141.
13. V. I. Lenin, *Polnoe sobranie sochineniy* (Moscow, 1963) vol. 41, p. 404. For examples of the numerous citations of this passage, see N. M. Keyzerov, *Politicheskaya kul'tura sotsialisticheskogo obshchestva* (Moscow, 1982) p. 26; N. Blinov, Yu. Ozhegov and F. Sheregi, *Politicheskaya kul'tura i molodezh'* (Moscow, 1982) p. 3; A. K. Belykh, *Razvitoy sotsializm: suchnost' i zakonomernosti* (Leningrad, 1982) p. 123; and N. M. Lisenkov, *Politicheskaya kul'tura sovetskogo cheloveka* (Moscow, 1983) pp. 7–8.
14. V. G. Kalensky, *Politicheskaya nauka v SShA* (Moscow, 1969) esp. pp. 73–86.
15. F. M. Burlatsky, *Lenin, gosudarstvo, politika* (Moscow, 1970) p. 55. See also p. 327.
16. Whereas Kalensky discussed the term in the context of its use in American political science, Burlatsky made a more general case for its usefulness in research and political analysis. The fact that Burlatsky enjoyed considerable political standing, as a former head of Yuriy Andropov's group of consultants in the Socialist Countries department of the Central Committee of the CPSU, is also of relevance to the influence exerted by his 1970 book.
17. L. I. Brezhnev, 'Vse dlya blaga naroda, vo imya sovetskogo cheloveka', speech of 14 June 1974, published in L. I. Brezhnev, *Voprosy razvitiya politicheskoy sistemy sovetskogo obshchestva* (Moscow, 1977) pp. 306–21, at p. 315.
18. *Materialy XXVI s'ezda KPSS* (Moscow, 1981) p. 63.
19. Ibid, pp. 63–4.
20. Speech of 22 April 1982, reprinted in Yu. V. Andropov, *Izbrannye rechi i stat'i* (Moscow, 1983) 2nd edn p. 192.
21. Article, 'Uchenie Karla Marksa i nekotorye voprosy sotsialisticheskogo stroitel'stva v SSSR', *Kommunist*, no. 3, 1983; reprinted in Andropov, *Izbrannye rechi i stat'i*, ibid, p. 242. Andropov, in his speech to party veterans on 15 August 1983, spoke again of the need 'systematically to raise the political culture of the working people'. See *Pravda*, 16 August 1983, p. 1.

22. L. A. Onikov and N. V. Shishlin (eds) *Kratkiy politicheskiy slovar'* (Moscow, 1980) 2nd edn pp. 318–19.
23. Ibid, pp. 319–20.
24. Ibid, p. 318. For a very similar definition of political culture, see R. A. Safarov, *Obshchestvennoe mnenie v sisteme sovetskoy demokratii* (Moscow, 1982) p. 38.
25. *Kratkiy politicheskiy slovar'*, p. 318.
26. V. V. Smirnov, 'Razvitie politicheskoy kul'tury v usloviyakh zrelogo sotsializma' in G. Kh. Shakhnazarov and Yu. A. Tikhomirov (eds) *Aktual'nye problemy sovremennogo politicheskogo razvitiya (ocherki teorii)* (Moscow, 1982) pp. 109–24, at p. 111.
27. Ibid, p. 110.
28. G. Kh. Shakhnazarov and F. M. Burlatsky, 'O razvitii marksistsko-leninskoy politicheskoy nauki', *Voprosy filosofii*, no. 12, 1980, pp. 10–23, at p. 14.
29. Burlatsky, *Lenin, gosudarstvo, politika*, p. 55. A different characterisation of political culture is, however, given in a book co-edited by Burlatsky. See L. S. Mamut, 'Politicheskaya kul'tura i politicheskoe soznanie' in Burlatsky and V. E. Chirkin (eds) *Politicheskie sistemy sovremennosti* (Moscow, 1978) pp. 43–53.
30. Shakhnazarov and Burlatsky, 'O razvitii marksistsko-leninskoy politicheskoy nauki', p. 13.
31. V. G. Kalensky, *Gosudarstvo kak ob'ekt sotsiologicheskogo analiza (Ocherki istorii i metodologii issledovaniya)* (Moscow, 1977) pp. 139–40.
32. Smirnov, 'Razvitie politicheskoy kul'tury v usloviyakh zrelogo sotsializma', p. 112.
33. Ibid, p. 113.
34. Ibid, p. 114.
35. Ibid, p. 115.
36. Ibid.
37. Ibid, pp. 115–16.
38. Ibid, p. 116.
39. Ibid, p. 122. Other articles by V. V. Smirnov which are in whole or in part devoted to political culture include 'Kontseptsiya politicheskoy kul'tury v politicheskoy nauke SShA' in D. A. Kerimov (ed.) *Mirnoe sosushchestvovanie i sotsial'nopoliticheskoe razvitie* (Moscow, 1977) pp. 66–74; ' "Krugliy stol" po problemam politicheskoy kul'tury' in D. A. Kerimov (ed.) *Politicheskie otnosheniya: prognozirovanie i planirovanie* (Moscow, 1979) pp. 125–33; and 'Politicheskaya sistema sovetskogo obshchestva: aspekty issledovaniya' in *Sovetskoe gosudarstvo i pravo*, no. 3, 1982, pp. 13–21, esp. p. 19.
40. Blinov, Ozhegov and Sheregi, *Politicheskaya kul'tura i molodezh'*.
41. Keyzerov, *Politicheskaya kul'tura sotsialisticheskogo obshchestva*.
42. Lisenkov, *Politicheskaya kul'tura sovetskogo cheloveka*.
43. N. M. Keyzerov, *Politicheskaya i pravovaya kul'tura: Metodologicheskie problemy* (Moscow, 1983).
44. For the social breakdown of the sample, see *Politicheskaya kul'tura i molodezh'*, p. 6.
45. Ibid.

46. Ibid, p. 48.
47. Ibid, p. 132.
48. Ibid, p. 141. A majority of Soviet citizens appear to get their legal knowledge also mainly from friends, acquaintances and family rather than from the mass media, formal instruction or those in positions of authority. Valeriy Shchegortsov, in a sociological study of legal consciousness, cites a Leningrad survey which found that 28.5 per cent of respondents got such legal knowledge as they possessed from conversations at their place of work and 28.4 per cent got it from close friends and members of their family. Rather similar results emerged from Shchegortsov's own research. For his respondents, the major sources of legal knowledge were friends at their workplace or place of study (27.8 per cent), the family circle (26 per cent) or 'life's experience' (16.2 per cent). See V. A. Shchegortsov, *Sotsiologiya pravo-soznaniya* (Moscow, 1981) p. 69.
49. *Politicheskaya kul'tura i molodezh'*, p. 141.
50. Keyzerov, *Politicheskaya i pravovaya kul'tura*, pp. 144–5.
51. See, for example, M. T. Iovchuk, 'Nekotorye osobennosti politicheskoy kul'tury sotsializma' in D. A. Kerimov (ed.) *Problemy politicheskikh nauk* (Moscow, 1980) pp. 164–72, at p. 169; similarly, Iovchuk, 'Osobennosti politicheskoy kul'tury sotsializma' in V. E. Chirkin (ed.) *Razvitie politicheskikh sistem v sovremennom mire* (Moscow, 1981) pp. 86–94, at p. 88.
52. 'Social activity' writes Mikhail Lisenkov 'is the decisive indicator of a personality of the socialist type'. See M. M. Lisenkov, *Politicheskaya kul'tura sovetskogo cheloveka*, p. 56. See also V. A. Shchegortsov, 'The Essence of Political Culture' in D. A. Kerimov and Yu. A. Krasin (eds) *Papers on Some Problems of Political Science* (Moscow, 1982) pp. 44–9, esp. p. 49.
53. See, for example, the section, 'Zakonomernost' vedushchey roli politicheskoy kul'tury' of A. K. Belykh, *Razvitoy sotsializm: sushchnost'i zakonomernosti*, pp. 123–9; and N. M. Keyzerov, *Politicheskaya kul'tura sotsialisticheskogo obshchestva*, p. 17. Keyzerov speaks, however, of the possibility of a situation in which an individual may have a high level of political consciousness – 'knowledge, convictions, professional competence and skills, but not political culture'. That is because 'only in dialectical unity with political practice do political knowledge and convictions become political culture' (ibid, p. 18). Keyzerov is far from alone among Soviet authors in using, as he does here, 'political culture' as a synonym for 'high' political culture in terms of Soviet ideological norms.
54. D. A. Kerimov (ed.) *Politicheskie otnosheniya*, p. 218.
55. 'Problemy formirovaniya politicheskoy kul'tury' in *Politicheskoe samoobrazovanie*, no. 1, 1981, pp. 72–6.
56. Ibid., p. 76.
57. In addition to a number of the works mentioned earlier in this chapter, reference should be made to the writings of S. A. Egorov. See, for example, the section on 'Kontseptsiya politicheskoy kul'tury kak faktora sotsial'no-politicheskoy stabil'nosti' in his book, *Politicheskaya sistema, politicheskoe razvitie, pravo: kritika nemarksistskikh politologicheskikh kontseptsii* (Moscow, 1983) pp. 117–28.

6 Czechoslovak Political Culture: Pluralism in an International Context

H. GORDON SKILLING

It has been argued by certain Western specialists that pluralism has been a prominent and enduring feature of the political culture of Czechs and Slovaks. Archie Brown and Gordon Wightman, for instance, have observed 'A belief in the virtues of political pluralism has almost certainly been a dominant one throughout the existence of the Czechoslovak Republic'.[1] David Paul, who broadened his purview to cover a longer historical period, has written of political pluralism as a 'recurrent tendency' and 'a pattern well-known' in Czechoslovak history, has discerned 'a thin thread' of continuity linking manifestations of this tendency under capitalism and under socialism and has described 'the re-emergence of deeply rooted patterns' in the 1960s.[2] The present author, on the other hand, while referring to pluralism as a 'deeply rooted national tradition,' has placed greater emphasis on the heterogeneity, and the discontinuity of Czech and Slovak traditions. He has noted certain defects or weaknesses in the pluralist tradition, and the presence of a contradictory tendency toward authoritarianism which has markedly influenced the behaviour and the thinking of the two nations.[3]

Pluralism is but one component of the multiplex phenomenon of Czech and Slovak political culture, and can be separated only arbitrarily from others equally important. A more systematic analysis of pluralism would, however, be useful in testing the utility of the concept of political culture in understanding and interpreting the essence of politics in Czechoslovakia. It would also help in assessing the validity of the several approaches adopted by scholars employing the concept and in evaluating their differing interpretations of Czech and Slovak politics.

115

My own views were given a preliminary exposition in a paper prepared for the sixtieth anniversary of the Czechoslovak Republic and published in somewhat revised form in a special issue of the *International Journal* on Prague 1968 and its aftermath.[4] These thoughts were developed more fully in a paper presented in Moscow at the congress of the International Political Science Association in 1979.[5] The present essay, like its Moscow predecessor, on which it is partly based, has a threefold purpose. In the first place, it re-examines the dialectic of continuity and discontinuity of pluralism in the Czech and Slovak past, subjecting my earlier expositions to revision in the light of criticism and further consideration.[6] In the second place, it puts the theme of pluralism in the context of the international environment, analysing the crucial role of international factors in a country as small and as weak as Czechoslovakia. In the third place, recognising that external and domestic factors are so interwoven as to make a clear separation sometimes difficult, if not impossible, the essay seeks to estimate the relative weight of each set of factors in determining the fate of pluralism, and the degree of responsibility of those persons having domestic power and influence in the ultimate outcome.

For the purpose of the following analysis, pluralism is taken to mean 'the diffusion and dispersion of power in a political system from central authorities to more or less autonomous groups, organisations and individuals'.[7] In more specific terms, pluralism, in my judgement, may embrace *some* or *all* of the following elements: competing political parties, independent interest organisations, such as trade unions; an active representative and legislative assembly; autonomous organs of local and regional self-government, perhaps taking federalist forms; a market economy (either capitalist or socialist); uncensored newspapers and journals, radio and television; workers' participation in management; and individual human rights, including freedom of expression and association and of scholarship and publication.

One might usefully distinguish, as does David Paul, lower and higher levels of pluralism. 'First-stage' pluralism,' in his analysis, consists of the differentiated political behaviour of citizens arising from the existence of differentiated social groups,[8] and, I would add, of divergences in values and beliefs. A 'higher stage of political pluralism', again in Paul's usage, is one in which there are 'competing forces in the political system – parties or other organised groups capable of sharing in, or challenging, the established power structure'.[9] To avoid confusion, it should be noted that the amorphous and unorganised 'interest groups' which sometimes exist in a dictatorial or authoritarian society, such as Communist Czechoslovakia, are regarded as a primitive form of 'quasi-pluralism' and not as genuine pluralism.[10]

POLITICAL CULTURE

The search for an understanding of the essence of Czechoslovak politics has adopted many guises and has not been eminently successful. Throughout their modern history Czechs have been, one might say, obsessed with the attempt to identify 'the meaning of Czech history' (*smysl české historie*), as Masaryk expressed it. His own 'philosophy' of Czech history, rooted deeply in the religious values of certain historical episodes, such as the Hussite reformation, and embodied in the idea of 'humanist democracy', was subjected to scholarly criticism by his contemporaries and successors, and is now acknowledged, even by an ardent admirer, to be 'in ruins'.[11]

During the First Republic, Masaryk's ideas were often distorted by his followers into a romantic interpretation of the 'national character.' Karel Čapek, for instance, writing at a high point of the Republic's fortunes, declared that a 'democratic spirit' and a 'love of liberty and peace' were 'part and parcel of the very character of the Czechoslovak nation'.[12] In the same volume Ferdinand Peroutka praised the 'humanitarianism' of the Czechs, a quality which separated them off from Russia and made them 'essentially part of the West'.[13] These words were written presumably in 1937, the year of Masaryk's death, and published in 1938, the year of the death of the Republic and of the ideas it was presumed to embody. Subsequent blows to Czech national fortunes in 1939, 1948 and 1968, dispelled all illusions as to the meaning of Czech history or of Czech national character and led Czechs to indulge in what I have called elsewhere 'almost an orgy of self-criticism or even of national denigration'.[14] Haunted by a sense of repeated failures, Czechs, writing with an intense emotional involvement and often in a moralising vein, have painted the 'national character' in the darkest colours, quite the opposite of the bright hues of 1937, and perhaps equally exaggerated and unjustified.

A few foreign scholars, not personally involved in the tragedies of recent Czechoslovak politics, have been wrestling with the same problem of interpreting the Czech past and present. Their approach, as might have been expected, has been somewhat more dispassionate than their Czech and Slovak colleagues, but occasionally has verged on almost complete neglect of the controversial issues which dominate the latter's discussions. An American historian, for example, has written of Czechoslovak 'traditions', including those in politics, in entirely positive terms, as though nothing had happened to challenge or change them.[15] Several political scientists, grappling more realistically with the problem, have shunned such metaphysical terms as 'the meaning of Czech history', or the ambiguous notion of 'national character', or even the more neutral word, 'tradition', and have turned to another concept, derived from anthropology and applied more recently in political studies, namely 'political culture'.[16]

This concept seeks to identify and define as precisely as possible the salient features of the orientation of a given nation (or a group within the nation) to politics as expressed in its values and/or actions over an extended period of time. It is something more than an examination of 'traditions' since it embodies not only the old, but also elements of change, and represents a kind of synthesis of the two. It is quite distinct from 'national character', which is often a subjective and impressionistic picture derived from slender historical evidence. Nor is it a mere 'philosophy' of the past which is sometimes not founded on solid empirical facts. Have the students of Czechoslovak politics, employing the concept of political culture, been successful in finding a definition of the realities of politics in that country which is more comprehensive than a mere description of traditions, more detached and precise than national character, and more objective and reliable than a philosophy of history? Have they in particular resolved the problem of continuity and change? Have they been able to clarify the difficult question of 'congruence' or 'dissonance' between what has been called the 'real' and the 'ideal' culture, and between the so-called 'official' culture of the regime and the 'dominant' culture of the people?[17]

Without discussing the matter exhaustively, one should note certain handicaps of the concept of political culture, both in the way it has been defined, and in the manner in which it has been applied by the authors cited above. Unfortunately, the term has been used in two opposed senses, as noted in earlier chapters of this book. One approach concentrates on the 'subjective orientation' to history and politics, namely 'beliefs and values' about politics.[18] The other expands the term to embrace also 'objective phenomena', the actual behaviour patterns of a group or nation.[19] This variation in usage has had a direct impact on the definition of Czechoslovak political culture, and in particular on the formulation of the problem of continuity and change. Those who emphasise inner values rather than outward behaviour tend to disregard the more negative experiences of the past and to stress the enduring character of the ideas and beliefs of the people. They tend to discern, and to emphasise, a lack of congruence between values and behaviour, and between official and dominant culture, under Communist rule. Those who are more concerned with the actual deeds of Czechs and Slovaks in politics, are struck by the elements of change and discontinuity, at least in 'official culture', and are to varying degrees sceptical of 'values' which are not translated into action.

It is admittedly difficult to identify the political culture of a group or a nation. The choice of methods, or sources, will influence the conclusions reached. In the case of Czechoslovakia, survey data or public opinion polling data are available and have been used extensively by Brown and Wightman as the chief source of their conclusions. Do the replies of individuals in polls reflect deeply held and persistent political values, or are they merely spontaneous and transient attitudes expressed in response to questions which are themselves selective and often ambiguous?

Apart from those of 1968, the polls make no direct reference to pluralism, so that beliefs on this subject can only be inferred from attitudes to the First Republic or to Masaryk, on the assumption that both embody the values of pluralism. Yet poll results – which showed a positive attitude to the First Republic, among Czechs, of only 8 per cent in December 1946, and 39 per cent in October 1968 – neither confirm the 'enormous importance' of the First Republic, nor a continuity of the values of that period, but rather the contrary.[20] In 1968, the poll cited by Brown and Wightman demonstrates a strong commitment to the 'pluralism of ideas', but other polls, which are not cited, reveal a divided and ambivalent attitude toward the pluralism of political parties.[21] Nor does the enthusiasm for the Action Programme in 1968, which, as one of its authors later admitted, advocated a 'restricted' conception of pluralism, document an unambiguous commitment to genuine pluralism.[22]

Moreover because of the absence of opinion polls from the nineteenth century and the First Republic, as well as the 1950s and the 1970s, we are left with data from 1946 and 1968 which give evidence of what Czechs and Slovaks thought in those years only, and cannot mirror what they thought in earlier periods (nor, of course, how they actually behaved earlier). This makes it difficult to gauge the degree of dissonance between 'dominant' and 'official' values in the 1950s or the extent of continuity of pluralist values.[23]

One is on more solid ground, at least in identifying 'real political culture', if one studies the actual historical experiences of a given people or nation. In comparison with public opinion polls, the evidence thus garnered offers a finer and more discriminating instrument of analysis which brings out the complexity, the heterogeneity and the changing character of a country's political culture. David Paul, for example, is able to probe deeply into the rise of 'a pluralistic culture' during the nineteenth century, its continuance after the war, and the 're-pluralisation' of Czechoslovak politics in 1968 after the years of Stalinism.[24] Such a historical approach facilitates the analysis of the weaknesses as well as the strengths of the First Republic, and indeed the negative and positive features of Czech history over a longer period; it makes it possible to distinguish the dominant or official cultures of the First Republic from important 'sub-cultures', such as the Slovak or the communist, as well as to analyse the heterogeneity and ambivalence of each of the latter. The historical approach may also document the degree of congruence between subjective and objective aspects of political culture, and between official and dominant versions of culture. Under undemocratic conditions, however, when 'a minority sub-culture of authoritarianism and anti-pluralism',[25] such as communism, rules, the historian may find himself almost as helpless as the analyst of survey data in his attempt to offer convincing proof of a continuity of values or a dissonance between official and dominant values.

PLURALISM – CONTINUITY OR DISCONTINUITY

The historical record demonstrates a remarkable degree of continuity in Czechoslovak political culture during the first seven decades of Czech and Slovak politics, that is, from 1867 to 1938.[26] During five decades of semi-constitutional political experience within Austria–Hungary the Czechs gradually and steadily developed a genuine and meaningful pluralist society and polity, which comprised both a large number of interest groups and associations, and a multiplicity of political parties. Although Slovak politics of this period was less developed and was distinctive, it shared many of the features of the pluralistic culture of its more mature Czech counterpart.[27] After a temporary interruption during World War One these traditions re-emerged, forming the basis of the First Republic which in many ways constituted a projection of the pluralist tendencies of the preceding half-century. There was a flowering of pluralist values and ideas, and they were embodied in actual practice to a large degree. Despite this substantial congruence of official and dominant political culture, there were dissonant elements, even distinct sub-cultures, such as the Slovak or the Communist, but each of these was itself divided and neither could challenge the dominant or official culture (at least not until 1939 and 1945, respectively).

This was not a pure and undefiled pluralism, however, but one which was restricted and distorted by other authoritarian tendencies. Austro-Hungarian bureaucratic absolutism not only set limits to a genuine pluralism before 1918 but left its mark on Czechoslovak politics between the wars, for example, in the bureaucratisation of political parties and trade unions, and in the dominant position of the coalition oligarchy, the *Pětka*. The injunction of Masaryk to Czechs to 'de-austrianise' (*odrakouštět*) themselves was not completely fulfilled.[28] The anonymous author of a samizdat volume, *Sixty Eight*, although recognising the value of the experience of 'plurality' under Austria, criticised the 'particularism', the attention to special interests, which had characterised both the interest associations and the political parties under the Monarchy and which had continued under the Republic.[29] Another anonymous writer, in reviewing my article in the special issue of the *International Journal*, and speculating on the reason for the ease with which pluralism was destroyed in the 1950s, wondered whether this lay in the 'undeveloped political pluralism' of the past and in the fact that the tradition had not been deep or free of defects.[30]

One of the most corrosive influences on pluralism under the Hapsburgs and in the First Republic was the force of nationalism, which often led to the subordination of special group interests to the 'superior' national interest, and to intolerance of heretical or unorthodox views (such as those of Masaryk in the 1890s). It also resulted in the failure of the Czechs, under the Republic, to recognise fully the interests and demands of Slovaks or Germans, thus curbing the full pluralism of nationalities. Petr Pithart, reflecting on this concentration on the 'nation', as an entity based solely on the community of language, concluded, in a controversial samizdat article, that the Czechs had been unable to accept the 'state' as a community based on the voluntary association of 'citizens' loyal to common ideas and ideals.[31] As a result, the people did not show themselves capable of defending themselves (in 1938) because they had nothing of their own to defend'.[32]

The pluralist tradition, whatever strengths or defects it may have had, was interrupted by the Munich *diktat* in 1938. This event represented a decisive turning-point in Czechoslovak political culture and ushered in four decades of step-by-step deterioration in the quality of pluralism and the increasing saliency of a contradictory authoritarian tendency.[33] The successive stages of this transformation, as set forth in my earlier paper, need only be mentioned: the damaging blow to pluralism during the Second Republic (1938–9); its temporary destruction during the German occupation of the Czech lands and Slovak statehood; its brief revival, in seriously attenuated form between 1945 and 1948; its drastic liquidation during the Stalinist years; the gradual resurgence of the pluralist tradition in the 1960s and its flowering, although in highly qualified form, in 1968; and its forcible elimination again in the 1970s and 1980s.

The brief historical excursion leaves little doubt that in the realm of actual political behaviour ('real political culture') discontinuity, not continuity, was the cardinal feature of Czechoslovak political culture for more than forty years. The temporary restoration of a diluted and limited pluralism from 1945 to 1948 and in 1968–9 was overshadowed by the anti-pluralism of the other years.

Much more baffling is the question as to whether there was a continuity of subjective political culture, that is, whether the values of pluralism survived beneath the surface, so to speak, in the hearts and minds of the people. Brown and Wightman are confident that the official political culture of the communist period, apart from brief intervals such as 1968, was out of harmony with the subterranean traditional values, and was quite unable to replace them in spite of persistent efforts to do so.[34] David Paul seems to share this view in writing that Czechs, 'while conforming outwardly, managed to keep alive their sense of values'. Under Stalinism, survival required 'an ongoing effort at living one's life according to the demands of the system, even when that involves a conflict with one's values', thus resulting in 'a constant dissonance between what the individual believes and how he acts'.[35] On the other hand, he wrote of the 'repluralisation' of Czechoslovak politics in the 1960s and the 're-emergence' of pluralism in 1968, as though this tradition of Czech politics had in fact died out and had to be resurrected or reborn in a new form.[36]

It would be foolish to deny that, throughout the changing fortunes of Czech and Slovak life, there was a certain continuity of values which expressed itself in renewed tendencies towards pluralism when conditions permitted or encouraged it. It is more open to question as to whether these values, even during the worst years of Stalinism, represented the 'dominant political culture', accepted by the majority of the population. In the words of the old saw, 'actions speak louder than words', or in this case, 'thoughts'. One may question whether values which are not acted on, for whatever reason, are really deeply held and whether they are in any case politically relevant, except in the long run.[37] The self-repression of inward values and outward conformity with official ideology, prolonged over many years (in this case some thirty-eight of the forty-three years since Munich) perhaps reflect more accurately the subjective political culture than 'high thoughts' not translated into deeds.

Furthermore, prolonged subjugation to foreign occupation or dictatorial oppression is likely to affect not only outward behaviour and public expression of attitudes, but the innermost realm of values and beliefs. Václav Havel, in his eloquent portrayal of the moral crisis of Czech society, wrote that 'self-preservation' has become the only aim of the citizen, requiring 'external adaptation' and producing political apathy, outward conformity, materialism, escapism, corruption, lying and deceit. A profound inner conflict ensued, within the individual and within society, between what Havel calls 'these contrary tendencies that slumber in society'. The future depended on whether 'the worst in us – egotism, hypocrisy, indifference, cowardice, fear, resignation and the desire to escape every personal responsibility – is activated and enlarged', or whether it is 'the better side' which prevails.[38]

Milan Kundera, celebrated Czech novelist, now in exile, was even more pessimistic when he wrote of the efforts of the Husák régime to destroy the nation's history, to make the nation 'forget what it is and what it was', and concluded 'In moments of clairvoyance the Czech nation can glimpse its own death at close range. Not as an accomplished fact, not as the inevitable future, but as a perfectly concrete possibility. Its death is at its side'.[39]

These gloomy warnings do not, of course, mean that values such as pluralism are forever dead or that the people have accepted, or internalised, the official values of the régime. Traditional values have, however, been gravely weakened and will be resuscitated only by supreme effort at a more favourable time.

THE INTERNATIONAL CONTEXT

All countries are subject in varying degree to international influences in the forming of their foreign and domestic policies and in the evolution of their political systems. It has been argued indeed that 'International relations and domestic politics are so interrelated that they should be analysed simultaneously, as wholes'.[40] The experience of Czechoslovakia, like all small countries, and perhaps more than many others, confirmed what Rosenau termed the linkage of domestic and international systems, according to which behaviour originating in one system is reacted to in another.[41] It has been a classic example of what he called 'a penetrated political system', in which non-members of the national polity 'participate directly and authoritatively' in its decision-making process.[42] In the case of Czechoslovakia, what Rosenau terms 'environmental outputs' (actions originating in the external environment) have frequently been decisive in crucial decisions affecting basic policy lines and even the very existence of the country as an independent entity. Czechoslovakia was often able to influence the international environment only in a negative or passive sense by yielding to international pressures, and only occasionally succeeded in having a positive or active impact on the course of events. Moreover it was often impossible to distinguish clearly between domestic and international factors, for example, the Sudeten German Party and Nazi Germany, or the Communist Party of Czechoslovakia and the Soviet Union.

Paradoxically, the study of political culture has tended to neglect the international factors which may condition or even determine the evolution of a country's culture. It seems generally to have been assumed that a political culture is formed in an international vacuum and is the product exclusively of the actions of the people involved. David Paul, however, has cogently argued that the critical variable determining the nature of politics in Czechoslovakia has been the degree of freedom from outside interference.[43] Independence, either complete or partial, has favoured the organic growth and development of a coherent political culture, in particular one which tended in the direction of a pluralistic democracy. Conversely, prolonged dependence on a foreign power has been unfavourable to such a tendency and has been 'counter-pluralist' in its effect.[44] Yet, as he has pointedly noted, 'of the entire period since the beginning of the Czechoslovak Republic, fewer than twenty-four years have been independent in any meaningful sense of the word'; 'independence has been the exception rather than the rule in Czechoslovak history'.[45]

Space permits only a cursory examination of the interplay of domestic and international factors at successive stages of Czechoslovak history, and the effects of this on political culture, in particular on pluralism.[46] The Austro-Hungarian framework within which Czech and Slovak politics was for many years conducted was not, strictly speaking, 'foreign' or 'international'. It was, however, a non-Czech, non-Slovak context which set strict limits on the mode of politics of the two peoples and was in many respects hostile to genuine pluralism. Moreover Habsburg foreign policy, notably the alliance with Germany, was supportive of German and Magyar dominance of the state and hence restrictive on the attainment of Czech and Slovak national or group interests. Independence was unthinkable to almost all Czech and Slovak political leaders, and the invocation of foreign assistance in the struggle for the national interests or for home rule, was limited to vague appeals to Paris and Moscow by František Rieger, the romantic pan-Slavism and pro-Russianism of Karel Kramář, and the more realistic and pragmatic critique of the Austro-German alliance and Balkan expansionism by Thomas Masaryk. None of these constituted a real challenge to non-Slav hegemony or imperial despotism.

The achievement of independent statehood, a sharp breach in Czech and Slovak historical continuity, was largely a result of Allied military victory and great power diplomacy, which produced a temporary vacuum of power in central and eastern Europe and made possible the creation of a tier of independent states in the area. Yet Masaryk and Beneš, in wartime exile, made a decisive contribution to the outcome through their able diplomacy during the war years and at Paris, supported by military action of the Czechoslovak legions on various war fronts. In other words, the rare combination of a favourable international balance of power and the active influence of domestic actors made possible the creation of an independent state and the moulding of its political institutions in the image of Western democracy. The adoption of the values and practices of an essentially pluralist system reflected long intellectual associations with the West and Masaryk's admiration of American, French and British models of government, and was not the result of outside interference or foreign imposition.

The triumph was shortlived, however. A new balance of power resulted from the revival of German strength, the lack of British and

French interest in Czechoslovakia's fate, and the exclusion of the Soviet Union from the councils of Europe. The policy of appeasement followed by the West led to the partition of Czechoslovakia at Munich. Domestic factors, such as the hostility of the Sudeten Germans, the enmity of minority Poles and Magyars, and the disaffection of Slovaks, became elements of the international context and contributed to the final result. President Beneš saw no alternative but to surrender to a dictate imposed upon him by enemies and allies together and supported by powerful domestic forces. During the brief interregnum between September 1938 and March 1939, the traditional pluralism of inter-war politics was severely curbed, reflecting a reluctant accommodation to outside pressures and shifts of attitude by Czech and Slovak party leaders toward more authoritarian ideas.[47]

Continuing German pressure, and capitulation to it by Czech and Slovak leaders (President Hácha and Father Tiso) led to the occupation of Bohemia and Moravia by the Reich and the establishment of a separate Slovak state. Once more, as in 1918 and 1938, this was the product of an interweaving of domestic and international factors, this time an unfavourable international environment and weak Czech and Slovak leadership. The domestic consequence was the destruction of the pluralist society and government which had been developed during the two decades of independence and the forced imposition of a Nazi political culture.

In 1945 the defeat of Germany and the emergence of a new balance of power, in which Soviet Russia assumed the dominant role in Eastern Europe, made possible the restoration of Czechoslovakia to the map of Europe, but in a position of dependence on its Eastern ally. The wartime liberation struggle abroad, led by Beneš, contributed to the achievement of liberation, but his close collaboration with the USSR enhanced the Soviet influence in the liberated Republic. This tipped the scales away from traditional pluralism in an authoritarian direction. During the early post-war years when Soviet influence was not overwhelming, a partial and limited pluralism was established, but it was diluted by authoritarian elements, thus facilitating the seizure of total power by the communists in 1948. Again, the outcome was produced by a combination of international factors (Soviet hegemony in Eastern Europe and Western withdrawal) and domestic factors (Communist strength and deceit; the weakness and ineptitude of Beneš and the non-communists). The February coup led to complete subjugation of Czechoslovakia to its Soviet 'ally'; the liquidation of all traces of pluralism in the 1950s and the imposition of Soviet political culture in its Stalinist form, suffused with all its historic Russian antecedents. The régime, although it broke with all past traditions, enjoyed massive and enthusiastic support, not only from the rank-and-file of the party, but by prominent intellectuals and even by some non-party political forces.

The rebirth of some crude elements of pluralism during the 1960s can be attributed to indigenous forces, reacting against the Soviet political culture imposed during the preceding decade, but was encouraged in some degree by Khrushchev's de-Stalinisation drive. This culminated in 1968 in the blossoming of pluralistic tendencies in the form of a free press, a revival of interest groups, minority rights, etc. In some respects the Prague Spring represented a return to the limited pluralism of the period 1945–8; in others, to the more genuine pluralism of the First Republic; in others, for instance, federalism, it went beyond its predecessors. Yet it remained a pluralism qualified by the leading role of the Communist Party and the dominance of the National Front. Even more crucial was the lack of real independence of spirit, and of action, on the part of Dubček and his associates. The failure to resist intense Soviet pressures, to grasp the danger of possible Soviet armed intervention, and prepare for resistance to the use of force, brought about a repetition of the 1938 scenario. Dubček, like Beneš, before him capitulated to *force majeure*, a surrender which was accepted by the ordinary Czech and Slovak after a week of passive resistance.

History seemed to repeat itself. After a short period of strictly limited pluralistic politics in the months after the occupation, a new surrender, in April 1969, prepared the ground for the eradication of the pluralising tendencies of the 1960s, in this case willingly, by Gustáv Husák. Once again lack of independence brought about the erasure of all vestiges of a pluralistic political culture and the total destruction of more ancient traditions of pluralism.

DOMESTIC RESPONSIBILITIES

It has sometimes been argued that Czechoslovakia's fate was irrevocably determined by international or outside forces and that there was nothing that Czechs or Slovaks could have done to alter the outcome. But international influences, no matter how powerful, do not eliminate the possibility of an alternative response in times of crisis, even though the options may at times seem to be marginal. 'However compelling external pressures may be', wrote Gourevitch 'they are unlikely to be fully determining, save for the case of outright occupation. Some leeway of response to pressure is always possible, at least conceptually. The choice of response therefore requires explanation.'[48]

After Munich Czechs were inclined to place the blame for failure on the international environment and the smallness of the country. In the post-1968 period of introspection and self-flagellation there has been a greater tendency to seek the explanation in domestic failings, and to lay the responsibility, or 'guilt', on their own leaders and even on the national character. The anonymous author of *Sixty Eight* even discerned in Czechoslovak political culture an ever-repeating tendency to yield, which he calls 'some kind of capitulationist complex in the Czech nature'.[49] The Czech journalist, Pavel Tigrid, tracing the events of successive crises from 1918 to 1968, identified a basic constant of the Czech response, the 'unwarlikeness' (*nebojovnost*) of their leaders which led to capitulation in each case. He discerned a cycle constantly recurrent in this non-violent tradition – enthusiasm, capitulation, despair, a search for blame, an effort to survive.[50] Another Czech, Christian Willars, who lives in Vienna, in a bitter critique of Czech failures, detected a similar sequence of events: great ideas, inconsistent efforts to realise them, confrontation, capitulation, and catastrophe. He ventured an explanation in the fact that the Czechs were an 'a-historical' nation, a nation 'which had lost a sense of its own history', and traced this back to the defeat at the White Mountain in 1620 and to the experience of Hapsburg rule.[51]

The successive instances of Czechoslovak capitulation to outside pressures and assaults offers what seems to be compelling evidence for these harsh judgements and proof of the culpability of leaders and the responsibility of their people. In the episodes cited, the Czech or Slovak leaders chose to surrender to what they regarded as an overwhelmingly unfavourable balance of international forces which left them no alternative. They yielded with greater or less reluctance, even with full assent in some cases (for example, Tiso and Husák). There were usually powerful domestic forces which reinforced, or even represented, the outside factor. If there were domestic forces which urged a policy of resistance, they were not strong enough to override the decisions of the leaders. The people at large soon acquiesced in the surrender and accommodated themselves to the new order, however distasteful. David Paul, after a careful examination of the historical record, concluded that the Czechoslovak tradition has been to yield to superior external force without a struggle, and to reject a policy of violent resistance.[52] In the years between the crises, he argued, outward accommodation on the surface was combined with inward spiritual and intellectual rejection of foreign rule, an attitude of mind which Paul termed 'Švejkism,' a mixture of collaboration and resistance, in the interests of 'survival'.[53]

This leaves open the question as to whether there *was* an alternative to surrender – non-compliance or resistance, whether violent or passive. The case of Masaryk has been cited above as an example of such an alternative course which produced favourable results. Could Beneš, in 1938 and 1948, or Dubček, in 1968, under very different circumstances, have followed a similar path, leading to an outcome less tragic for the nation? Both Beneš and Dubček, in all three crises, sought desperately, it should be noted, to utilise factors in the domestic and international environments to ward off the danger confronting the country. When this failed, neither took seriously the option of resisting by force, or even threatening to do so. Yet it was argued by some at the time, and by others later, that resistance, or preparation for resistance, was not only possible but desirable, and might have averted catastrophe.[54] Even ultimate defeat, after violent resistance, might in the long run have enhanced the ability to face a future crisis more resolutely. Successive capitulations reinforced the tradition of compliance and reduced the option of resistance in the future, and thus introduced a new element into the nation's political culture.

It is beyond the scope of this chapter, or the competence of the author, to make a definitive judgement on this controversial issue. This would require a careful empirical examination of each case, and its unique conditions, domestic and international. Surrender, or resistance, might have been more or less justified in the individual case. At the same time it would be helpful to broaden the scope of the analysis by examining a wider sweep of Czechoslovak history, the changing international setting, and the varied Czech and Slovak reaction in successive situations, ranging from voluntary adaptation to coerced accommodation to outside pressures and influences, and from passive to violent resistance.

Generalisations about Czechoslovak patterns of behaviour should also take into account the experiences of other small countries in Eastern Europe and elsewhere in formulating their domestic and foreign policies within a confining international context.[55] Although the range of options and the margin of independence have been narrow, resistance was not excluded, and capitulation not preordained, as the examples of Poland in 1939, Finland in 1940,

Yugoslavia in 1948, Hungary in 1956, and perhaps Poland in 1980–1. prove. Nor has resistance always failed to achieve results, sometimes in the short run, sometimes in the longer run. Each country's political culture, in its manifold variety, has contributed to the action taken in each case, and has in turn been profoundly influenced by that action and its results.

CONCLUSIONS

Conclusions can only be modest and must leave many questions open for further research and discussion. Pluralism, it is clear, has been a significant and enduring element of Czechoslovak political culture. The historical record, however, excludes a simplified interpretation of continuity, even in the realm of values, but documents a dialectic of continuity and discontinuity, as well as of heterogeneity. The fate of pluralism has been decisively influenced by international influences, but not to the exclusion of domestic determinants. Those who shared in the making of policy, whether leaders, specialised élites, or ordinary citizens, could not escape responsibility for the outcome. There *were* options to capitulation to external pressures, or accommodation to foreign rule. In explicating the shifting destiny of pluralism neither side of the medal, the international nor the domestic, can be ignored.

Political culture is a useful concept, but does not offer a magical key to the understanding of a country's politics. That culture is a complicated phenomenon, embracing a wide array of ingredients, all mutually affecting each other, some mutually supporting and others contradicting one another. Pluralism is part of a complex whole and must be evaluated accordingly. It can only be fully grasped if its subjective and objective aspects, and their interrelationship, are comprehended. Subjective judgements, as revealed in public opinion polls, are not a sufficient, and may not even be a reliable, source of evidence. Only concrete historical research, using all possible sources, including survey data if available, can offer even an approach to a solution of the problem.

NOTES AND REFERENCES

1. Archie Brown and Gordon Wightman, 'Czechoslovakia: Revival and Retreat', in Archie Brown and Jack Gray (eds) *Political Culture and*

Political Change in Communist States (London, 1977) p. 170 and the whole of chap. 6.

2. David W. Paul, *The Cultural Limits of Revolutionary Politics; Change and Continuity in Socialist Czechoslovakia* (New York, 1979) pp. 132, 136, 153, 51. Pluralism, he writes, is 'rather firmly embedded in the consciousness of Czechs and Slovaks' (p. 175) and is 'a long, if broken tradition' (p. 131).

3. H. Gordon Skilling, 'Stalinism and Czechoslovak Political Culture', in Robert C. Tucker (ed.) *Stalinism, Essays in Historical Interpretation* (New York, 1977) esp. pp. 278–9.

4. Skilling, 'Sixty-eight in Historical Perspective', in 'Prague 1968: the Aftermath', special issue of *International Journal*, XXXIII, no. 4, Autumn 1978. This was originally presented as a paper at a conference of Opus Bonum on the sixtieth anniversary of the founding of the Czechoslovak Republic, held in Wildbad Kreuth near Munich, October 19–22, 1978, and at the annual convention of the American Association for the Advancement of Slavic Studies, held in Columbus, Ohio, October 13–15, 1978.

5. Entitled 'Pluralism in Czechoslovak Political Culture: Continuity and Change in an International Setting', August 12–18, 1979.

6. Appreciation is here expressed to Milan Hauner, Stanley Winters, and David Paul, and to several historians in Czechoslovakia who must remain anonymous.

7. This is Stephen White's definition, derived from Robert Presthus and used by White in his article, 'Communist Systems and the "Iron Law of Pluralism" ', *British Journal of Political Science*, vol. VIII, no. 1, January 1978, pp. 101–17, and in his book, *Political Culture and Soviet Politics* (London, 1979).

8. Paul, *Cultural Limits*, p. 134.

9. Ibid, p. 135.

10. Skilling, 'Pluralism in Communist Societies; Straw Men and Red Herrings', *Studies in Comparative Communism*, XIII, no. 1, Spring 1980, pp. 82–90.

11. Václav Černý, 'Dvě studie masarykovské' (Two Studies of Masaryk) (typewritten) published abroad in *Svědectiví*, (Paris) XIV, no. 56, 1978, pp. 665–80, esp. pp. 668, 677.

12. *At the Cross-Roads of Europe, A Historical Outline of the Democratic Idea in Czechoslovakia* (Prague, 1938) pp. 19–20.

13. Ibid, pp. 256 *et seq.*

14. Skilling, 'Sixty-eight', pp. 679–80. For examples of such self-criticism, see Christian Willars, 'Znovu; smysl českých dějin' (Once Again – the Meaning of Czech History) *Svědectví*, XII, no. 46, 1973, pp. 289–301; Pavel Tigrid, 'Jací jsme, když je zle' (What Kind of People Are We when Things are Bad) ibid, no. 46, 1973, pp. 301–20; Jan Příbram, 'Příběh s nedobrým koncem' (An event with a Not So Good Ending) ibid, XIV, no. 55, 1978, pp. 371–95; Petr Pithart, 'Pokus o vlast', (A Search for a Homeland) ibid., XIV, no. 59, pp. 445–64.

15. Bruce Garver, 'The Czechoslovak Tradition', in H. Brisch and I. Volgyes,

Czechoslovakia: The Heritage of Ages Past (Boulder, Colorado, 1979) esp. pp. 48 ff.

16. The works cited in notes 1, 2 and 3 above.
17. See above, in earlier chapters.
18. Brown and Wightman, 'Czechoslovakia', p. 159.
19. Paul and Skilling, cited in notes 2 and 3 above.
20. Brown and Wightman, pp. 159, 164–5. The evaluation of Masaryk, on the other hand, is very high in each poll (pp. 179–80).
21. Ibid, p. 170. Cf. polls cited by Skilling, *Czechoslovakia's Interrupted Revolution* (Princeton, 1976) pp. 363–6, 550–5.
22. Brown and Wightman, pp. 174, 188–9. See Z. Mlynář, 'Notions of Political Pluralism in the Policy of the Communist Party of Czechoslovakia in 1968', Working Paper no. 3, *The Experiences of the Prague Spring 1968* (July, 1979) esp. pp. 2–6.
23. Brown and Wightman, pp. 189–90.
24. Paul, *Cultural Limits, passim.* See also Stanley Z. Pech, 'Political Parties in Eastern Europe 1848–1939: Comparisons and Continuities', *East Central Europe*, vol. 5, no. 1, 1978, pp. 1–38.
25. David Paul's phrase, *Cultural Limits*, p. 175.
26. The following summarises the longer treatment in my Moscow paper (note 5 above); see also Skilling, 'Sixty-eight'.
27. David W. Paul, 'Slovak Nationalism and the Hungarian State, 1870–1910', unpublished paper.
28. Josef Korbel, *Twentieth Century Czechoslovakia* (New York, 1977) pp. 82–4.
29. *Osmašedesátý: Pokus o kritické porozumění historickým souvislostem* (Sixty Eight, An Attempt at Critical Understanding in an Historical Context) typewritten (Prague, June 1977–August 1978) p. 178; later published abroad under this title and under the pseudonym, J. Sládeček.
30. *Svědectví*, XV, no. 60, 1980, esp. pp. 732–3.
31. Pithart, 'Pokus o vlast' 59, p. 463.
32. Ibid, p. 458. Cf. also the anonymous reviewer cited above who referred to 'an unwillingness (in 1968) to assume responsibility for the state or at the very least to defend it' (ibid, no. 60, p. 734).
33. The sharpest critique of Munich was made by Příbram, 'Příběh', pp. 378, 383, 394. See also V. Prečan, 'Probleme des Tschechischen Parteiensystems zwischen München 1938 und dem Mai 1945', in *Die Erste Tschechoslowakische Republik als multinationaler Parteienstat* (München, 1979) esp. p. 531; Milan Hauner, 'Recasting Czech History', *Survey*, 24 no. 3 (108) Summer 1979, pp. 219–20.
34. Brown and Wightman, pp. 172–3, 187–9. Cf. also Mlynář, *Nachtfrost* (Köln, 1978) pp. 148–9 on the Communist régime's failure to destroy the values of Masaryk and the First Republic; English edition, *Night-frost in Prague, The End of Humane Socialism* (New York, 1980) pp. 117–18.
35. Paul, *Cultural Limits*, pp. 277–9.
36. Ibid, pp. 172–3.
37. The anonymous reviewer cited above wrote 'Values for which we are not willing to sacrifice much are evidently not real values for us' (*Svědectví*, no. 60, p. 734).

38. Havel, 'An Open Letter from Prague', *Encounter* (London) September 1975, esp. pp. 15, 18, 28. The letter, dated 8 April 1975, and addressed to President Gustáv Husák, circulated in typescript in Czechoslovakia.

39. Kundera, *The Book of Laughter and Forgetting* (Harmondsworth, 1983) p. 159.

40. Peter Gourevitch, 'The Second Image Reversed: the International Sources of Domestic Politics', *International Organization*, 32, no. 4, Autumn 1978, p. 911.

41. James N. Rosenau, *The Scientific Study of Foreign Policy* (New York, 1971) chap. 9, esp. p. 318.

42. Ibid, pp. 127–8, 319 (also cited by Paul, *Cultural Limits*, pp. 12, 302).

43. Paul, *Cultural Limits*, p. 82.

44. Ibid, pp. 56, 81–2, 287–90.

45. Ibid, p. 252.

46. See my comments on the international factor, 'Sixty-eight', pp. 680–2, 698–9, and the more expanded treatment in the Moscow paper.

47. Prečan, 'Problem des Tschechischen Parteiensystems', pp. 536, 549, 551–52.

48. Gourevitch, 'Second Image', p. 911.

49. *Osmašedesátý* (see note 29), p. 165.

50. Tigrid, 'Jaci jsme', pp 312 ff, esp. p. 317.

51. Willars, 'Znovu', pp. 290, 296. In 1938, 'the body of the nation was preserved at the cost of its soul' (p. 293).

52. Paul, *Cultural Limits*, pp.253–6, 269 ff.

53. Ibid, pp. 256 ff.

54. For a severe criticism of Beneš' actions in 1938 and 1948, see Korbel, *Czechoslovakia*, pp. 147–9; for a defence of Beneš, see E. Taborsky 'Tragedy, Triumph and Tragedy: Czechoslovakia 1938–1948', in Brisch and Volgyes, *Czechoslovakia*, esp. pp. 114–17, 133. See the sharp critique of Beneš and Dubček by Příbram and Tigrid in works cited above. For a balanced assessment of 1938, 1948 and 1968, see Paul, *Cultural Limits*, pp. 271–6, 106–7; of 1968, Skilling, *Interrupted Revolution*, pp. 843–6.

55. Paul, *Cultural Limits*, p. 280. See also Dalimil, *Obrana národa* (Defence of the Nation) *Listy*, VII, no. 5, October 1977, pp. 1–3.

7 Czechoslovakia's Political Culture Reconsidered

DAVID W. PAUL

The preceding chapters reflect a creditable development in recent years within the field of communist studies, namely the intense dialogue centring on the political cultures of communist-ruled societies. With respect to Czechoslovakia, as well as to the Soviet Union, this dialogue has reached a high level of sophistication and advanced the cause of political science measurably. Simplistic assertions have fallen under well-aimed criticism, and polarised positions on this or that issue have been gradually replaced by increasingly subtle and balanced analyses.

Four problems to which allusion has already been made in earlier chapters will be taken up in this one (which contains not only a response to the preceding contribution by H. Gordon Skilling but also a reassessment of earlier writings on the subject, including my own). These embrace (i) continuity and discontinuity in Czechoslovakia's political culture, especially in the tradition of pluralism; (ii) heterogeneity; (iii) the impact of outside (that is, foreign) forces; and (iv) the problem of persistence versus change. A fifth section will briefly consider some broader, comparative issues relating to power, weakness, and penetration.

CZECHOSLOVAK POLITICAL CULTURE: THE DIALECTIC OF CONTINUITY AND DISCONTINUITY

H. Gordon Skilling's phrase, 'the dialectic of continuity and discontinuity', is an excellent formulation of an important question and serves to resolve a major discrepancy among previous analysts of the Czechoslovak political culture.[1] There is, of course, no disagreement among scholars that the political history of Czechs and Slovaks has been most discontinuous. The years of authoritarian rule in the twentieth century now outnumber the years and months of more liberalistic political orders in which pluralistic values could find expression in institutional structures and mass behavioural patterns.[2] The long gestation of Czechoslovak democracy from 1867–1918 and the solidification of pluralistic norms from 1918–38 may indeed have set certain patterns that subsequent autocracies were unable to snuff out, but it is undeniable that the disillusioning realities of 1938–45, 1948–68, and 1969 to the present have had their own strong influence on the political culture. The political activists of 1968 had learned something about democracy from their parents' recollections; now another generation is growing up, and what it knows about democracy will have been learned only from parental recollections of the eight-month 'spring' of 1968. In the meantime, the reality of contemporary life, replete with lessons in the 'proper' interpretation of Marxism–Leninism and relentless pressures to conform politically, will have their effect on the development of youthful attitudes.

Yet history has been full of surprises. Who would have predicted, say, 150–250 years after the defeat of Bohemia on White Mountain, that a Czech nation would arise and assert itself in the course of the nineteenth century – or, even more remarkably, that a Slovak nation would consolidate itself from among those primitive, parochial Slavic communities of northern Hungary? Similarly, the movement within Communist Czechoslovakia that culminated in the events of 1968 startled those who had presumed the spirit of democracy to have died twenty years earlier.

Certainly, the Habsburg conquest destroyed historical Bohemia. Indisputably, the cataclysmic events of 1938–9 shattered the political structures that had developed among the Czechs since 1860 and among the Slovaks since 1918. Of course, the wartime despotisms and the equally dictatorial system introduced in 1948 radically altered citizens' political behaviour and undoubtedly changed some of their ideas about the nature of politics. In the light of these realities, it is all the more remarkable that today's scholars can seriously discuss continuities in the political attitudes and behaviour patterns of Czechs and Slovaks – continuities that appear to connect, albeit vaguely and precariously, underlying political orientations across several generations reared in starkly different political environments. Without in any way denying the salience of the obvious discontinuities, one must therefore account for the continuous elements of democracy and pluralism that have survived the attempts of several governments to weed them out.

Have these elements of democracy and pluralism indeed survived? One can only speculate about the present and future. So long as a democratic opposition exists, whether in the form of the persecuted Charter 77 movement or in less visible circles, one can be confident that the tradition is kept alive – though how widely the democratic and pluralistic outlook of the Chartists is shared cannot be empirically known given the constraints on scholarship in current-day Czechoslovakia. Looking to the future, one must of course be even less confident and more speculative in one's assessment. Perhaps the historically-minded would be tempted to guess that if pluralistic tendencies survived earlier assaults, they will outlive the current political reality and emerge again at a more propitious time; we must admit, however, that this is no more than an optimistic speculation.

What we can say is that, looking back at the reform movement of 1968, we can surely find grounds for arguing that the events of that year constituted the reawakening of a longer tradition, however generally that tradition is defined.[3] And perhaps, when referring to Czechoslovak pluralism, it is best to keep the discussion in relatively unspecific terms. Thus, the continuous element of pluralism in the Czechoslovak political culture is a general assumption, widely shared among Czechs and Slovaks of at least two generations, that politics should be an arena of organised group competition. In this vein, the extent to which the political system envisioned by the reformers of 1968 resembled that of the First or Third Republic is immaterial. What matters is the proposition that the movement toward a pluralistic institutional structure was fuelled by an ingrained pattern of orientations which construes politics as an inherently pluralistic phenomenon – a notion apparently so widespread that it affected the viewpoint of many influential Communists who had once been Stalinists.

One final point about pluralism should be made. It would be useful to draw a distinction between pluralistic *structures*, *behaviour* and *orientations*. It is common among political scientists to consider the three to be inseparable components of pluralism. However, their interrelationship can be rather complex. Obviously, pluralistic political structures facilitate and encourage pluralistic behaviour; yet we know of many instances in which pluralistic political structures have broken down because the attraction of anti-pluralist movements was apparently more compelling than the preservation of pluralism – as, for example, in the collapse of the Weimar Republic. Weimar

Germany, it seems, existed as a set of pluralistic structures without a sufficiently strong base of popular orientations; in its final years, it struggled unsuccessfully for survival against political behaviour patterns that became increasingly anti-pluralistic. Conversely, pluralistic behaviour can take place in the absence of a pluralistic institutional structure: such was the case in the Czechoslovakia of 1968, where political reformers sought to devise the proper institutional framework for this as yet amorphous pluralism. The Dubček regime hoped to absorb the public impulse to pluralism and channel it into the construction of socialism. Whence came that pluralistic impulse? From something in the nation's underlying political orientations – 'a belief in the virtues of political pluralism', as Brown and Wightman have expressed it.[4] If those orientations existed prior to 1968, they might still exist today, underlying the anti-pluralist structures that bespeak a persisting incongruence between governmental norms and public preferences.

HETEROGENEITY

Skilling has advanced our understanding of the Czechoslovak political culture greatly by exploding the myth of an unambiguously democratic and pluralistic culture that, somehow, has preserved its purity despite years of anti-pluralistic rule. Many different factors have shaped the political culture, giving it a mixture of features that are not altogether compatible. Contradictory tendencies abound, and in certain historical periods political sub-cultures have become particularly notable: the best examples are the Communists and the Slovak populists (L'udáks) in the time of the First Republic.[5]

One can also see important differences between the political traditions of Czechs and Slovaks, the two major nationalities of the republic. (I prefer not to speak of a Slovak political sub-culture, for the term smacks of deviation or marginality.) Scholars, especially those of earlier periods, have often underestimated the significance of those differences, assuming that Slovaks are really like Czechs, only not as far advanced; that Slovak nationalism (sometimes referred to as 'ultranationalism') is deviant; and that the Slovaks, lacking any deep political traditions of their own, owe their twentieth-century political development to the Czechs, without whose tutelage they would still be a rather primitively organised people. To correct these misconceptions, it must be pointed out that the Slovak national tradition now reaches back nearly two hundred years. That tradition was of course formed and developed amid constant strains and pressures, often more severe than those acting upon the Czechs. It is true that the Hungarian system before World War One obstructed Slovak political development, but it is inaccurate to say that Slovak politics hardly existed 'except in embryonic form'.[6] It would be an equal exaggeration to argue that Slovak politics had reached an advanced stage by 1918, or even that its degree of development was equal to that of the Czechs, who were more favourably situated within the Austrian half of the Dual Monarchy; however, Slovak political activities during the twenty years preceding independence had shown a liveliness, a tenacity, and a strength of organisation sufficient to persevere in spite of determined efforts to eradicate the movement.[7] Although independence brought a generally more propitious climate for the development of Slovak politics, some pressures and constraints continued to be present in the First Republic, which in Skilling's apt phrase was 'stamped by Czech traditions and experiences'.[8] Nor was the World War Two Slovak state unaffected by distorting political pressures; Msgr Tiso, Adolf Hitler's compliant puppet, led a regime that snuffed out all but the most extreme chauvinistic, anti-pluralist political impulses among his countrymen and thus moulded his state according to the values of an excusive élite.

This history left its own imprint on the political consciousness of the Slovaks. If Czechs cannot take their national existence for granted, as Milan Kundera has stated, Slovaks have even less reason for doing so. Most reformers among the Slovak Communists in 1968 felt it necessary to remind the Czechs repeatedly that Slovakia had its own problems which required separate solutions. While Czechs were rehabilitating the memory of Masaryk and Beneš, Slovaks were rehabilitating Štúr and Štefánik. The resurgence of Slovak nationalism in its Communist form bore witness to a political culture that has its own unique flavour.

It is tempting to say that Slovak attitudes about pluralism are different from those of Czechs, less supportive, on the whole, or that Slovaks are perhaps more inclined to accept authority. These propositions cannot be verified. What can be said is that the *tradition* of pluralism in Slovakia is not as pronounced, and is probably weaker, than in the Czech lands. Looking back at the First Republic, Slovak politics tended to be more polarised and bitterly fissiparous than Czech politics; Slovak parties were more hierarchically organised and generally dominated by single leaders; Slovak party divisions followed blunt ideological lines, with the largest portion of the Slovak vote consistently divided up among the L'udáks (on the far right wing), the Communists (on the far left), and the centrist Agrarians.[9] In contrast, the Czech electorate splintered in every parliamentary election after 1920, and by 1935 one would have to say there were at least seven viable Czech parties.[10] Moreover, the tone of Slovak politics was more polemical; there was a pervading atmosphere of hostility between the two most powerful parties, the Catholic-nationalist L'udáks and the Czechophile, Protestant-dominant Agrarians. Politics was less 'secular' in Slovakia than in the Czech lands, and the ideological differences among the major parties were intensified by popular stereotypes linking them with religious groupings: the 'Catholic' L'udáks, the 'Protestant' Agrarians, the 'atheistic' or 'Jewish' communists. If one can confidently say that the experience with political pluralism during the First Republic left Czechs with a dominant strain of positive orientations toward pluralism, one must be sceptical of any similar judgements about the Slovaks.

Let us not exaggerate this contrast, however. It would be simplistic to characterise Czechs as overwhelmingly democratic and inclined toward pluralism, just as it would oversimplify the issue for us to see Slovaks as authoritarian and tending toward political polarisation. Here again, a dialectical understanding of the political culture is most helpful. It is not unusual for a political culture to contain contradictions, and it should not be difficult to understand that the Czechoslovak political culture, in both its Czech and its Slovak variants, is both pluralistic and unpluralistic, both democratic and authoritarian.

One can find analogous contradictions in other societies. For example, Paul Warwick has noted an oscillation in the French political culture between tendencies to ideological purity and non-compromise, on the one hand, and tendencies to putting aside ideological differences in a spirit of pragmatism, on the other hand. Both tendencies are integral to the French political culture, but historical realities may encourage the momentary expression of one or the other under relatively predictable conditions.[11] Such would appear to be true in the case of pluralism and anti-pluralism in Czechoslovakia: both have their place in the political culture, but one or the other will tend to dominate depending on the historical circumstances. Experience suggests that the determining variable in this Czechoslovak oscillation is the presence or absence of a controlling foreign power.[12]

With this in mind, the present author disputes the usefulness of the distinction, sometimes made, between the 'ideal political culture' and the 'real political culture'.[13] Certainly, one needs to distinguish between ideals and realities, but political cultures are composed of both; that is, they consist of values which can be thoroughly idealised and behavioural patterns which can often violate stated values. The gap between ideal and reality can separate citizens (or certain groups of citizens) from a regime; or, as Jack Gray has rightly pointed out, there may be a pronounced gap between the regime's proclaimed ideal – especially the image of the new socialist man – and the often cynical, sometimes corrupt, always power-conscious 'operational code' of the ruling personages.[14] Mary McAuley has suggested that the gap between ideal and reality thus cuts through the middle of what has been called the 'official political culture' in Communist states, leaving us with the problem of determining just what the official political culture really is and how best to describe it.[15] In Czechoslovakia, for example, there is much evidence to argue that the regime has long abandoned the goal of creating new socialist men and, for reasons of maintaining tranquillity, is satisfied with a populace that abstains from politics and seeks material self-gratification. From the current regime's perspective, such a populace is preferable to the one in 1968 that became widely politicised, contested the party's monopoly over policy ideas, and contributed to the rationale for a Soviet military intervention.

Thus in noting the dissonance within Czechoslovakia's political culture between the behavioural model of the new socialist man, drawn from what one might call the 'ideal' image in the official political culture, and the 'real' behaviour of the citizenry, one must add that this is not simply a matter of dissonance between actual political behaviour and ('ideal') values; rather, it is a case of discrepancies and contradictions running throughout all elements of the political culture, 'official' and 'dominant', 'ideal' and 'real', Czech as well as Slovak and historical as well as contemporary. Professor Skilling has suggested that the abortive political systems of 1945–8 and 1968–9, had they lasted, might have provided opportunities to reconcile these contradictions;[16] the reality, however, has turned out otherwise. If there is a dialectical pattern in the dynamic of Czechoslovakia's political culture, it has been interrupted and short-circuited by the intervention of outside forces. The dissonances and contradictions remain, therefore, and the predominant character of the political culture is incoherence.

THE IMPACT OF OUTSIDE FORCES

Since 1968, as so often in the past, outside forces have intervened to determine which of the contradictory elements in Czechoslovakia's political culture dominate political reality. If the experience of the First Republic indicated the strength of Czech-pluralist values in a society left alone to order its politics of itself, the experience of World War Two and its aftermath has demonstrated the thoroughness with which the pluralist values could be submerged by the realities of imposed authoritarianism.

Professor Skilling has correctly stressed the decisive influence of international factors in Czechoslovakia's political culture and has aptly described the role of the Communist Party of Czechoslovakia as a conduit through which elements of the Russian and Soviet political cultures have been transmitted to Czechoslovakia.[17] Elsewhere, I have argued that the Czechoslovak Communists arose from a political sub-culture on the fringe of First Republican politics, and as they moved into power, they assumed the role of a colonial élite beholden to the foreign power that would permanently dominate Czechoslovakia in the post-war era.[18] Today, Soviet power is the critical factor that has determined the victory of autocratic and anti-pluralist strains in Czechoslovakia's political reality.

To restate this point: left mostly to themselves, Czechs and Slovaks have tended toward relatively democratic patterns of government and sought to institutionalise their impulse to pluralism. Under the impact of outside forces – and this is true of both Nazi Germany and the USSR – highly authoritarian sub-cultures have come to the surface, embodied in the colonial élites entrusted by their foreign masters with the power to rule. In this broad sense, the governments of Hácha and Tiso had something in common with those of Gottwald and Husák. The oscillating pattern of democracy and autocracy, pluralism and anti-pluralism, is thus attributable to the historical ebb and flow of foreign control. If there have always existed groups in Czechoslovakia who are ready to support authoritarian regimes, it is important to recognize that these groups have never gained dominance without the strong backing of foreign powers.

PERSISTENCE VERSUS CHANGE

Repeatedly in this century, underlying tendencies to democracy and pluralism have percolated to the surface of what had been autocratic political orders and, in moments of freedom from outside interference, have become the dominant cultural influence in Czechoslovakia's politics. Repeatedly, the outside forces have intervened in support of anti-democratic ruling groups, imposing an arbitrary resolution of the contradictory tendencies in Czechoslovakia's political culture. Surely this recurrent suppression of democracy and pluralism has coloured Czech and Slovak orientations to politics. One might justifiably expect that, by now, Czechs and Slovaks should evince some attitudinal effects of this frustrating history. Would that we could answer the question – empirically unanswerable for the time being – of whether or not the long tradition of pluralistic values will survive yet another lengthy period of political suppression. Already, we read pessimistic forecasts by some, such as Milan Kundera, of the death of the Czech nation under the rule of Gustáv Husák, 'the president of forgetting'.[19] It is ironic that the brilliant writer Kundera, endowed with a great gift of insight into the collective mind of his nation, should now be making this fatalistic prediction, for in the 1960s Kundera had so eloquently reminded his people that they had been able to escape cultural extinction in earlier eras of their history.[20] Have they now forfeited their last chance?

What we know about political cultures suggests that they are relatively resistant to large-scale changes except over long periods of evolution or in unusually disturbing circumstances.[21] Is there something in Czechoslovakia's current situation that might lead us to predict the end of that long pluralistic tradition forever? Certainly the reform period of 1968–9 saw the re-emergence of that old pluralistic impulse, but in a form that was conditioned by the preceding twenty years of socialist authoritarianism; there were in 1968 no serious discussions of any non-socialist political alternatives. If this fact reflected a change in the Czechoslovak political culture from the unlimited pluralism of the First Republic, or even the limited pluralism of the Third Republic, can we not expect to see a continued narrowing of the public ideological spectrum in the years beginning with 1969 and extending into the indefinite future?

The answer to this depends on the development of political attitudes among members of a generation that is now growing up. Today's younger generation will, in all likelihood, have heard their parents' stories of the 1968 'spring'. These stories might very well sound like those of the First Republic told by the parents of the generation which mobilised for the movements of 1968. Will they be as compelling? Or will the stories of 1968 be filtered through a veil of scepticism, bitterness, and despair so powerful as to overwhelm all youthful propensities to optimism? Alas, we do not have access to any meaningful research on the attitudes of youth in the Czechoslovakia of the 1970s and 1980s, but such impressionistic evidence as we have suggests little to indicate a widespread, burning desire to reform the political system. One generally gets the impression that Czechoslovak youth tend to be apolitical, materialistic, and inclined to self-gratification rather than to higher social causes.[22]

And if the nation is ever to be uplifted once again, who will serve as spokesmen and conscience for another renascence? Maybe the courageous activists of Charter 77 will not only keep the spirit of democracy alive in the interim but also emerge, eventually, in the role played by the intellectual 'awakeners' of the 1800s and the 1960s. Certainly, the fortitude and tenacity of the chartists have impressed many citizens and kept alive some of the grander national traditions. On the other hand, one might just as persuasively predict the eventual dying-out of the dissent movement under the protracted strain of harassment, persecution, and forced emigration. Add to this the dearth of genuine historical writing – meant, according to Kundera, as a purposeful strategy on the part of 'the president of forgetting' to erase the nation's memory – and the meaning of earlier political experiences may ultimately be lost, leaving nothing to guide the future but the dictates of those in power.

One does not like to make such a prediction as the one immediately foregoing, but one must consider both the scenarios to which allusion has been made – another Czechoslovak renascence and the exact opposite, the death of political alternatives – as real possibilities. Again, the role of that ubiquitous outside force is crucial. No one can accurately predict the limits of Soviet tolerance, and this would seem to be particularly true now that the USSR has entered a period of leadership transition. It is possible that the next generation of Soviet leaders will not only allow but also encourage political reform in Eastern Europe, but it is also possible that the opposite will occur.

One should also consider the possible impact of political and economic trends within Hungary and Poland, Czechoslovakia's other neighbours. Hungary, by most standards of measurement, is not yet a worker's paradise, but its economic successes in recent years have shone like a diamond amid the darkening economic outlook of the CMEA countries. Hungary's political stability, moreover, seems to confirm the wisdom of the prevailing moderate reformism.

Poland, on the other hand, serves as a lesson in economic and political mistakes. Throughout 1980–1, the Czechoslovak leaders looked on in horror as Polish workers seized control of their own union activities and pressured the state to share economic and political power with them. The Prague regime could not restrain its glee as martial law descended upon Poland in December of 1981; yet it soon became clear that the military crackdown reimposed order only on the surface of a still uncontrolled society. Surely the unresolved problems of economic mismangement, shattered workers' morale, and a persisting society-wide disaffection – the reality of Poland – are also sharp reminders of similar, if as yet less severe, difficulties confronting Czechoslovakia.

Will the future see the spread of political reform and renewal to other countries in an increasingly uncontrollable Soviet bloc – including Czechoslovakia? Clearly, any significant renewal of the Czechoslovak political system must come in the context of a relaxation of Soviet control over Czechoslovakia. This author is not bold enough to make any prognostications about the future of Soviet control in East-Central Europe generally.

SOME BROADER CONSIDERATIONS

The idea that political systems are penetrated by forces outside a country's boundaries, and that these external forces can significantly influence domestic politics, is relevant to both great powers and mini-states. To appreciate this, we need only recall the centuries-long response of Russian rulers, from Peter the Great to Leonid Brezhnev, to the generally more advanced ideas and technologies of the West. Yet great powers are in many respects far less susceptible to outside forces than smaller states – far less penetrable, that is. Peter the Great found western technological ideas fascinating and worthy of copying, but he did not see fit to import into Russia the social and political concepts that led to the French Revolution and the evolution of British parliamentary democracy. Likewise, Brezhnev, with one eye on the development of American military technology, led his country into a position of strategic parity with the United States; but yet, notwithstanding the wide appeal of western pop culture, there is no evidence that western political ideas have been attractive to more than a relatively small part of the population of the Brezhnev and post-Brezhnev USSR.[23] Thus, the large and powerful Russian society has for centuries demonstrated a substantial capacity to resist penetration, and the Soviet political culture has proved to be rather resilient in its confrontation with foreign ideas.

The same can be said, perhaps in differing terms and degrees, of such inherently strong societies as those of China and Japan. Both cultures have been penetrated by outside forces, particularly those coming from the West; both have absorbed certain ideas and modes of the foreigner, but they have also displayed a capability of resisting penetration. For example, the forced adoption by the Japanese of a constitution modelled after many in the West, as well as the conscious borrowing from and mimicking of western industrialisation models, have not by any means obliterated Japanese cultural patterns. To some extent it can even be said that the penetration of Japan by the West has not reached certain core areas of the culture; western political structures and western-influenced business norms merely overlie peculiarly Japanese patterns of authority in both governmental and corporate organisational systems, the 'inscrutable' functioning of which often bemuses westerners.[24]

Czechoslovakia is obviously an example of a very different syndrome. Czechs and Slovaks have long been self-consciously aware of their country's smallness and weakness. Outside forces have persistently penetrated their societies deeply, inescapably. The results have not always been destructive of the national cultures, but all too often they have been; therefore, a strain of profound humility and, indeed, shame runs through the collective consciousness. Whatever possibilities there may at times have been for resistance to outside penetration have been rendered even less plausible than one might expect by a widespread tendency to yield rather than fight against heavy odds. Exceptions must be noted; the ancient legacy of the Hussites, the courageous efforts of the Czechoslovak legionaries, the short-lived Czech resistance in the Second World War, and the valiant Slovak uprising of 1944 all stand as monuments to a heroic spirit. Yet, the result of past resistance has been defeat more often than victory, and in the moments of crisis that lie within the memory of Czechs and Slovaks living today, surrender, rather than resistance, has been the prevailing course of national action.

We cannot empirically say that Czechs and Slovaks are psychologically predisposed against violent resistance; we do not know exactly what the response would have been had Beneš called his people into battle in 1938, or had he asked them in 1948 to repudiate the Communists' illegal bid for total power, or had Dubček mobilised the populace in 1968 for an armed resistance. We do know that various forms of non-violent resistance were practised on a wide scale after the German occupation of Bohemia and Moravia in 1939 and the Warsaw Pact's occupation of the entire country in 1968. These acts of non-violent resistance, as I have argued at length elsewhere, served to keep alive something of the national spirit in times when it was most seriously endangered.[25] If this was true, however, the path chosen – non-violence – has not demonstrably succeeded in overcoming or subverting the power of the outsider; and, moreover, the path chosen is hardly the stuff of a valorous national tradition which inspires pride in the hearts of patriots.

When we consider the prospects for change in the Czechoslovak political culture, we must take into account the experiences with outside powers and the accumulated national humiliations. This author has heard individual Czechs and Slovaks wonder aloud, for example, whether the exuberant attempt to create a 'socialism with a human face' was worth the troubles visited upon them in August 1968 and thereafter; life during the last few years of the Novotný regime, after all, had not been so bad in comparison with the repression of Husák's 'normalised' Czechoslovakia. How serious or widespread this sentiment is cannot be judged, but in our range of future scenarios we must include the possibility of a generalised reluctance on the part of the public (as well as of the ruling élite) to disturb whatever marginally tolerable conditions may exist for fear that the alternative will be not better, but even much worse, than the status quo. Thus, in this most pessimistic of scenarios, we must admit it is conceivable that the long strain of democracy and pluralism in the Czechoslovak political culture could wither away or become totally irrelevant because society, penetrated so thoroughly, had succumbed to an unhappy inertia.

Perhaps, however, a new generation of rulers will find the courage to explore political alternatives once again. It may be they will discover some viable manoeuvring room within the constraints of the Soviet empire, having learned something from the experiences of neighbouring Poland and Hungary, and perhaps at that point a conservatively reformist party élite will be able, figuratively speaking, to reach its hands out and grasp those of a populace whose political orientations have changed enough to accept and celebrate the resulting breath of limited freedom. At that point, a thoroughgoing re-evaluation of the Czechoslovak political culture will be in order.

NOTES AND REFERENCES

1. See H. Gordon Skilling, chapter 6 of this volume. In several earlier writings, Skilling tended to argue the saliency of discontinuities in the make-up of Czechoslovakia's political culture, in contrast to the relative emphasis placed by Archie Brown, Gordon Wightman and the present author on continuities. Cf. Skilling, 'Pluralism in Czechoslovak Political Culture: Continuity and Change in an International Setting', a paper presented at the congress of the International Political Science Association in Moscow, 1979; Archie Brown and Gordon Wightman, 'Czechoslovakia: Revival and Retreat', in Archie Brown and Jack Gray (eds) *Political Culture and Political Change in Communist States* (London and New York, 1977, 1979) chap. 6; and David W. Paul, *The Cultural Limits of Revolutionary Politics; Change and Continuity in Socialist Czechoslovakia* (Boulder, Colorado and New York, 1979).

2. This is true even if we consider the years 1900–14, a time when Czech pluralism thrived in Austria. (It did not do so after the outbreak of World War One, when strict political controls were enforced throughout the Empire.) The years of imperial autocracy (1914–18), German domination (1939–45) and Communist dictatorship (1948–68, 1969–present) now add up to more than one-half the years in this century.

3. David W. Paul, 'The Repluralization of Czechoslovak Politics in the 1960s', *Slavic Review*, vol. 33, no. 4 (December, 1974) pp. 721–40. See also *idem, The Cultural Limits of Revolutionary Politics*, chap. 5.

4. Brown and Wightman, 'Czechoslovakia: Revival and Retreat' (1977) p. 170.

5. For example, see my discussion of the Communists as a sub-culture that rose to élite status in *The Cultural Limits of Revolutionary Politics*, chap. 3; cf. Skilling, 'Pluralism in Czechoslovak Political Culture'. Ethnic minorities have also represented political sub-cultures about which very little has yet been written.

6. This is Skilling's phrase (ibid., p. 4). See also Victor S. Mamatey, 'The Establishment of the Republic', in Mamatey and Radomír Luža (eds) *A History of the Czechoslovak Republic 1918–1948* (Princeton, New Jersey, 1973) pp. 7–10.

7. I have begun to explore the dimensions of this movement in a separate research project. For a preliminary statement, see David W. Paul, 'Slovak Nationalism and the Hungarian State', in Paul R. Brass (ed.) *Ethnicity and the State* (London, forthcoming).

8. Skilling, 'Pluralism in Czechoslovak Political Culture', p. 4.

9. In the 1925 elections, these three parties attracted more than 82 per cent of the total vote cast for Slovak parties. By 1935, the Social Democrats had moved into a contending position in fourth place, and the four largest parties attracted 86 per cent of the Slovak vote in a field of approximately ten parties.

10. The Agrarians, Social Democrats, People's Party, National Socialists, Communists, Tradesmen's Party and the National Democrats.

11. Paul V. Warwick, 'Ideology, Culture, and Gamesmanship in French

Politics', *Journal of Modern History*, vol. 50, no. 4 (December, 1978) pp. 631–59.

12. Paul, *Cultural Limits*, pp. 82, 287–90. See also Skilling's argument in this volume.

13. See, for example, Skilling's use of such a distinction in this volume.

14. Gray, in *Political Culture and Political Change in Communist States* (1977) p. 260.

15. Mary McAuley, in Chapter 2 of this volume.

16. Skilling, 'Pluralism in Czechoslovak Political Culture', pp. 1–2, 11–12, 14–16.

17. In addition to the preceding chapter in this volume, see also Skilling, 'Stalinism and Czechoslovak Political Culture', in Robert C. Tucker (ed.) *Stalinism: Essays in Historical Interpretation* (New York, 1977), pp. 257–80.

18. See chapters 3–4 of Paul, *Cultural Limits*, as well as the broader discussion of Czechoslovakia's international position in David W. Paul, *Czechoslovakia: Profile of a Socialist Republic at the Crossroads of Europe* (Boulder, Colorado, 1981) chap. 2.

19. Milan Kundera, *The Book of Laughter and Forgetting* (New York, 1980) p. 158.

20. See, for example, Kundera's speech to the Fourth Congress of the Czechoslovak Writers' Union (1967), printed in English translation in Dušan Hamšík, *Writers Against Rulers* (New York, 1971) pp. 167–77.

21. Cf. Sidney Verba, 'Germany: The Remaking of Political Culture', in Lucien W. Pye and Verba (eds) *Political Culture and Political Development* (Princeton, 1965) pp. 130–70, in which the author emphasises the difficulty and long-term nature of remoulding German citizens' political orientations; and Robert E. Ward, 'Japan: The Continuity of Modernization', in ibid, esp. pp. 52 ff, in which the effects of Japan's military defeat and the American occupation are juxtaposed against longer-term influences and developmental patterns in the making of the modern-day Japanese political culture.

22. This is admittedly an impressionistic judgement. Unfortunately, there have been no significant studies of Czechoslovak youth since the 1960s.

23. This is not to discount the likelihood that increased contacts with westerners may be having their effect over the long run, creating a differentiation of political generations as yet not completely observable. See Stephen White, *Political Culture and Soviet Politics* (London and New York, 1979) pp. 182–8.

24. For a lucid study of Japanese politics, see Robert E. Ward, *Japan's Political System*, 2nd edn (Englewood Cliffs, New Jersey, 1978), especially the chapter on political culture, pp. 58–73.

25. Paul, *Cultural Limits*, chap. 8.

8   Conclusions

ARCHIE BROWN

The essential purpose of this book has been to ventilate argument concerning the scope of the concept of political culture, to question whether the notion should be applied in the study of Communist systems, to ask what (if anything) it has to offer by way of explanation or interpretation of political life in such systems, and to attempt to show how it or its component parts can be elucidated or refined in such a way as to provide greater insight into Communist politics. Some formidably large questions have been raised – among them, the nature of the relationship between a people and their history; the ways in which political beliefs are acquired, maintained, changed and transmitted; and the relationship between values and attitudes, on the one hand, and political behaviour, on the other.

In the formulation and exploration of these and other questions in the pages that follow, I take up some of the arguments of other contributors to this volume, more often than not when I disagree with them. It would be otiose to repeat all the numerous points in the previous chapters which seem to me pertinent and well-taken. I have, moreover, not limited myself to the lines of enquiry followed by my co-authors. In particular, I find it useful not only to recognise that disciplines other than political science and history have much to offer towards an understanding of the problem of political culture and Communist studies, but also actually to discuss some of the most relevant anthropological and social psychological literature.

CULTURE AND POLITICAL CULTURE: THE SCOPE OF THE CONCEPTS

Mary McAuley writes (Chapter 2, p. 14) that 'the political culturalists are divided between those who are *interested in*' (my italics, A.B.) the subjective perception of history and politics, in beliefs, values, political knowledge and expectations and 'those who argue for a definition of political culture which embraces behaviour as well'. To *define* political culture in such a way as to exclude behaviour in no way, however, implies lack of *interest* in behaviour. It is in considerable measure because they wish to be in a position to consider the relationship between the complex of subjective factors, on the one hand, and political behaviour, on the other, that a number of scholars prefer not to group the subjective and the behavioural factors under the same overarching concept. As John Miller notes in Chapter 3 (p. 41) the authors who began to apply the term 'political culture' in Communist studies 'believed that they were redirecting attention to an area of the subject which had been woefully neglected and that this neglect was vitiating a balanced understanding of Communist societies', but they did *not* claim 'that political culture was a more important field of investigation than others, nor that it was a label for what the authors found to be the essential features of Communist systems'. Some poetic licence is, therefore, involved in McAuley's use of the term, 'subjectivists', for those who favour a non-behavioural *definition* of a concept which they see as in no way supplanting the study of structures, interests and political activity within a Communist (or any other) system.[1]

Though I have taken up earlier in this volume (Introduction, pp. 3–6) the problem of the scope of the concept of political culture, it is one to which it is necessary to return, since two of the other five authors (Mary McAuley and John Miller) take the view that even the 'subjective' definition of political culture blurs too many important distinctions and hold that it would therefore be better to eschew the term altogether, whereas Stephen White (Chapter 4, p. 62) and David Paul (Chapter 7, p. 140) prefer a broader version of the concept, whereby it explicitly embraces behavioural patterns as well as values and beliefs. This is a position towards which Gordon Skilling also leans, and Skilling suggests (pp. 118–19) that the choice of the broader or the narrower version of the concept appears to affect subsequent assessments of the issue of historical continuity and discontinuity within Communist countries, in the case at least of Czechoslovakia.[2]

It is unlikely that complete agreement will ever be reached by students of politics on how the concept of political culture should best be delineated any more than we can expect unanimity concerning the scope of the concept of culture among anthropologists. Discussing the two main ways of characterising the concept of political culture,

Robert Tucker observes 'Admittedly, it is ultimately a matter of scholarly expediency which position we take. But this seems to be one of those issues of expediency which carry significant implications for research orientation and for theory'.[3] Though I agree with Tucker that what matters most is how useful a particular delineation of the concept is likely to be in subsequent analysis of Communist (or other) polities, I disagree with him on where the balance of usefulness lies. Tucker is by no means unaware of differences of view on the concept of culture among anthropologists,[4] but he nonetheless characterises subjective and cognitive definitions of political culture, such as those of Verba[5] and Pye[6] as a 'deviation from anthropological usage'.[7]

It may be instructive to take a closer look at what has been happening within anthropology, since the 'subjective' definition of political culture has its close parallels there. It is especially – though not only – among anthropologists who have turned from the study of primitive to more complex societies, and from an emphasis on social homeostasis to a concern with social change, that there has been a reaction against the earlier tendency within anthropology to include under the rubric of culture everything except the kitchen sink. (Indeed, the kitchen sink is not necessarily excluded either. As an artefact, it is, after all, part of 'material culture'.)[8] Extended discussion of the concept of culture occurs much more in the American than in British anthropological literature. Edmund Leach, who makes a sharper distinction than many authors 'between social anthropology (mostly British) and cultural anthropology (mostly American)'[9] suggests that the crux of the difference is that 'the social anthropologists are still carrying on a dialogue with Durkheim and Max Weber', while 'the cultural anthropologists are still arguing with Tylor'.[10]

Many cultural anthropologists do, indeed, find it necessary to dissociate themselves from what Leach calls Tylor's 'celebrated catch-all definition'[11] and, as Leach notes, 'the anthropologist's concept of culture has undergone transformations' since Tylor's day and 'there is now no present-day consensus on how the term should be used'.[12] Yet there has been a strong tendency towards excluding patterns of behaviour and artefacts from the anthropological definition of culture. Thus, in an article comparing the nineteenth-century approaches to culture of Arnold and Tylor, George W. Stocking writes:

Arnold's culture . . . was, both for the individual and for society, an organic, integrative, holistic phenomenon. Tylor's analytic evolutionary purpose forced him to place great emphasis on the artefactual manifestations of culture, on those objects of 'material culture' which were easily and convincingly arranged in hierarchical sequence; Arnold's culture, *like that of most modern anthropologists, was an inward ideational phenomenon* (italics mine, A.B.).[13]

Ward Goodenough, in common with virtually every anthropologist who has written on this subject, has recognised that 'one of our major problems is that culture is a vague and rather ill-defined term in anthropology, meaning different things to different people'.[14] He has noted that much of what is called 'cultural' change in social scientific literature is in fact 'change in a community's real or phenomenal conditions, only incidentally including changes in the criteria by which people discern things, their beliefs about things, their purposes in relation to them, or their principles for dealing with them'.[15] Yet these cognitive and evaluative factors are among those that 'most anthropologists seem to have in mind, some precisely and some more vaguely, when they speak of a community's culture'.[16] For Goodenough:

> Culture, then, consists of standards for deciding what is, standards for deciding what can be, standards for deciding how one feels about it, standards for deciding what to do about it, and standards for deciding how to go about doing it. A community's culture in this sense should never be confused with its culture in the sense of patterns of recurring events and arrangements that characterize the community as a relatively stable system.[17]

That such a view of culture is acquiring an increasing acceptance in anthropology is scarcely in doubt. Clifford Geertz, who tries to steer a course between the broad view of culture which embraces behaviour patterns and the Goodenough position which he sees as an attempt to attribute to culture 'a self-contained "super-organic" reality with forces and purposes of its own',[18] implicitly notes that the more subjective delineation of the concept has gained much ground. Thus, in a chapter first published in 1966, he writes that 'culture is best seen not as complexes of concrete behaviour patterns – customs, usages, traditions, habit clusters – *as has, by and large, been the case up to now*, but as a set of control mechanisms – plans, recipes, rules, instructions (what computer engineers call "programs") – for the governing of behaviour' (italics mine, A.B.).[19] Writing in 1973, he describes the view of culture which locates it 'in the minds and hearts of men' as one which is *'right now very widely held'* (italics mine, A.B.).[20] That is not to say that Geertz agrees with this position of which he regards Goodenough as the leading proponent. On the contrary, he sees it as amounting to a reification of culture and as 'the main source of muddlement in contemporary anthropology'.[21]

Geertz admits that 'at first glance this approach may look close enough' to his own 'to be mistaken for it' and he sets out at some length what he sees as the distinction between his own approach and that of Goodenough.[22] In a brief characterisation of his own position as of 1973, Geertz writes:

> The concept of culture I espouse . . . is essentially a semiotic one. Believing, with Max Weber, that man is an animal suspended in webs of significance he himself has spun, I take culture to be those webs, and the analysis of it to be therefore not an experimental science in search of law but an interpretive one in search of meaning.[23]

Those anthropologists, however, who wish to get away from the omnibus concept of culture cite *both* Goodenough and Geertz on their side.[24] (Given Geertz's opposition to the more eclectic definitions of culture – including patterns of behaviour and sometimes much else – this is understandable.) Keesing and Keesing, who are among those who draw on the arguments of Geertz as well as of Goodenough, use the term, 'culture', to refer to 'the ideational codes of a people with which they conceptualize their world and interact with one another'.[25] Arguing the importance of separating analytically culture and social structure, they note that 'especially in a world of rapid change, the cultural order and patterns of social organization slip far out of fit with one another'.[26]

The point applies *a fortiori* in Communist systems where after a Communist revolution or seizure of power, changes in political institutions (including the prohibition or emasculation of any parties which might act as a rival to the ruling Communist Party and the subordination of the legislature and the judiciary – insofar as these had any prior independence – to the wishes of that ruling Party) and changes in social structure (including the prohibition of capitalists and landowners and the expansion of the working class and of the bureaucracy) have usually followed with exceptional rapidity as compared with political and social change in most non-Communist systems. Yet, as Lenin knew well and as Soviet writers on political culture such as Smirnov acknowledge (see Chapter 5, p. 108) changes in values and beliefs do not take place with anything like a corresponding rapidity. Even conformist *behaviour* can be achieved by a new leadership, especially in an authoritarian political system, without the standards on which that behaviour is based – those set by the political authorities – being fully internalised by the mass of participants (at a mundane level) in the political process.

Looking at the same problem from a different angle and in a quite different context, Ladislav Holy has written: 'New insights into the working of social systems have been achieved in anthropology through following the implications of an analytical distinction between the conceptual and cognitive world of the actors and the realm of events and transactions in which they engage'.[27] Holy regards as an important part of this cognitive or conceptual world the norms (or standards) to which people subscribe and observes that 'the recognition of the fallacy that the relationship between norms and observable social events is neatly congruent has led to the increasing questioning of the assumption hitherto implicit in most anthropological and sociological writing, that norms through their internal compelling force determine actual behaviour'.[28] He further suggests that anthropological approaches which have explicitly rejected an assumption of neat congruence between 'the norms to which the actors subscribe or which they recognise and the social transactional processes in which they engage' have considerably enhanced understanding of the 'dialectical relationship' between norms and behaviour and emphasised the usefulness of the analytical distinction between the conceptual and cognitive world of the actors, on the one hand, and their actions, on the other.[29]

There is, then, within the newer body of anthropological literature a strong intellectual tendency to exclude from the scope of culture not only laws and formal institutions (which were sometimes included in the past) but also behaviour patterns. This does not mean that there is any less interest in behaviour, but rather it represents a recognition that making an analytical distinction between 'the cognitive world of the actors and the realm of events and transactions in which they engage' points up the problematic nature of the relationship between the subjective and cognitive realm, on the one hand, and the behavioural, on the other, in a way conducive to reflection and research on the nature of the interaction. As I noted in the Introduction to the present volume, this closely parallels the preference of most political scientists who employ the concept of political culture for making a clear distinction between beliefs, values and subjective perceptions of history and politics, on the one hand, and political behaviour, on the other, and renders somewhat dated the rebuke that this represents a departure from anthropological usage (which was considered significant, it would appear, partly on the grounds that anthropologists are the people who know about culture, just as political scientists know about power, sociologists about social stratification and economists about scarce resources).

Though political scientists need feel under no obligation to follow anthropologists in their use of the concept of culture if its scope is defined by the latter in a way which is unhelpful for political analysis, it is certainly not without interest that many anthropologists have found their analyses both of social change and of belief change enhanced by making an analytical separation between beliefs and behaviour. The very large literature in social psychology on values, beliefs and attitudes and the relationship between these and behaviour, to which attention will be paid in the next section of this chapter, provides more compelling evidence of the desirability of maintaining such a distinction.[30]

If political culture is considered as that part of a culture (in the newer anthropological sense) which bears relevance to politics,[31] it can be particularly valuable as a concept which cuts across disciplinary boundaries and brings together, and organises, insights to be found in the work of historians, anthropologists, social psychologists and sociologists (as well as of students of politics). In the following pages attention is drawn to some significant discussions and findings in these cognate disciplines, and brief consideration is paid to their pertinence to the study of continuity and change in Communist political cultures.

VALUES, BELIEFS, ATTITUDES AND BEHAVIOUR

Even with every possibility to conduct experiments under 'controlled' conditions, and with no obstacles placed in their way by governmental authority, Western social scientists who have devoted serious attention to the study of attitude and value change, of the relationships among an individual's various beliefs and of the relationship between attitudes and values, on the one hand, and behaviour, on the other, have reached comparatively few conclusions which are readily generalisable and not 'situation-specific'. Indeed, this entire literature (mainly social psychological[32] but also sociological[33] and anthropological[34]) indicates the futility of supposing that in the present state of knowledge it is possible in the study of Communist countries to do more than attempt to provide tentative accounts of the dominant political culture within these societies. Yet, as I shall argue later in the chapter, it remains important to make such attempts, even though the accounts provided will, naturally, be modified and improved upon in the light of criticism and the availability of further evidence. Hypotheses are most unlikely to be definitively confirmed or refuted, but understanding should be enhanced and an element in the political life of a society which is always of great potential importance, even though its salience varies according to time and circumstance, may be brought into clearer focus.

In writing of the 'dominant political culture', I have in mind – as was made clear earlier – *subjective* perceptions of history and politics, fundamental political beliefs and values, foci of identification and loyalty, and political knowledge and expectations. But we would do well to bear in mind that subjective though these perceptions, beliefs and expectations are in the case of the individual citizen, in the aggregate they become an important part of the objective reality which confronts Communist political leaderships (as well as Western students of Communist politics). The extent to which they can be controlled by these leaderships is one of the issues which has concerned the authors of this volume and on which differing views exist, but the fact that vast resources are devoted by Communist rulers to a conscious political socialisation effort is beyond dispute, even though the scale of this effort varies over time and from one Communist state to another.

In a seminal article published twenty years ago, Philip Converse wrote: 'Belief systems have never surrendered easily to empirical study or quantification. Indeed, they have often served as primary exhibits for the doctrine that what is important to study cannot be measured and that what can be measured is not important to study'.[35] Though significant progress has been made since then, it is still the case that though attitudes can be measured with considerable sophistication the study of the relationship between one attitude and another, between knowledge and belief, and the investigation of the intensity and consistency with which particular beliefs are held, are more complex matters, even when the object of study is the ideational world of individuals,[36] and more difficult still when the aim is to generalise about nations and social groups. The findings of scholars who have addressed themselves to these questions in the context of Western societies provide suggestive leads for the student of Communist political cultures, but the conclusions of the latter are still likely in a number of respects to fall short of the precision which can at times be achieved by the former, since political scientists studying Communist systems are, after all, dealing with authoritarian systems in which limits are placed upon the empirical research of foreigners and upon the publication of the results of research by indigenous social scientists. McAuley, following Mann,[37] rightly points to the likelihood of inconsistency within the belief systems of citizens of Communist countries and to the probability that the inconsistency is greater among the less educated than among the more educated (Chapter 2, p. 28). There is much evidence from studies of Western countries (and, in particular, the USA) to suggest that such a pattern exists in these societies and it is more than likely (though still not proven) that the same holds good for Communist states. Yet, *pace* Miller (Chapter 3, p. 46) the point that the same people act on the basis of different motives or on the basis of inconsistent beliefs and the fact that the word 'perceptions' covers 'a broad spectrum of things' including calculations of interest as well as those values which can be divorced from interest, do not constitute grounds for abandoning the term, 'political culture', to embrace the entire complex of subjective orientations to politics. *Perception* of interest is surely affected by people's political experience, knowledge and expectations, so that, as Barrington Moore has put it, 'what looks like an opportunity or a temptation to one group of people will not necessarily seem so to another group with a different historical experience and living in a different form of society'.[38] That is not to say that interests cannot be studied separately from culture, but rather that in the study of political culture it would not be particularly useful to attempt to separate *perceptions* of interest from other political perceptions or from political knowledge, beliefs and expectations, since there is a strong case for regarding them as interlinked.

Joel Cooper and Robert Croyle are unusual among social psychologists in actually referring, in a recent article, to political culture. They write:

> No domain of attitude research has more relevance to modern political culture than the study of persuasion. While sociologists have long been concerned with the study of charisma and the dynamics of social movements, the mass of accumulated data on the persuasion process is largely a product of experimental social psychology.[39]

The social psychological literature on persuasion and on the resistance or openness of attitudes and beliefs to change undoubtedly has relevance to the attempts of Communist rulers to change the beliefs of citizens in those countries. In that context, it is worth noting in passing the importance of perceptions of the *source* of information and of attempts at persuasion. A source who is regarded as an expert, or as disinterested, or who evokes strong positive emotional feelings (the link between affect, or emotion, and cognition has been much stressed lately)[40] will be more successful in producing attitudinal change than one who is not perceived as either authoritative or attractive.[41] If this seems unsurprising, and scarcely, indeed, requiring the confirmation of experimental social psychology, perhaps less obvious but equally relevant to the question of the relative success or failure of political socialisation in Communist states is the finding that to get someone to commit himself publicly to a particular belief which he has not hitherto held is an especially effective way of producing an internalisation of that belief. More precisely, to succeed on the basis of very modest rewards or very moderate sanctions in getting a person to engage actively in persuading others to a view which the persuader has previously not held, or only weakly held, will make considerably more likely a change of attitude (or, in the case of the weakly-held belief, a strengthening of the belief) on the part of the proselytiser.[42]

Thus, those Soviet writers on political culture who stress the importance of active participation in approved socio-political work for a strengthening of the beliefs which they deem appropriate for citizens to possess may well be right in terms of their own goals.[43] Similarly, it seems probable that the Chinese Cultural Revolution which Mao Zedong encouraged in the mid-1960s and which led to sustained proselytising, and public criticism on a massive scale of people who showed insufficient revolutionary zeal, did indeed strengthen the convictions of those – in particular, the tens of millions of young people – who took part. In terms of increasing belief in that variant of Marxism–Leninism known as 'Mao Zedong Thought', it was almost certainly much more effective as a means of inculcating a form of Marxism–Leninism than the willingness to settle for a much higher degree of political quietism – epitomised in Kádár's 'He who is not against us is with us' – in much of Eastern Europe during the post-Stalin years. (Needless to say, that is not to suggest that Maoist-style Cultural Revolution is a *better* way to run a Communist – or any other – country or, indeed, to imply that the convictions of the young activists were to remain with them years later, by which time they had had an opportunity to assess the negative consequences of the turmoil they helped to create.)

In the Chinese case, it is important that, at least in the early stages of the Cultural Revolution, millions of young people entered voluntarily into what they say as an opportunity to assert themselves and to attack established authority.[44] Even when citizens of a Communist state participate politically under conditions in which they feel they have no choice but to comply (the act of voting may be a case in point), this is likely to result in *some* attitudinal change, but it is unlikely to result in as much change in beliefs as behaviour which does not appear to the participant to be mandatory. Social psychological experiments in which subjects had to write counter-attitudinal essays (that is to say, essays in which they argue against the attitudinal position they held immediately prior to undertaking this task) under conditions of 'choice' and of 'no choice' have found greater attitude change in cases where participants were given options than when they had 'no choice' instructions.[45] Such experiments belong to the vast and controversial literature on cognitive dissonance[46] which has a number of other suggestive insights to offer the student of Communist politics on belief change,[47] as well as on the broader question of the relationship between values and attitudes, on the one hand, and behaviour, on the other. It is to that question which I now turn.

There are many examples in the cognitive dissonance literature of the way in which attitudes may be modified or changed following counter-attitudinal behaviour as one way of reducing the stress which, in certain conditions and for some people, would otherwise be involved.[48] Indeed, for some time it seemed almost as if behaviour was a better predictor of attitude than attitude of behaviour, while numerous studies found no significant correlation at all between values and attitudes, on the one hand, and behaviour, on the other.[49] The attitude–behaviour discrepancy problem was vividly brought to light in a much-cited study by LaPiere conducted as long ago as 1934. LaPiere wrote to various restaurants and hotels throughout the United States, asking them 'Will you accept members of the Chinese race as guests in your establishment?' Of the eighty-one restaurants and forty-seven hotels which replied, 92 per cent said that they would not accept Chinese guests. But when six months later, LaPiere travelled across the United States with a Chinese couple, visiting these self-same hotels and restaurants, they were refused service only once. This case has been extensively re-analysed and some problems with the methodology and LaPiere's interpretation have been noted.[50] One source of the attitude–behaviour discrepancy, it has been suggested, is that in 1934 the *stereotype* of the Chinese in the minds of American hotel and restaurant managers was doubtless far removed from the reality of the particular well-dressed, middle-class Chinese couple who arrived on their premises.[51] Yet, as Schuman and Johnson have put it 'the essentially zero agreement between attitude (actually, behavioural intention) and action in LaPiere's study makes even important criticisms of its method appear somewhat inadequate to explain the results'.[52] One point which emerges from the LaPiere study and from a host of more recent ones is that it is impossible to predict *specific* behaviour in *particular* contexts on the basis of a person's *general* attitude on an issue.[53]

The social psychological literature on the relationship between attitudes and behaviour has moved over half a century from the assumption that to know a person's attitude was tantamount to being able to predict his or her behaviour (LaPiere in his day was unusual in his scepticism concerning this) through the position that attitudes are but epiphenomena and 'cannot be expected to bear any directive influence on behavior', to a recognition that a much higher degree of specificity of the nature of the attitude or belief, on the one hand, and of the behaviour to be performed, on the other, is required if one wishes to show the influence of the former on the latter.[54] As Fazio and Zanna put it 'Rather than asking whether attitudes relate to behavior, we have to ask "Under what conditions do what kinds of attitudes held by what kinds of individuals predict what kinds of behavior?" '[55]

So far as the predictive usefulness of particular kinds of attitude is concerned, it is worth noting that the link between attitudes and behaviour has been shown to be greatly strengthened by *vested interest*; on the other side of the coin, when actions are likely to have little impact on the subsequent lives of those concerned, attitude–behaviour consistency tends to be lower.[56] A different point, but one which is also of relevance to students of Communist politics, is that attitudes which are based upon direct behavioural experience tend not only to be more persistent over time than attitudes based upon indirect experience but also, as a consequence of this relative strength, the former are more likely to serve as guides to behaviour than the latter.[57]

The terms 'attitudes' and 'values' are variously used. While in much psychological writing 'attitudes' is used broadly, so that 'values are regarded as components of attitudes',[58] in recent years there has been a greater insistence on the need for specificity in determination of the attitude and of the behaviour to which it is supposed to relate. In most writing on political culture, the term 'value' is regarded as by definition something more basic to a person's belief system than an 'attitude'. Support for such a position comes from Milton Rokeach who writes:

> An attitude differs from a value in that an attitude refers to an organization of several beliefs around a specific object or situation . . . A value, on the other hand, refers to a single belief of a very specific kind. It concerns a desirable mode of behavior or end-state that has a transcendental quality to it, guiding actions, attitudes, judgements, and comparisons across specific objects and situations and beyond immediate goals . . . a value is a standard but an attitude is not a standard. Favorable or unfavorable evaluations of numerous attitude objects and situations may be based upon a relatively small number of values serving as standards.[59]

Viewing both values and attitudes as 'intervening variables',[60] Rokeach suggests that social psychologists have devoted more attention to attitude change than value change (though here he ignores the extent to which they have often subsumed values within their notion of attitudes) because they assume that 'the centrally located values are more resistant to change than attitudes'. The reason why attitude changes are frequently short-lived is that 'the more central values underlying them have been left intact'.[61] Thus, while one way of removing dissonance between attitude and behaviour is to change the attitude to bring it into correspondence with the behaviour, such a process can lead to dissonance of a different sort with the new attitude having become more discrepant with the underlying value or values. There is, therefore, for Rokeach a paradoxical sense in which 'values may be easier to change than attitudes', by which he appears to mean that if the change is effected it is likely to be more lasting.

This last observation could be seen as a practical justification for the strategy of 'cultural revolution' adopted at various times by Communist regimes as a way of changing attitudes and beliefs by altering the fundamental values which underlie them. In fact, it may well be the case that greater change in values and fundamental beliefs has taken place in the Soviet Union and China where under Stalin and Mao such 'revolutions' took place than in Czechoslovakia, Hungary or Poland where the upheaval was on a lesser scale. Even in China, though, as has become clearer under Mao's successors, the transformation of values was apparently incomplete and, in general, Rokeach's paradoxical argument notwithstanding, specific attitudes would appear to have changed more than basic values. Insofar as the latter *have* changed radically, as distinct merely from certain values acquiring a somewhat greater weight and others being accorded a reduced weight, this may have more to do with the spread of basic education to areas which lacked it than to anything else.

The likelihood of more fundamental change in the way of thinking of large sections of the population in the Soviet Union and China in the course of the Communist period, as compared with their counterparts in the Communist countries of East-Central Europe, is, indeed, greatly increased by the fact that the former entered Communist rule with much lower literacy rates and have only in the Communist era made the transition to high literacy. The effects of this transition were illuminatingly studied by a Soviet psychologist, the late A. R. Luria, in research carried out in the villages and mountains of Kirghizia and Uzbekistan during 1931–2, the results of which, however, were published only in the 1970s.[62] Luria shows, with many examples, the enormous advance in the capacity for generalisation and abstract thought, for deduction and inference, which occurred within a short period of time in Soviet Central Asia. He writes of 'the fundamental psychological shifts that had occurred in human consciousness during a vigorous revolutionary realignment of social history – the rapid uprooting of a class society and a cultural upheaval creating hitherto unimagined perspectives for social development'.[63] Though it can hardly be doubted that the vast change which took place in people's social relations and working lives had an impact on their consciousness, the most important difference in their way of thinking would appear – on the basis of Luria's evidence – to have been achieved, quite simply, by schooling. As Luria puts it 'The significance of schooling lies not just in the acquisition of new knowledge, but in the creation of new motives and formal modes of discursive verbal and logical thinking divorced from immediate practical experience'.[64]

It does not follow from this, however, that people who have acquired literacy during the Soviet period and whose working relations have been greatly changed will necessarily adopt the norms and values of the Soviet official political culture (which is itself by no means unchanging). Some of the best evidence comes from the important study by the British anthropologist, Caroline Humphrey, of the Buryats, a Mongolian-speaking people in Siberia, based on her own field-work as well as on extensive use of Soviet ethnographic litera-ture.[65] Discussing religion among the Buryats, Humphrey notes that it would be 'too simple to see Soviet ideology as merely replacing Lamaist or shamanist thinking. What has occurred is a much more complex cross-cutting of ideas, in which Soviet elements and ideals enter into folk structures – ways of thinking which survive even though their previous strong institutional supports in society have virtually disappeared'.[66] During the 1960s and 1970s, she observes, Buryat collective farm workers 'continued to explain many aspects of the Soviet world to a great extent by their own patterns of thought'.[67] Making it clear that this strong element of cultural continuity does not exist in a social vacuum, Humphrey elaborates:

> Rather than the insertion of a Buryat native content into Soviet modes of explanation, we find the reverse: the phenomena of the Soviet world appear, disconnected from their theoretical origins, structured by a Buryat consciousness. Those Buryat social institutions which exist are wholly adapted to Soviet circumstances, but this is not recognised and they continue to be explained as though there had been no break with the past. In this, the nature of rural economic organisation has probably played an important part, since it has preserved intact the Buryat communities of the remote countryside, and even the exodus of up to 50% of the younger generation has not, given the extremely high birth-rate, had the effect of destroying them.[68]

If, on this account, the Buryats have found their own way of dealing with the potential tension between two different ways of looking at the world (in psychological terms, of eliminating cognitive dissonance), it would appear that elsewhere the effect of the co-existence within the minds of the same people of two different ways of speaking, and to some degree of thinking, can cause more unease. Some of the most useful insights on this from writers who have lived all or most of their lives in the Soviet Union come in creative literature rather than in social scientific works. What compartmentalised thinking can mean in intelligentsia circles is incisively and wittily portrayed in the novels of Aleksandr Zinoviev.[69] But discordant manners of speech and even modes of thought can be a source of stress also in Russian rural communities if Aleksandr Yashin's short story, *Levers*, published in Moscow in 1956[70] and illuminatingly discussed by Robert Tucker several years later,[71] is accepted as the accurate observation it has been taken to be (even though almost three decades have passed since its publication caused a minor sensation in a year of major political sensations, and much may have changed down on the Soviet farm since then). For Tucker, one of the significant themes, not only in Yashin but in the literature of the Khrushchev era more generally, was that 'the line of division between the two Russias may run through the individual person'.[72] By 'the two Russias' he means 'official and popular Russia',[73] the dissonance between which finds a place even within the minds of the members of the Party organisation in the collective farm described by Yashin who move from talking naturally and critically among themselves to an utterly different way of speaking when their meeting begins. They immediately adopt the official phraseology they had mocked a moment before, but the meeting over, with 'a sense of duty done, but at the same time of uneasiness', they revert to their normal mode of speech and become again, in Yashin's concluding words, 'honest, sincere, direct people – people and not levers'.[74] For Yashin, as Tucker notes, the 'real' selves are the unofficial ones.[75] There is apparently a dissonance between the values of the collective farm members and their political behaviour and certainly a great discrepancy between their assessments of the same person and same experience when they are speaking informally and when they are speaking in their official Soviet voices.

If we turn to the question of the relationship between attitudes, values and political behaviour in the context of post-war Czechoslovakia, we are confronted by a whole series of objections from McAuley (Chapter 2, pp. 23–7) to the way the political cultural aspect of this has been treated,[76] and also by Skilling's scepticism (Chapter 6, p 119) concerning 'values' which are 'not translated into action'. It is unnecessary to defend the view that no change in the political culture of Czechs and Slovaks – with particular reference to their values, fundamental political beliefs and political knowledge – took place between the end of the Second World War and the 1970s. Such a position would be absurd and it is *not* adopted in the chapter on Czechoslovakia in *Political Culture and Political Change in Communist States*. What does seem reasonable to contend is, first, that there was significantly more attitudinal change and behavioural change than change in the underlying values and fundamental political beliefs; second, that insofar as there was change in the dominant political culture, it was at times in a quite different direction from that favoured and emphasised in the official political culture; and third, that while, ultimately, a test of values and of basic political beliefs is that they should be reflected in behaviour, it is unrealistic to expect that this should occur regardless of the circumstances and constraints.

The 1946 elections in Czechoslovakia were a triumph for the parties on the left of the Czechoslovak political spectrum, with the Communist Party doing best of all. To vote Communist on this occasion, rather than for the Social Democratic Party or the National Socialist Party (a democratic socialist party and not to be confused with the pre-war German National Socialists) meant for many voters a change of attitude, but how great a shift did it represent of values and fundamental political beliefs? These are beliefs at the level of whether people think that they have a right, in association with others, to choose those who will govern their country and to hold them accountable for their actions – not at the attitudinal level of voting for one party of the left rather than another. They did not jettison 'Masarykism' for socialism (McAuley, Chapter 2, p. 24) since these were not seen by the average Communist voter to represent conflicting values. There was indeed a Communist Party sub-culture, in which authoritarian strands were fairly strong, and within the Party there were many who rejected, as well as many who accepted Thomas Masaryk's attachment to pluralism and libertarianism and his view of democracy as 'a conversation among equals, the thinking of a free people open to complete publicity'.[77] But to identify the authoritarian sub-culture with the dominant political culture within Czechoslovakia even in those early post-war years would be to make a mistake which the Communist leadership itself did not make at a time when they still had to compete for support within the country and could not use the coercive apparatus of the state to impose compliance. The esteem in which Thomas Masaryk was held was such that the attacks on Masaryk and 'Masarykism' came only after power had been secured. At the Eighth Congress of the Communist Party of Czechoslovakia, held in March 1946 just two months before the elections to the National Assembly, even the hardline party ideologist, Václav Kopecký, found it expedient to speak of 'the great personality and great historical role of T. G. Masaryk', particularly in the formation of the first Czechoslovak state.[78]

The elections of 1946 were the last free elections to be held in Czechoslovakia; some 40 per cent of the electorate voted Communist in the Czech lands and 30 per cent did so in Slovakia (where the Democratic Party obtained 62 per cent of the votes). But the implications of a Communist vote at that time were far from clear to many of the voters (or, indeed, to many of the more idealistic socialists among the Party members). As Vladimir Kusin has put it: '. . . these voters and supporters of the "Czechoslovak road to socialism" . . .

voted in 1946 to make the Communist Party the strongest in the country but not to endorse its monopoly of power for all times to come. If such monopoly had been at issue in a democratic election, the result would certainly have been different'.[79] Even *if* we make the highly unlikely assumption that every Communist voter in 1946 wished to see an end to party competition, the fact remains that, though the Communists emerged as the largest single party, approximately two-thirds of the electorate voted for parties which supported a competitive party system and other features of political pluralism. It is harder, if not impossible, to *prove* that a majority of citizens of Czechoslovakia retained a belief in the virtues of political pluralism throughout the years of harshest oppression – the end of the 1940s and especially the early 1950s. It is plausible to suggest that the authoritarian sub-culture was strengthened during that time, gaining as it did the full support of the official political culture, and given the atmosphere of fear of enemies at home and abroad which the party leadership, with some success, attempted to engender. If a move in that direction occurred among those who had voted Communist in 1946, this would not be surprising. It would be one way of eliminating the stress which the knowledge of their vote for the Communist Party might otherwise have caused them. What would be much more surprising would have been such a shift in the basic political beliefs of those (the majority) who had voted *against* the Communist Party. Since we have no survey data from those years (and since the political atmosphere and institutional constraints were such that these data would be meaningless, even if they existed) we are left to make inferences. High levels of coercion wielded by the holders of political power are very effective means of getting people to change their behaviour patterns. They are much less effective in promoting change of values and beliefs in the direction desired by the power-holders. Indeed, the psychological theory of 'reactance' has produced a good deal of evidence of a tendency for individuals who feel their freedom or autonomy threatened to move further away from the attitude they are coming under pressure to adopt.[80] (This theory, it should be noted, concerns not just attitude change or, more precisely, resistance to persuasion, but points to the attachment which people, once they have enjoyed certain *freedoms*, acquire to these freedoms as such.)[81]

The second point made on page 164 – that the direction of change in the dominant political culture during the Communist era was at times in a direction quite different from that favoured and stressed in the official political culture – could be argued in detail, but a brief elaboration here must suffice. The whole reform movement of the 1960s was one which began in the Party intelligentsia, though in 'cultural life', in the everyday sense of literature and the arts, the distinctions between Party and non-Party members which had been so important in the 1950s gradually ceased to matter. For the mass of the people, however, there was little opportunity to make their voices heard until 1968 itself. For many thousands of Party intellectuals, who had suppressed their doubts about the show trials and other ugly aspects of the early post-1948 years, Khrushchev's 'secret speech' of 1956 came as a great shock. In the course of interviews and conversations with some fifty members of the Czechoslovak Communist Party in the 1960s, I found that all but a handful mentioned 1956 – and, in particular, the Khrushchev speech – as the beginning of a process for them of reappraisal of their political beliefs. The change was a gradual one, though faster for some than for others, and the reinforcement provided by Khrushchev's speech to the Twenty-second Congress of the Communist Party of the Soviet Union in 1961 was also important. Information already available, but which, because it came from 'bourgeois' sources regarded as untrustworthy and had, therefore, either been consciously rejected or less consciously screened out in the selective process of political perception, could not be ignored when it came from the lips of the leader of the most important Communist Party in the world. What Czech Party intellectuals heard from Khrushchev about torture and rigged political trials in the Soviet Union under Stalin forced them to reflect on the oppression and trials in Czechoslovakia, too, during the last years of Stalin's life – and even beyond it.

Though Khrushchev had spoken of some at least of the crimes which had been committed in the name of the Party, the conclusions which Czech Party intellectuals drew from this were much more radical than those drawn by Khrushchev himself or, indeed, by the Party intelligentsia in the Soviet Union. For Czech intellectuals, the 'cult of personality' explanation was not an explanation at all. Abuse of power on such a scale raised basic questions about a political system which was incapable of holding its leaders accountable or curbing the activities of the security police. The reappraisal which was going on in the minds of many Czech Party intellectuals from 1956 onwards was not, in most cases, reflected in political behaviour until the early or mid-1960s when, gradually, the limits of what could be said in public and in print were pushed wider. A change, that is to say, had by the mid-1960s already taken place in the political culture of the élite (broadly defined), but only to a very much more limited extent in the official political culture. (That the 'official' and the 'élite' political culture are not necessarily synonymous is a point to which I shall return in the next section.) The fact that Party intellectuals generally had a standard of comparison to draw upon – first-hand knowledge of what a pluralistic political system of a social democratic type could be like – was important in turning their attention to the kinds of institutional changes which would provide checks upon the abuse of power. They had no faith in the notion that merely to change a bad 'Stalinist' leader for a good one who would adopt a 'Leninist style' of rule (the solution offered in the Soviet Union and in a number of other East European countries) would meet the problem.

The 'Prague Spring' was not a manifestation of a 'quite extreme nationalism' which McAuley (chapter 2, p. 34, citing Szelenyi) suggests it might be. Even anti-Soviet and anti-Russian feeling was very mild (certainly in comparison with Poland or Hungary) until after the Soviet-led military intervention of August 1968. It was, however, the most far-reaching and most carefully thought-about attempt at reform of a Communist political system which had ever been undertaken. The most active reformers consciously thought, and publicly stated, that they were creating what the Party's April 1968 Action Programme called 'a new model of socialist society, one which is profoundly democratic and conforms to Czechoslovak conditions'.[82] This was not an attempt simply to replicate the First Republic, but to do what had never been done before – to combine political pluralism (though there was argument between those who wished to try to institutionalise a one-party pluralism and those who held that the freedom to create or recreate other political parties was an essential right and one of the best bulwarks of pluralism) with a welfare state and a socialist market economy.

But very widespread emotional attachment on the part of Czechs in 1968 to the memory of the First Republic also existed, though both McAuley and Skilling appear to wish to cast doubt on this. It is most unlikely that it was 'the limitations of parliamentary democracy' (McAuley, Chapter 2, p. 25) which postponed the culmination of the reform movement until twenty years after the Communist seizure of power in Czechoslovakia and twelve years after 1956.[83] On the contrary, non-Communist Czechs and, in the course of the 1960s, even many Communist Czechs acquired an idealised view of the First Republic and overlooked its inadequacies which had been apparent enough in 1946,[84] but which had paled into insignificance once they had been given the opportunity of comparing it with a Soviet-type system.[85] Skilling (Chapter 6, p. 119) referring to the survey data (quoted in *Political Culture and Political Change in Communist States*) on the evaluations of Czechs of the First Republic in 1946 and again in 1968, says:

> Yet poll results – which showed a positive attitude to the First Republic, among Czechs, of only 8 per cent in December 1946, and 39 per cent in October 1968 – neither confirm the 'enormous importance' of the First Republic, nor a continuity of the values of that period, but rather the contrary.

The first of these points is based upon a misapprehension. Neither in 1946 nor in 1968 were respondents asked whether they evaluated positively or negatively the First Republic. In 1946 they were offered a restricted choice among eight named periods and were allowed to nominate only *one*. Three periods only, of which two were remote in time, had a higher percentage support than the First Republic. These were 'The Hussite wars' (19 per cent), 'The reign of King Charles IV' (17 per cent) and 'The present time (1945–46)' (16 per cent). When in 1968 Czech respondents were allowed to name *any two* periods in answer to the question 'When you contemplate the history of the Czech nation, which period do you consider to be the most glorious, a time of advance and development?', the First Republic came ahead of all other periods, including the age of Hus, the reign of King Charles IV and the period after January 1968. Given the eras respondents were forced to reject, including some which had been regarded as glorious both in pre-war and in post-war Czechoslovakia, the support for the First Republic is remarkable, and it is entirely reasonable to infer that, with the removal of the 'two period' restriction, support for it would have been overwhelming.[86] This is not to deny that distance had lent enchantment to the view, but, then, the age of Saint Wenceslas, the age of Hus, the reign of King Charles IV and even the National Revival of the nineteenth century were still more distant. There was no one alive who could remember how hard a time he or she had in those days!

In the second of his points – that this shifting evaluation of the First Republic – confirms not 'a continuity of the values of that period, but rather the contrary' – Skilling is, it would be fair to say, pushing against an open door. His argument is in line not only with that presented here but also with that to be found in the 1977 volume to which he refers where, in my chapter with Gordon Wightman, I wrote:

Neither the new economic base nor the new institutional structures succeeded in changing the political cultures of Czechs and Slovaks in the direction which the holders of institutional power desired. If anything, the opposite happened. The old values and beliefs were reinforced. Masaryk became more highly esteemed than ever and by 1968 the First Republic was perceived both far more positively than was the post-1948 political system and far more than it had been in the immediate post-war period when Czechoslovak citizens were not yet in a position to compare it with a system modelled on that of the Soviet Union. If a Czech 'new man' had been created by 1968, he was, ironically, one more firmly devoted to social democratic and libertarian values than the Czech of 1946.[87]

This brings me to my third contention set out on page 164 – that while, ultimately, a test of values and of basic political beliefs is that they should be reflected in behaviour, we should not expect to find congruence between values and beliefs, on the one hand, and political behaviour, on the other, regardless of specific circumstances and of the sanctions against particular courses of action. McAuley (Chapter 2, p. 27) asks 'Has Czechoslovakia since 1948 been, *or is it today*, more of a democratic society than Hungary, Yugoslavia or Poland?' (my italics, A.B.). Skilling (Chapter 6, p. 123) observes 'One may question whether values which are not acted on, for whatever reason, are really deeply held and whether they are in any case politically relevant, except in the long run'. Both authors – McAuley, by implication, and Skilling, more directly – are suggesting that if, for example, democracy and political pluralism are valued by a majority of citizens within Czechoslovakia, this should be reflected in their actions.

One cannot object to this as a moral judgement, but if it is intended to be an empirical generalisation, it is highly questionable. As noted earlier in this chapter, there is a wealth of evidence indicating that on the basis of values or general attitudes it is impossible to predict specific behaviour in particular contexts. Though sociological or social psychological investigations of attitudes in the West as well as in the East are of varying quality and even when well conducted can at times produce responses which are superficial, it would be rash to assume that the way a person behaves in public even in Western society is necessarily a better guide to what he or she thinks than attitudinal and value research. As Schuman and Johnson put it:

The possibility that elicited attitudes are sometimes inconsistent with behavior because the former are 'truer' makes good sense in many situations. Thus when professors are evaluated by students through anonymous questionnaires, the assumption is that these attitudinal expressions may be inconsistent with the student's overt behavior toward the professors because the behavior, not the attitude, is deceptive . . . The general point that behavior rather than attitude may be insincere has been noted by Merton[88] and reiterated by others from time to time, though probably seldom taken as seriously as it deserves.[89]

We do not assume that a Western politician in an election campaign who makes a point of kissing babies necessarily loves babies or that shaking hands with every stranger within reach reflects the politician's exceptional friendliness and feelings of benevolence towards all mankind.[90] The behaviour is, on the contrary, in all probability calculated to make a certain impression upon potential voters. In countless everyday situations in even the most liberal of societies, people's behaviour may be a misleading guide to what they are thinking. Thus, notwithstanding the difficulties of uncovering or eliciting attitudes and beliefs, they may be 'of value precisely because behavior is so constrained as to conceal wishes'.[91]

If this is the case in societies with a high degree of institutionalised freedom and tolerance, it should be evident that it applies much more strongly to authoritarian political systems when it is *political* behaviour which we have in mind. This is still more true when we take account of the international context on which Skilling rightly lays emphasis and which is stressed also by Paul (Chapter 7, p. 141). The fact is that Czechoslovakia was invaded in August 1968 by a superpower. The direct intervention in the affairs of a fairly small country (and Czechs and Slovaks are conscious of 'smallness' to the extent that they might be said to have a 'small country complex' – there are, after all, many smaller countries) by the largest country in the world, and one with a population sixteen times that of Czechoslovakia, could hardly escape the attention of even the most politically apathetic citizen. To expect Czechs and Slovaks to demonstrate in their political behaviour in the 1970s and early 1980s the attachment to pluralist and democratic values they showed in 1968 is more than a little unrealistic. Most people are not heroes most of the time. Even in Western countries political activism is highly correlated with a sense of political efficacy.[92] The sense of political efficacy of reformist-inclined Czechs and Slovaks is at present close to zero. Having failed for a variety of reasons – the most important of which, however, was the military strength and political determination of the Soviet Union – to preserve the *de facto* political pluralism of 1968, a majority of Czechs drew the conclusion that reformist political activity would have to await change within the Soviet Union.[93] A minority of citizens have remained willing to accept the risks of acting according to convictions which are utterly at odds with the norms of the official political culture, but an entire hierarchy of sanctions is available, and used as necessary against them.[94]

In a recent social psychological study, Eiser and van der Pligt point to some missing links in the argument associated with Fishbein and Ajzen,[95] which has attempted to close the attitude–behaviour theoretical gap by suggesting that 'a person's attitude towards an act is predictable from the sum of his or her "salient evaluative beliefs" about that act' and that 'intention to perform the act is then predictable jointly from the attitude towards the act and "subjective norms" concerning such behaviour'.[96] Choice and preference, as they note, entail comparison, and this means that the relationship between attitudes and evaluations, on the one hand, and behaviour on the other, must be seen 'in the frame of reference or context in terms of which each object or option is evaluated and any choice is made'.[97] As Eiser and van der Pligt also put it:

> If a weight is judged heavier or lighter depending on whether it is presented with a light or heavy comparison stimulus, it is surely a strange sort of psychological theory that would suggest that, say, a person's evaluation of a job offer (let alone the criteria on which such an evaluation is based) is unaffected by whether (among many other things) the alternative is no job at all or a more enjoyable job at twice the salary.[98]

Equally clearly, the relationship between values and political beliefs and political behaviour in Czechoslovakia must be seen in the context of the choice facing Czechs and Slovaks and of the political constraints upon their actions. The degree of deviant political behaviour tolerated by the authorities from the beginning of the 1970s onwards has been less than that in Hungary, Poland or Yugoslavia. Citizens in Czechoslovakia are well aware of what the choice is. If they abide by the official norms, they can live lives free of police harassment, have a choice of occupation, a secure if moderate standard of living and the prospect of their academically able children going on to higher education. If they attempt to engage in autonomous political activity, they will be expelled from the Party (if they are already in it), lose their job, lose their material and personal security and their privacy and find that there are no places available in higher education for their children (with obvious implications for *their* career prospects). These sanctions usually suffice, but when they do not, there are the alternatives of prison or foreign exile. Such 'rules of the game' apply in varying degrees in other Communist systems also.[99] The difference is that they have been applied more rigorously in Czechoslovakia and that Czechs and Slovaks are too close to the experience of Soviet military intervention to feel that it is within their power to change the rules. Many Party intellectuals in the 1960s felt that the rules could be changed and their optimism was shared by a majority of the people in the eight months of the 'Prague Spring'. In a political context which offered hope that the results of autonomous political action in defence of pluralist or libertarian values would be cumulatively efficacious, values and beliefs were translated into political action with a speed which surprised many foreign observers. In a political context in which citizens have the expectation that autonomous political action in defence of these same values will bring endless troubles for them and their families and change nothing in the political system, foreign observers should not be surprised that a majority of people have chosen to retreat into their private lives and go through the motions of behaving politically in the officially approved manner. It would be rash, indeed, though, to regard their relatively conformist behaviour as much of a guide to their values and political beliefs.[100] The question of whether a gulf between the official and dominant political culture actually matters if the latter is not immediately translated into political behaviour is one to which I shall return.

Having considered in this section values, beliefs and attitudes and some of the complexity of their relationship to behaviour, I remain unpersuaded by the argument that there is not enough cohesion or interlinkage in the subjective orientation to politics for this to deserve a separate label, 'political culture', and I am still further from being convinced that explanation or interpretation of Communist politics is enhanced by adopting such a broad concept of political culture as to blur some of the important distinctions which concern social psychologists, which increasingly concern anthropologists, and regarding which, political scientists studying Communist countries need to be particularly alert. Terms such as 'dominant' and 'official' political culture have been used in this and other chapters and it may be useful now to attempt to clarify more explicitly what is meant by these and other concepts employed in the analysis of politial culture and to examine some of the interrelationships between different categories of political culture.

CATEGORIES OF POLITICAL CULTURE

The question of the relative success or failure of official attempts to effect political cultural change within Communist countries has been raised by several contributors to this book. In political science literature there has often been an assumption that this effort has met with a very high degree of success, at least in the case of the Soviet Union and, in the view of some authors, in Communist states generally. Thus, for instance, Huntington and Dominguez have written:

> Many states, old and new, try to plan change in their country's political culture. The *most dramatically successful case of planned political cultural change is probably the Soviet Union* . . . To date, *other than in communist systems*, planned political cultural change through mobilization has been rare and has fared poorly. Political culture tends to resist change and, when it changes, it does so more slowly than ideologues may desire (italics mine, A.B.).[101]

Juan Linz, who counts Communist systems in general as totalitarian, has come to a somewhat similar conclusion on the outcome of the conscious political socialisation efforts within such systems:

> If we keep in mind the findings about opinion leaders as mediators between the mass media and the individual in democratic societies and the impossibility of creating any comparable network of personal influences, except in some cases the churches, we can understand *the success of propaganda*, the appearance of enthusiasm and support, and the pervasive conformity in totalitarian systems (italics mine, A.B.).[102]

Linz is doubtless well aware of differences among Communist systems, but he does not make such a sharp distinction between the Soviet Union, on the one hand, and the East European systems, on the other, in terms of the success of propaganda and the official political culture as does another prominent writer on this theme, Seweryn Bialer. But Bialer, though he contrasts what he sees as the success of the official political culture in the Soviet Union with its relative failure in Eastern Europe (most notably, in Poland, Hungary and Czechoslovakia) argues strongly for viewing the Soviet Union as an example of an almost unified political culture. As he puts it:

> It is the Soviet participatory system on the one hand and the closed character of the information system and the massive directed propaganda effort on the other hand which account for the phenomenon of which we are becoming more and more aware: the pervasiveness of the official political culture in the civil society. There are not two political cultures in the Soviet Union, one élite and the other popular. The dominant political culture is accepted by both the élites and a very large part of the population.[103]

Bialer speaks also of 'the pervasiveness and unconscious acceptance of the official political culture among all strata of Soviet society', though he observes that the 'acceptance is weakest among the intelligentsia'.[104] He leaves open the question of whether 'paternalistic and autocratic Russian traditions reinforce the process' of acceptance, but suggests that in the process of the 'intergenerational persistance' of public identification with the Soviet system 'this acceptance has been internalised'.[105]

Mary McAuley, in her contribution to this volume, regards the success or failure of the official political culture as a much more open question or, to be precise, series of questions (see Chapter 2, pp. 35–6). She regards 'the treatment of official values by our subjectivists' as 'cavalier indeed' (p. 29) and calls for analysis of 'changing official values and their content' (p. 33). She raises the possibility (pp. 33–4) that 'official culture has been remarkably *successful* in instilling its values in society at large' but this is because 'it is the *leadership* which reverts to traditional values and imposes them upon society, which in turn is receptive towards them'. But this she regards as still a matter for investigation: 'If we are interested in the relationship between official values and society's values, we must dissect official values'. Though I cannot claim to speak for all 'subjectivists', I am in full agreement with McAuley on the desirability of undertaking detailed analyses of the official political culture (or cultures) of Communist systems.

We need, however, to distinguish some of the categories in which the discussion is conducted and which are often confused. When the term 'political culture' is used, without any qualifying adjective, as it often is in this book or in the title, *Political Culture and Political Change in*

Communist States,[106] reference is being made, in a conscious simplification, to 'the' political culture of a society, meaning usually a nationwide or state-wide society.[107] As I have argued in the above-mentioned book to which this one is, in some respects, a sequel, four possible configurations of political culture may, in principle, exist within societies: (i) a unified political culture; (ii) a dominant political culture which co-exists with various sub-cultures; (iii) a dichotomous political culture; and (iv) a fragmented political culture – that is to say, one in which no state-wide political culture has emerged to dominate the numerous political cultures or sub-cultures based upon tribe, locality, national or social group.[108] I suggested in that work that the first of these configurations was the *goal* of almost all of the societies included in the study, but that in none of them had it been realised. Seweryn Bialer, as noted above, has come close to saying that it has been achieved in the Soviet Union. While the possibility in principle of a unified political culture should not be ruled out, it would be surprising to find this in practice if by 'political culture' we have in mind the subjective orientation to politics. Some evidence suggesting that the Soviet case is more complex than Bialer allows for when he is explicitly discussing political culture (even though his general contrast between the Soviet Union and East-Central Europe remains valid) is provided in several of the contributions to this volume and by Stephen White in his book on Soviet political culture.[109]

The second configuration – that of a dominant political culture which co-exists with various sub-cultures – is what we can most commonly expect to find when we study political culture on a state-wide basis. Though I prefer to eschew the term 'national character', and see the concepts of 'culture' and of 'political culture' as better suited to bringing out the historically-conditioned differences between one nation and another while, at the same time avoiding the connotation of immutability which is often attached to national character, it is worth noting Geert Hofstede's conclusions on the basis of a remarkable comparative study of forty countries:[110] 'modern nations do have dominant national character traits which can be revealed by survey studies and by the comparison of measurable data on the society level. The mental programs of the members of the same nation tend to contain a common component'.[111] He goes on to note that there are also other components which are 'subcultural' – shared only 'by others of the same educational level, socio-economic status, occupation, sex, or age group' – and that (as one would expect) some countries are more culturally homogeneous than others.[112]

The third configuration, that of a dichotomous political culture, is one in which there are two salient political cultures within the society and neither has achieved dominance over the other. As Dennis Kavanagh has observed, Northern Ireland comes close to exemplifying that pattern.[113] A society in which there is a particularly sharp cleavage between 'élite' and 'mass' political cultures might also be fitted into such a category. This may be the case with some of the poorest 'Third World' countries. It is, however, worth examining differences between and within 'élite' and 'mass' political cultures in other types of society as well, including those where a dominant political culture may be located.

The fourth type of configuration is that of the fragmented political culture, in which no state-wide political culture has gained sufficient adherence by groups or internalisation by individuals to dominate the variety of political cultures, or sub-cultures, based upon tribe, locality or social or national group. Among Communist countries, Yugoslavia hovers uncertainly betwen the second configuration – dominant political culture and various ethnic sub-cultures – and this last category of fragmentation.[114] Not surprisingly, in view of the country's history and ethnic diversity, in which no one nationality enjoys clear numerical preponderance, there is a less dominant 'Yugoslav' political culture than there is, for example, a dominant national political culture in Hungary.

In this particular classification no mention has been made of 'official political culture', for its status is somewhat different. It represents official norms, desiderata and political goals rather than societal values and beliefs. Thus, a distinction should be drawn between 'official political culture' and 'dominant political culture' and neither of these is necessarily the same thing as 'élite political culture'. In theory, it is possible that the three concepts could in the case of a particular society involve one and the same set of beliefs and norms. But in practice the interrelationship among the three is likely to be much more complicated and should be studied. It is fair to say that no such detailed study has been undertaken yet.[115]

On the need for this, I am – as already noted – in agreement with McAuley. McAuley, while calling for attention to be paid to the 'crucial question of changing official values and their content' (Chapter 2, p 33) takes note of 'the regularity with which the different Communist party leaderships, or sections of them, in countries with very different earlier political traditions have come up with similar types of answer as to what is needed to run the country or economy more efficiently' and she suggests that 'the institutions of power are crucial here' (p. 30). It is worth noting, however, that the institutions of power in all Communist states were modelled to a greater or lesser degree on those of the Soviet Union and that the same was the case with the official political culture. This has been especially true of the earliest years of Communist power in what are now established Communist systems, though Cuba is something of an exception inasmuch as its adaptation towards the Soviet model took longer and it is closer to it today than in the early post-revolutionary years.

It can certainly be argued that national variations in the official political culture from one Communist state to another have become increasingly apparent over time, and yet the variation is not so great as in the 'dominant' political cultures of these societies – that is to say, as that to be found between the fundamental political beliefs and values, political knowledge, foci of identification and loyalty, and subjective perceptions of history and politics of a majority of people within these various societies. The variation tends also, it could be argued, to be less than that between the 'élite' political cultures of the various Communist states. The élite as a whole – especially if it is defined sufficiently broadly as to include the creative and technical intelligentsia – is much more open to influence from the dominant political culture (should that happen to be at variance with Marxist–Leninist political cultural norms) than is the narrower stratum within the élite which acts as guardians and arbiters of the official political culture.

The official political culture, consisting of the norms laid down by the party leadership and those responsible for establishing ideological standards and guidelines within the state (among whom one should certainly count the employees of the Department of Propaganda of the Central Committee) can and does change. In the process of interaction between the official and the 'traditional' political culture, however, one cannot assume that even in the Soviet case the influence comes almost entirely from the one ('official') side. Nor, *pace* McAuley (Chapter 2, p. 34) is it particularly plausible to argue that 'it is the *leadership* which reverts to traditional values and imposes them upon society, which in turn is receptive towards them'. Before the Communists came to power in the states which are today ruled by Communist Parties, Communists represented a quite distinctive sub-culture. They are an embattled minority and in the Eastern European Communist states, with the exceptions of Czechoslovakia and Yugoslavia, a fairly small minority. Among the general features which marked them off from other political parties and from the dominant political culture within their respective societies were (i) the fact that they looked to the Soviet Union for guidance and inspiration; (ii) the doctrine of class struggle and theoretical attachment to the establishment of a 'dictatorship of the proletariat'; (iii) a strictly hierarchical and disciplined party organisation (in comparison at least with 'bourgeois' parties) to which the name, 'democratic centralism', was given; (iv) commitment to the view that the Communist Party, by virtue of its ability to interpret and act as an instrument of the 'science of society', Marxism–Leninism, had a unique entitlement to rule; (v) a determination to alter fundamentally property relations within the economy and society whereby private ownership of industry (and in time of agriculture) would be largely abolished; and (vi) the claim that their ultimate goal was that of building a classless society to be known as 'communism'.

Most of this *remains* part of the official political culture of most ruling Communist Parties. Some of the terminology is different. Thus, the phrase 'leading role of the working class' takes the place of 'dictatorship of the proletariat' once socialism, as defined by the party leadership, has been developed. The one phrase is as meaningless or as meaningful as the other. They are both equally meaningless in the sense that to move out of the proletariat or working class in order to wield bureaucratic power, or even to join the ranks of the intelligent-sia, was and is regarded as promotion, as an instance of *upward* social mobility. Only insofar as the doctrine establishes the superior status and (usually) superior material rewards of the *workers vis-à-vis the peasantry* and insofar as it supports what has at times amounted to an affirmative action programme for the admittance of workers and the sons and daughters of workers to higher educational institutions can either phrase be taken, to some degree, at face value. They are meaningful, however, inasmuch as both the 'dictatorship of the proletariat' and the 'leading role of the working class' can be used, and have been used, by party bureaucrats (especially those whose func-tional responsibilities make them ideological guardians) as sticks with which to beat reformist, 'revisionist' or 'bourgeois nationalist' intellec-tuals within the ranks of the Communist Party itself as well as critics and potential critics outside the Party.

There have been various accretions to the official political culture, and some parts of it are emphasised more at some times than at others and in some countries than in others. Yet there are still many common threads to be found in the official political cultures of ruling Com-munist Parties and this is so for a variety of reasons. Among these reasons are the influence at best and the potential or actual coercive power at worst of the Soviet Union *vis-à-vis* other European Communist states; the fact that this official political culture by and large serves the interests of Party officials as they perceive them; and the fact that an unquestioning acceptance of these norms was for most high party officials in most Communist states a *sine qua non* of their ascent to the topmost rungs of the political ladder.

Among the specific components of the official political culture (which follow from the general features already mentioned) are the attitudes towards authority to be fostered in the mass of the population; the type of political participation which is encouraged; the interpretation of the country's history which is favoured; the attitude adopted towards political organisation other than organisations subordinate to the Communist Party; the view taken of religion; the nature and extent of the political information deemed appropriate for citizens to possess; and the goal, or goals, in terms of which present labours and sacrifices are justified or legitimised. To locate the official political culture we might look, *inter alia*, at the speeches of top party leaders; at resolutions of the Central Committee; at the proceedings of party Congresses; at school textbooks; at the editorials in the main official daily newspaper of the Communist Party; and at writing explicitly devoted to the theme of the characteristics of the 'new man' or 'new socialist person'.[116] These are, on the whole, documents with a greater official authority, which have to pass more rigorous tests of political orthodoxy, than works of creative literature or small-circulation books and journals in the social sciences, though even the latter are not, needless to say, immune from censorship and self-censorship. It is of interest that the Secretaries of the Central Committee responsible for ideology within those ruling Communist Parties which maintain an alliance with the Soviet Union (that is to say, the great majority of ruling Parties) meet regularly in an effort to co-ordinate their viewpoints and strategy and in so doing help to maintain an official Communist political culture which is international and is not merely the sum of the dominant political cultures within the various societies ruled by Communist Parties. As already noted, the status of the concept, 'official political culture' is different from political culture in the normal sense of the subjective orientation to politics. By reading certain authoritative documents, we can generalise about the main and recurring features of the official political culture and also draw attention to changes in it. In principle, indeed, it is easier to identify than are the 'dominant political culture' or sub-cultures, since it represents the official standards for a political culture which may, up to a point, be located in *authoritative texts*. To generalise about the values and beliefs which dominate the *minds* of members of social and national groups is – as the disagreements aired in this book illustrate – much more difficult.

The official political culture is not necessarily merely synonymous with Marxism–Leninism, though Marxism–Leninism lends itself to different emphases and interpretations, since both Marx and Lenin wrote voluminously and can be quoted against themselves and since, moreover, Communist theoreticians are enjoined to 'creatively develop' Marxism–Leninism. These are, it is true, in the case of Communist states, substantially *overlapping* concepts and bodies of doctrine. However, the official political culture can also embrace norms which, by no stretch of the imagination, could be called Marxist–Leninist, and which have included at times the attribution of almost superhuman powers to the country's top leader (Stalin, Mao), glorification of the national past and present (of which Romania provides one of the most striking contemporary examples) and the sanctioning and abetting of suspicion of foreigners (which reached its apogee in the Soviet Union in the last years of Stalin's lifetime, including even a ban on marriage to foreigners which lasted from February 1947 until January 1954).[117]

The 'dominant political culture' (where, as in Poland, for example, it involves a rejection of many of the values and norms of Marxism–Leninism and sees Catholicism as one of the badges of Polish national identity) tends to have a substantially greater influence within the élite as a whole than within the narrower circle of political leaders who are the guardians of the official political culture. A Stalin could at a stroke make concessions to 'traditional' elements in Russian political culture which had remained part of the dominant, though not hitherto of the official, Soviet political culture. Thus, he could restore to favour the word (*rodina*) and concept of the motherland and, as Stephen White (Chapter 4, pp. 88–9) reminds us, during the Second World War he could readily identify 'the Soviet cause with heroic figures from the Russian past such as Alexander Nevsky, Suvorov and Kutuzov, many of whom had been revered by patriots and conservatives in the pre-revolutionary period'. While this was, indeed, an initiative from the very top of the Soviet system, it required little or nothing by way of imposition, so far at least as the Russian majority of the Soviet population were concerned. It is also more typical of Stalin than of the way dominant and official political cultures more generally interact within Communist systems. It would appear to be more usual for elements of the dominant political culture (including often traditional features) to gain ground among the broader élite before they seep upwards and become, to a more limited extent, incorporated in the official political culture.

There is a percolation up as well as a handing down of political attitudes and beliefs and this is one of the sources of contradiction within the official political culture. Even in 'polyarchical' political systems, the political beliefs, perceptions and knowledge of political activists differ markedly from those of the majority of the population.[118] Robert Dahl, while noting that 'many of the beliefs held by political activists can be regarded as a part, or a product, of a country's political culture' nevertheless draws attention to the distinctive nature of other beliefs of activists.[119] This is a feature likely to be all the more true of the Bolshevik minority in pre-revolutionary Russia and of the Communist activists in pre-Communist Eastern Europe. Once in power, however, the Parties had to find ways of making the societies they ruled responsive to their policies and goals. They have chosen different methods of doing so (compare Stalin's and Khrushchev's, Rákosi's and Kádár's) but a rather widespread feature, once the immediate post-revolutionary years are over, has been some incorporation of, or accommodation with, traditional values and symbols.

This is, however, only one of the sources of contradiction within the official political culture. The way Jack Gray, quoted by McAuley (Chapter 2, p. 30), puts it is to suggest that 'there are two Communist Party political cultures', the first of which is 'represented by the long-term aspirations and expectations grouped round the idea of "new socialist man" ', while the second is 'the operational code of the hierarchical, self-perpetuating party, enjoying a monopoly of political power'.[120] This is, indeed, a structural, rather than a cultural, problem of Communist systems, and a more fundamental one than McAuley brings out. The second element in the official political culture – the 'operational code' – which in reality is given a higher priority than the idea of the 'new man' does not merely reflect the voluntarism and vested interests of the power-holders (though the vested interests of Party and other officials do, indeed, rapidly become a powerful constraint upon any challenge to the system) but is a direct result of the endeavour to 'force men to be free', to impose Utopian goals on a recalcitrant and unprepared society.[121]

McAuley has observed that 'official ideology', while not creating men in its own image '*is* responsible for the values that emerge. It is not that it is simply irrelevant or that it is waging a losing battle against a consistent set of unchanging traditional values (as the political culturalists would have us believe)' (Chapter 2, pp. 34–5). In similar vein, she has written 'Because of the assumption that official culture is unchanging and easy to identify they [the 'political culturalists'] dispense with any analysis of it' (p. 35). I detect here the rustle of straw men being knocked over. McAuley and I are agreed that the task of detailed analysis of the official political culture has yet to be undertaken, and that it should be, but I am not aware of ever having held the view that either the 'traditional values' or the 'official culture' within Communist countries are 'unchanging'. Some values are superseded, others are very persistent components of a dominant political culture; some elements of the official political culture are changed, others remain. Part of the task of a closer investigation both of the dominant political cultures and the official political cultures of Communist countries – insofar as these are at variance – will be to specify more precisely what has changed and what has persisted. This is desirable not only to overcome the comparative neglect of their content and interconnections but also to transcend false dichotomies. There is simply no need to assume that the choice before us is to regard Communist political cultures either as quite unchanged or as totally transformed.

The fact that different values and political beliefs may be found within the élites (broadly defined) of Communist societies and the fact that the official political culture contains contradictory elements and inconsistent goals need not surprise us. Nor is it a reason to regard as unworthy of note the relative failure of 'planned political culture change', including that of the overt attempt to create a new socialist person.[122] Though a far greater variety of conflicting beliefs may be aired within Western societies, though the political élites there, far from presenting a unified front to the 'masses', are openly divided in their values and political attitudes, and though access to information inconvenient to the power-holders is incomparably easier to come by than in Communist systems, many Western Marxists do not find it odd to suggest that these same Western élites have carried out a successful process of political socialisation and have created a 'false consciousness' in the minds of the mass of the people. If, then, in Communist countries, all television and radio programmes, newspapers, and college and school textbooks purvey, broadly speaking, the same values and political line, and yet there remains a gulf between what is purveyed and what is believed, that is a matter of interest. Those writers on political culture who have pointed to the limited success of Communist political socialisation efforts have, in fact, been writing against a scholarly background in which it has been assumed that in Communist systems, if nowhere else, planned political cultural change really has worked and that propaganda there has been particularly effective.[123] To the extent that there is evidence suggesting that in the case of some Communist countries that assumption was simply wrong and in the case of others an oversimplification, we need to try to explain the inefficacy of the official political socialisation efforts and also ask whether it is, indeed, of any consequence if there is a lack of harmony between the dominant political culture, on the one hand, and political structures and overt political behaviour, on the other.

POLITICAL CULTURE AND POLITICAL CHANGE

Authors who employ the concept of political culture have been variously accused of failing to explain *everything* (attention is drawn to political events on which political culture has little bearing) or of trying to explain *anything* with a concept which some of its critics – and even a few of its proponents – have suggested can explain nothing. When, however, those who reject the 'all-or-nothing' view of political culture make the point that after a period of dissonance between the dominant political culture within a society and an authoritarian political system, a crisis triggered off by other stimuli may produce a more open political situation in which part of an adequate *explanation* of particular political conduct is likely to be in political cultural terms (with Czechoslovakia in the 1960s cited as a clear example), this is dismissed as a 'milk-and-water claim'![124]

The task of satisfying the critics is evidently not an easy one and there is, in any case, a limit to the number of questions which can be answered at chapter length, since answers occupy more space than questions. A good many issues raised by the concept of political culture have already been discussed in the first seven chapters of this volume and from several different standpoints. But in this penultimate section of the concluding chapter, I turn to a problem which has been raised and which has not yet received the attention it deserves, namely: what does political culture matter if it can be shown that there is a dissonance between the political culture of the power-holders, on the one hand, and the political culture of the majority of the people in the society, on the other, and yet the power-holders nevertheless continue to govern on their own terms? Or, to pose the question differently (see Skilling, Chapter 6, p. 123), are values which are not acted on 'politically relevant, except in the long run'?

The 'long run' qualification is an important one, even if it will bring little comfort to those East Europeans who recall Keynes's aphorism that 'in the long run we are all dead!'. If there is anything on which scholars who use the concept of political culture actually agree, it is that this is a concept which is of long-term, rather than short-term, significance, and that the basic political beliefs and values which are vital components of a political culture tend to change slowly. Leaving aside for the moment the problem of the difficulty of ascertaining the values and beliefs of the majority of the people in an authoritarian political system, there is surely little reason to doubt that it is interesting in principle to know how they evaluate the political regime (or regimes) under which they have lived, their attitude to political authority, their beliefs as to whether political office-holders should be held accountable to, and removable by, the people as a whole or whether 'high politics' and what 'they' do in government is no concern of ordinary people. Knowledge of 'subjective orientations to politics' such as these helps us to understand contemporary politics in the countries concerned and also alerts us to the potential for, or – as the case may be – some of the obstacles to, rapid change from an authoritarian to a pluralist political regime.

It alerts us to possibilities – even, granted one important condition, to probabilities. Thus, in the case of Czechoslovakia, though Skilling and Paul have laid useful emphasis on the strength of authoritarian sub-cultures in Czechoslovakia during the present century and though they have noted that the period of time that Czechs and Slovaks have spent under authoritarian rule since the republic was founded greatly exceeds the extent of their experience of pluralistic political structures, both seem to be agreed that 'the critical variable determining the nature of politics in Czechoslovakia has been the degree of freedom from outside interference' (Skilling, Chapter 6, p. 124, citing Paul). The point applies, of course, to other East European countries also. Were the Soviet Union to allow anything approaching a 'Finlandisation' of Eastern Europe (to use a term which is, understandably, disliked by most Finns,[125] but is taken here to mean that a country retains a high degree of autonomy in its internal affairs, including the ability to determine the fundamental nature of its political and economic system, while accepting significant constraints upon its foreign policy and a measure of self-censorship in official comment on Soviet affairs), we could expect many changes in political behaviour in these societies which would reflect their dominant political cultures and currently repressed sub-cultures rather than the political culture of their present rulers which in most cases (there are partial exceptions, of which Hungary is one) are more consonant with Soviet official political culture (at least in its 'operational code' variant) than with the dominant political culture in their own society. If we return to the specific case of Czechoslovakia, we would expect to see the strong pluralistic strand in Czechoslovak political culture translated into political behaviour. That is not only because in the six and a half decades since the Czechoslovak state was founded 'groups in Czechoslovakia who are ready to support authoritarian regimes . . . have never gained dominance without the strong backing of foreign powers' (Paul, Chapter 7, p. 141) but because of the very different psychological impact of mandatory and voluntary behaviour (as I have noted earlier in this chapter).

The *affective* relationship[126] of citizens to their political system imposes limits on the *effectiveness* of the system in shaping the political culture of the people. It is much too simple to make the assumption which McAuley does that one government, and manner of governing, should have just as great a positive impact on the values and political beliefs of the citizenry as another. That at least appears to be the import of her observation that 'authors who claim that today's dominant . . . political culture – as discovered in surveys – is *not* the offspring of existing government practices can in no way suggest that it is appropriate to seek an earlier period's dominant political culture in that period's political practices'. A dominant political culture will never be merely 'the offspring' of existing government practices, but a result of a much more complex interaction between government and society. In particular cases, as when severely authoritarian rule is imposed upon a society with some years of experience of pluralistic and libertarian government or when the new political regime is perceived as having been imposed by a foreign power – the second case clearly applies to that of Polish perceptions of the Communist system in Poland and both cases apply to Czech perceptions of the post-1968 regime in Czechoslovakia – even the authorities' control over the major institutional instruments of political socialisation is unlikely to have the consequences the rulers intend.

The condition on which a pluralisation of Czech politics would again become a 'probability' is, however, a hypothetical one. There is no reason to suppose that in the near future the Soviet Union is going to be willing to accord the same autonomy to Czechslovakia that Finland possesses, though it is quite likely that even a smaller shift in Soviet policy (as happened in Khrushchev's time) would begin a movement which would lead to a much greater shift in Czechoslovakia than in the USSR. The international context is, however, as Skilling has emphasised, of crucial importance. The actual response of the Soviet Union to unrest in Eastern Europe has varied somewhat over time, and in ways that were not predictable, and the *perceptions* of Eastern European peoples of *likely* Soviet reactions vary from time to time also and from one country to another. This international factor, in its various aspects, is but one reason why McAuley's attempt (Chapter 2, p. 26) to introduce hypothesis-testing rigour into political cultural analysis is misplaced. Because of the international dimension and the many other related factors which in the real world cannot be controlled or predicted, there would be no point in setting up now, for the future, the hypothesis that 'the existence of a particular set of views at time *A* will lead to a particular pattern of disturbance at time *B* if official policy offends these views'.

The main value of the concept of political culture, however, is not primarily in relation to the future at all, but as an aid to understanding the present and as an element in the explanation of certain types of political change which have taken place. That, it must be emphasised, does not mean *all* political change or resistance to change. There is little to commend an explanation of the political change which has taken place in Czechoslovakia since Husák became Party leader in April 1969 in terms of indigenous Czech or even of Slovak political culture. But it is another matter with the reform movement within the Communist Party of Czechoslovakia in the 1960s and with the 'Prague Spring' of 1968 when, in those eight months, pluralisation and moves towards democratisation proceeded at a pace far greater than that desired by the Party leadership (many of whose members, indeed, disapproved not only of the pace but also of the direction of the change). No adequate explanation of 1968 can fail to include consideration of the dissonance between the political culture and the political system or at any rate (for those whose objection to the concise term 'political culture' remains deep-rooted) consideration of values and beliefs which were at odds with official norms, and cognisance of the perceptions of Czechs and Slovaks on the range of political options which the leadership change had opened up.

The importance of the political cultural dimension in the Soviet case need be discussed only briefly here, since it has been considered at length by White in Chapter 4, in what I find a balanced and largely convincing evaluation, notwithstanding our dissimilar definitional starting-points and some differences which follow from that. Earlier I suggested that the consonance between official Soviet political culture and the political culture of the mass of the people was not as great as had been claimed by several Western scholars[127] and by numerous Soviet scholars.[128] The political cultural differences between, for example, Estonians, Latvians, Georgians and Buryats would appear to be quite marked, with all of them different again from the Russians. Among Russians there are sub-cultural differences between neo-Stalinists and reformers and between Slavophiles and Westerners.[129]

Yet, by comparison with Czechoslovakia, there is far more consonance in the Soviet Union between the official and the dominant political culture. Three, in particular, of the common elements in the official (and, indeed, more broadly, the élite) political culture and the mass political culture are worth emphasising. The first and most important is fear of chaos. The second is patriotism, including love of the motherland and pride in Soviet superpower status. The third is a certain measure of official and popular agreement on the identity of national heroes.

The fear of chaos, described by Nadezhda Mandelstam as 'the most permanent of our feelings' and as something 'passed on from one generation to another',[130] has deep historical roots, but the high premium placed upon order and unity has almost certainly been strengthened in the twentieth century by the experience of the First World War, the chaos of the Civil War, and the enormous suffering during the Second World War. I have noted elsewhere the centrality of the value placed upon order, the strength of the fear of anarchy and the extent to which these values and emotions cut across social groups at least as far as the Russian majority of Soviet citizens are concerned.[131] On this aspect of Soviet (and, more specifically, Russian) political culture, I am at one with Seweryn Bialer who has written:

> If there is any single value that dominates the minds and thoughts of the Soviet establishment from the highest to lowest level, it is the value of order; if there is any single fear that outweighs all others, it is the fear of disorder, chaos, fragmentation, loss of control. . . . [And] fear of disorder and attachment to orderly society are valued not only by political leaders and élites but find strong resonance in the Soviet popular mind.[132]

On the second of the common elements of official and popular culture, White has referred (Chapter 4, p. 82) to the 'strong national pride' to be found in the Soviet Union, and in Chapter 5 (p. 103) I noted the tremendous stress placed on the 'Great Patriotic War' by Party leaders and propagandists, since there is no other shared experience which can evoke such a spontaneous emotional response. The success of propaganda which strikes a chord with people's direct experience is evidently very different from that which rests on theory alone. In the perceptions of Russian citizens in particular, the linkage between war memories and loyalty to the 'motherland', on the one hand, with loyalty to the Soviet system, on the other, amounts often to fusion. The strength of Soviet patriotism (again especially, but by no means exclusively, on the part of Russians) has been noted by countless experienced observers of the Soviet scene. Thus, the main conclusion reached by the Russian-born German specialist on the Soviet Union, Klaus Mehnert, to his original and enterprising study of Russians' favourite contemporary Soviet authors was of 'the over-whelmingly strong sentiment' of patriotism among both the writers and their readers.[133]

As far as national heroes are concerned, while Lenin may not command as much universal affection among Russians as Pushkin or the veneration which a section of the Russian intelligentsia reserve for Dostoevsky, his significance as a political symbol is very great. There is no other *political* figure to compare with him. Though the Lenin cult may provoke a satirical response from a minority of Soviet citizens, respect for Lenin (amounting at times to reverence) would appear to be widespread. That Lenin is admired at least as much as a great *Russian* as he is as a great revolutionary or enormously influential theorist is suggested by the incomparably higher degree of popular esteem for him than for Marx. One small indicator of this is the comparative emptiness of the Marx Museum in Moscow (except when parties of schoolchildren or delegations from the GDR are being taken round) which contrasts sharply with the enormously and consistently long queues of Soviet citizens waiting to pass through the Lenin Mausoleum. The role of teaching about Lenin would appear to be of considerable importance in the political socialisation of schoolchildren. As the author of a recent book on the Lenin cult has put it:

The cult of Lenin for children is as intense and high-pitched as ever. Journals on the Communist upbringing of children abound with articles on how best to inspire a love for Lenin in little ones, who are deluged from the earliest grades with stories and projects about Lenin. They cannot but be impressed by the legendary Ilich who forms such an important part of their school program.[134]

These three strands in Soviet political culture which cut across social strata, and to a more limited extent, ethnic groups, may certainly be regarded as part of the dominant political culture of the dominant nationality within the Soviet Union. As such, they are, on the whole, cultural supports for the systemic *status quo*, though they *can* be invoked by those who seek change, as the use of the patriotic theme by Solzhenitsyn (and Russian nationalists of his school) against the Soviet system and the use of Lenin against Stalinism by Khrushchev indicate. The contrast with Czechoslovakia in all three respects is instructive. First, neither intellectuals in Czechoslovakia nor the Czech and Slovak peoples as a whole feared that the rapid political change they had set in motion would lead to anarchy. There was no 'disorder' until it was created in August 1968 by the arrival of almost half a million foreign troops. Second, patriotism for Czechs and Slovaks, as for other East Europeans, tends to bring them into conflict with the official political culture as it involves an assertion of national distinctiveness and national traditions against the uniformist tendency of official Marxism–Leninism and the largely Soviet norms embodied in 'socialist internationalism'. Third, the Czechs and Slovaks are short of Communist heroes who command widespread recognition. The image of the first Communist leader of Czeckoslovakia, Klement Gottwald, is tarnished beyond repair and it seems more than likely that that symbol of Czech social democracy, Thomas Masaryk, as founder of the Czechoslovak state, remains the Czech 'Lenin', even if the contrast between his treatment in the official political culture and that of Lenin in the Soviet Union could scarcely be greater.

APPROACHES TO THE STUDY OF POLITICAL CULTURE: A SUMMING-UP

This book has been concerned with showing what contribution the study of the political cultures of societies ruled by Communist Parties can make to the understanding of political life within these countries and, in particular, with the relevance of the distinctive political cultures to diverse political developments in countries which have so much in common in terms of their political and economic systems and official ideology.[135] There has been much discussion of the vexed question of methodology and sources and a few final words on approaches to the study of political culture may be in order.

Useful in essence though Miller's distinction between what he terms 'research' and what he calls an 'account' is (Chapter 3, p. 43), it is also a little misleading inasmuch as it identifies 'research' with a particular kind of scientific research whereby hypotheses can be tested and falsified. When Skilling writes (Chapter 6, p. 130) that 'only concrete historical research, using all possible sources, including survey data if available, can offer even an approach to the problem', it is clearly not 'research' in Miller's limited sense which he has in mind, but it is none the less important for that.

Research in the context of Communist politics can also include interviews and conversations with citizens of the countries concerned which are of value for the qualitative insights they can provide, though insofar as they can be checked against survey data, this is desirable. However, given that the Western scholar cannot personally conduct statistically significant surveys within Communist countries, it behoves him or her to make judgements about the relevance to the study of political culture of particular indigenous surveys and to know something of the relative professionalism of the institutions or investigators involved. It is also important to be alert to the fact that the extent to which respondents will feel free to answer questionnaires frankly varies over time and from one country to another. Conditions are seldom so favourable to truthful answers as they were in Czechoslovakia in 1968,[136] but it is, nevertheless, of interest that elicited responses in surveys conducted by serious social scientists in the Soviet Union, for instance, tend to show a greater deviation from official norms and desiderata than does most overt political behaviour (and, in particular, voting behaviour). Where the survey data *are* different from what the authorities would like to hear, we shall usually not go far wrong if we assume that there is *at least that much* attitudinal deviation.

The study of political culture requires not only research but reflection. Memoirs and creative literature can be an aid to reflection as well as sources of evidence. The same is true of work in other social scientific disciplines. I suggested earlier in this chapter that the experience of anthropologists in handling (and 'paring down') the concept of culture can be instructive and that social psychology is of particular importance as a source of understanding the subjective and cognitive realm with which political culture is concerned. Indeed, many findings of social psychology provide insight into ways in which political cultures can be learned, transmitted and changed, for though the concept of political culture is only rarely invoked by psychologists, the study of the attitude–behaviour relationship and of attitudinal and value change is of central concern in that discipline.

There is also a growing body of writing in the Soviet Union and Eastern Europe which makes explicit use of the term 'political culture'. As will be clear from my account of some of this writing in the Soviet context, use of the *terminology* does not necessarily mean employment of the *concept*. This is particularly true of its use by Soviet politicians for whom the term is mainly evaluative – political culture is something which is 'high' or 'low'. Even serious Soviet and East European scholars also at times use the term in that way, but they use it, too, in description and explanation. That latter part of their work is, accordingly, of interest to Western students of Communist political cultures, as indeed, is some of the prescription which appears in the guise of description, such as accounts of the 'new socialist person' said to be already created. These are of relevance to the study of official political culture, though in its 'ideal' rather than 'operational code' aspect.

Reference to the official political culture brings us back, appropriately, to an aspect of McAuley's critique. One of the ways in which the study of political culture can move forward is by undertaking much more extensive research on the official political culture within particular Communist countries and by comparing these official norms over time and between one country and another. Also important (and this point is likewise stressed by McAuley) is the need to pay more attention to the ways in which political culture is transmitted.[137] Consideration has been given to that topic in this volume, but there is much more to be done. Other ways forward have been suggested throughout the book. Nothing is more useful for the study of political culture, however, than the exposure of existing analyses and syntheses to criticism and scrutiny. Thus, though the disagreements I have expressed from time to time in this chapter with Mary McAuley's arguments are not the only points on which I dissent from her views,[138] I am in no doubt about the value of her critique. She has brought many issues into sharper focus and stimulated further thought and work on the part of those she calls 'political culturalists'. Whether (see Chapter 2, p. 14) we remain 'hopelessly tangled in the brambles at the foot of the mountain' will be for the reader to judge.

NOTES AND REFERENCES

1. Mary McAuley, Chapter 2 (for example, at pp. 15 and 19, and p. 37, note 6). Are, then, those who see the task of political cultural analysis as that of 'thick description' (White, Chapter 4, p. 63, citing Clifford Geertz and Robert Tucker) to be called 'thick describers'? Perhaps a subjectivist is not such a bad thing to be after all!

2. Against that it is worth noting – as, indeed, Skilling himself does in Chapter 6, p. 115 – that there is a common emphasis on what Paul calls 'the persistence of pluralistic political orientations' (David W. Paul, *The Cultural Limits of Revolutionary Politics: Change and Continuity in Socialist Czechoslovakia* [Boulder, Colorado, 1979] p. 175) in Paul's writing and that of Gordon Wightman and myself on Czechoslovakia, notwithstanding the fact that Paul favours the broader and Wightman and I the narrower definition of political culture. See Brown and Wightman, 'Czechoslovakia: Revival and Retreat' in Archie Brown and Jack Gray (eds) *Political Culture and Political Change in Communist States* (London and New York, 1977) pp. 159–96.

3. Robert C. Tucker, 'Culture, Political Culture and Communist Society', *Political Science Quarterly*, vol. 88, no. 2, June 1973, pp. 173–90, at p. 178.

4. Ibid, pp. 176–9.

5. Cited, ibid, p. 176.

6. Cited, ibid, p. 177.

7. Ibid.

8. On 'material culture' and 'cultural materialism' see Melville J. Herskovits, *Cultural Anthropology* (New York, 1955) especially ch. 8, pp. 119–42; and Marvin Harris, *The Rise of Anthropological Theory: A History of Theories of Culture* (London, 1969) especially ch. 22 and 23, pp. 634–87.

9. Edmund Leach, *Social Anthropology* (Glasgow, 1982) p. 37.

10. Ibid, pp. 37–8. For a highly readable account of developments within British social anthropology over the past sixty years, see Adam Kuper, *Anthropology and Anthropologists: The Modern British School* (London, 1983, revised edn).

11. Leach, *Social Anthropology*, p. 38. Leach (ibid, pp. 38–9) cites Edward Tylor's definition given in his famous work, *Primitive Culture* (London, 1871) whereby 'Culture, or civilisation, taken in its wide ethnographic sense, is that complex whole which includes knowledge, belief, art, morals, law, custom, and any other capabilities and habits acquired by man as a member of society.'

12. Leach, ibid, p. 39.

13. George W. Stocking, Jr, 'Matthew Arnold, E. B. Tylor and the Uses of Invention' in *American Anthropologist*, vol. 65, no. 4, August 1963, pp. 783–99, at p. 795.

14. Ward H. Goodenough, 'Comments on Cultural Evolution' in *Daedalus*, vol. 90, no. 3, Summer 1961, pp. 521–8, at p. 521.

15. Ward H. Goodenough, *Co-operation in Change* (New York, 1963) p. 258.

16. Ibid.
17. Ibid, pp. 258–9.
18. Clifford Geertz, *The Interpretation of Cultures* (New York, 1973) in ch. 1, 'Thick Description: Toward an Interpretive Theory of Culture', pp. 3–30, at p. 11.
19. Ibid, ch. 2, 'The Impact of the Concept of Culture on the Concept of Man', pp. 33–54, at p. 44. This chapter was first published in J. Platt (ed.) *New Views of the Nature of Man* (Chicago, 1966).
20. Geertz, *The Interpretation of Cultures*, p 11. Geertz's objection may seem less than fair to the observations of Goodenough cited here, but they would appear to be directed more at the 'taxonomies, paradigms, tables, trees, and other ingenuities' which he sees as having flowed from them.
21. Ibid.
22. Ibid, pp. 11–30.
23. Ibid, p. 5.
24. See, for example, Roger M. Keesing and Felix M. Keesing, *New Perspectives in Cultural Anthropology* (New York, 1971) esp. pp. 20–1 and 24–5; and David Riches (ed.) *The Conceptualisation and Explanation of Processes of Social Change* (Queen's University Papers in Social Anthropology, vol. 3, Belfast, 1979) paper by Ladislav Holy, 'Changing Norms in Matrilineal Societies: The Case of Toka Inheritance', pp. 83–105, especially p. 83.
25. Keesing and Keesing, *New Perspectives in Cultural Anthropology*, p. 27.
26. Ibid, p. 26.
27. Holy, 'Changing Norms in Matrilineal Societies: The Case of Toka Inheritance', p. 83.
28. Ibid.
29. Ibid, pp. 83–4.
30. Some attention to the relationship between anthropology and psychology is paid in Ernest Gellner (ed.) *Soviet and Western Anthropology* (London, 1980). See Meyer Fortes, 'Anthropology and the Psychological Disciplines', pp. 195–215, and I. S. Kon, 'Ethnography and Psychology'. Neither author is, however, concerned with the body of social psychological literature to which some attention is paid in this chapter. Fortes, in particular, is concerned almost entirely with psycho-analytical writings, even though it could be argued that these had a somewhat baneful influence on earlier writing on culture and 'national character' (not least in the context of discussion of the USSR). For brief critiques of 'psycho-cultural' writing on Soviet politics, see Archie Brown, *Soviet Politics and Political Science* (London, 1974) pp. 101–3, and Stephen White, *Political Culture and Soviet Politics* (London, 1979) pp. 6–14.
31. A fuller study than is possible within the confines of a chapter might usefully pay as much attention to the adjective as to the noun in 'political culture'. In particular, it is worth noting that in Communist states, while in one sense of the term, 'political', there is a high degree of depoliticisation, in another sense the political realm is much more extensive than in pluralistic political systems. This point is touched upon later in the article – for example, in the brief discussion of the official political culture – but not fully explored.

32. Apart from the other books and articles (on the whole, more specialised) to which reference will be made in subsequent notes, attention should be drawn to the following books which include surveys of the literature as well as original work: Henri Tajfel (ed.) *The Social Dimension: European Developments in Social Psychology* (Cambridge, 1984) 2 vols; Jeanne N. Knutson, *Handbook of Political Psychology* (San Francisco, 1973) especially M. Brewster Smith, 'Political Attitudes', pp. 57–82; Robert E. Lane, 'Patterns of Political Belief', pp. 83–116; and Richard G. Niemi, 'Political Socialization', pp. 117–38; J. Richard Eiser, *Cognitive Social Psychology: A Guidebook to Theory and Research* (London, 1980); Neil Warren and Marie Jahoda (eds), *Attitudes*, 2nd edn (Harmondsworth, 1973); and Robert A. Baron and Donn Byrne, *Social Psychology: Understanding Human Interaction*, 4th edn (Boston, 1984).

33. One of the best surveys of the attitude–behaviour problem which draws on research from several different disciplines is by two American sociologists. See Howard Schuman and Michael P. Johnson, 'Attitudes and Behavior', in Alex Inkeles, James Coleman and Neil Smelser (eds), *Annual Review of Sociology*, vol. 2 (Palo Alto, 1976) pp. 161–207.

34. In addition to the works cited in notes 8–29, see Stephen A. Tyler (ed.) *Cognitive Anthropology* (New York, 1969); and Robert A. LeVine (ed.) *Culture and Personality: Contemporary Readings* (Chicago, 1974).

35. Philip E. Converse, 'The Nature of Belief Systems in Mass Publics' in David E., Apter (ed.) *Ideology and Discontent* (New York, 1964) pp. 206–61, at p. 206.

36. A classic exploration of the political beliefs of individuals is Robert E. Lane's in-depth study of just fifteen Americans, *Political Ideology: Why the American Common Man Believes What He Does* (New York, 1962).

37. Michael Mann, 'The Social Cohesion of Liberal Democracy', in *American Sociological Review*, vol. 35, no. 3, 1970, pp. 423–39.

38. Barrington Moore, Jr, *Social Origins of Dictatorship and Democracy: Lord and Peasant in the Making of the Modern World* (Harmondsworth, 1969) p. 485.

39. Joel Cooper and Robert T. Croyle, 'Attitudes and Attitude Change', in Mark R. Rosenzweig and Lyman W. Porter (eds) *Annual Review of Psychology*, vol. 35 (Palo Alto, 1984) pp. 395–426, at p. 413.

40. See, for example, Abelson *et al*, 'Affective and Semantic Components in Political Person Perception', *Journal of Personality and Social Psychology*, vol. 42, no. 4, 1982, pp. 619–30, who begin their article 'Suddenly it is fashionable to write about emotion' and note 'how powerfully affect patterns predict preference and evaluation by the public of politicians' (pp. 619 and 624). See also Baron and Byrne, *Social Psychology*, pp. 116–18.

41. See Cooper and Croyle, 'Attitudes and Attitude Change', especially pp. 416–18; and J. M. F. Jaspars, 'Determinants of Attitudes and Attitude Change' in Henri Tajfel and Colin Fraser (eds) *Introducing Social Psychology* (Harmondsworth, 1978) pp. 277–301, especially 290–93.

42. Thus, in a much-cited experiment reported in 1959, Festinger and

Carlsmith found that a greater change in a person's attitude towards a boring task would occur if he were paid one dollar, as compared with twenty dollars, for telling someone else that it was an interesting task. For brief discussion of this and of the subsequent literature on the magnitude of incentives which specifies more precisely the conditions in which 'less leads to more', see Eiser, *Cognitive Social Psychology*, pp. 139–46; Jaspars, 'Determinants of Attitudes and Attitude Change', pp. 292–3; and Baron and Byrne, *Social Psychology*, pp. 155–7. On the effects of active participation more generally, see C. I. Hovland *et al*, 'A Summary of Experimental Studies of Opinion Change' in Warren and Jahoda (eds), *Attitudes*, pp. 115–28, especially 123–5.

43. See, for example, the work of V. V. Smirnov as cited in Chapter 5 of this volume (p. 108).

44. Mark Elvin, enumerating fifteen points of similarity between the Cultural Revolution of the 1960s and the Boxer Uprising of 1899–1900, notes, as one of them, that 'the enthusiastic young were the most numerous recruits to the cause, and possibly those who eventually suffered most' (Elvin, 'Mandarins and Millenarians: Reflections on the Boxer Uprising of 1899–1900' in *Journal of the Anthropological Society of Oxford*, vol. X, No. 3, 1979, pp. 115–38, at p. 128. Stuart Schram has written that Mao's approach to revolution was characterised by 'a dialectical conception of the relation between social change and cultural change' and that he saw 'participation in struggle' as 'the most potent weapon for awakening revolutionary consciousness'. See 'Introduction: the Cultural Revolution in Historical Perspective' of Stuart R. Schram (ed.) *Authority, Participation and Cultural Revolution in China* (Cambridge, 1973) pp. 1–108, at p. 102; see also in the same volume Andrew J. Watson, 'A Revolution to Touch Men's Souls: The Family, Interpersonal Relations and Daily Life', pp. 291–330.

45. See Eiser *Cognitive Social Psychology*, pp. 149–53.

46. The work which began the debate and has stimulated much subsequent research is L. Festinger's *A Theory of Cognitive Dissonance* (Evanston, Illinois, 1957). For survey appraisals of the cognitive dissonance literature, see Eiser, *Cognitive Social Psychology*, ch. 5, 'Incentive, Dissonance and Justification', pp. 127–63; Elliot Aronson, 'The Process of Dissonance' in Warren and Jahoda (eds) *Attitudes*, pp. 100–12; and Cooper and Croyle, 'Attitudes and Attitude Change', pp. 395–426, esp. pp. 404–13. For critiques of cognitive dissonance theory, see Michael Billig, *Ideology and Social Psychology* (Oxford, 1982) pp. 135–66; and Daryl J. Bem, 'Self-Perception: An Alternative Interpretation of Cognitive Dissonance Phenomena' in Warren and Jahoda, *Attitudes*, pp. 74–99.

47. Among them, experimental evidence showing that an alternative to belief change as a way of reducing cognitive dissonance is drinking alcohol! See C. M. Steele *et al*, 'Dissonance and Alcohol: Drinking your Troubles Away' in *Journal of Personality and Social Psychology*, vol. 41, no. 5, 1981, pp. 831–46.

48. See, for example, Eiser, *Cognitive Social Psychology*, pp. 127–63; and Cooper and Croyle, 'Attitudes and Attitude Change', pp. 404–13.

49. See especially Schuman and Johnson's review of the literature on 'Attitudes and Behaviour'.
50. See, for instance, ibid, esp. 165–6, 172, 176, 181–2, 185–6, 197–8 and 201–2; Eiser, *Cognitive Social Psychology*, pp. 45–6 and 51; and Allan W. Wicker, 'Attitudes v. Actions: the Relationship of Verbal and Overt Responses to Attitude Objects' in Warren and Jahoda (eds) *Attitudes*, pp. 167–94, especially 167–71.
51. Eiser, *Cognitive Social Psychology*, p. 51.
52. Schuman and Johnson, 'Attitudes and Behavior', p. 165.
53. Russell H. Fazio and Mark P. Zanna, 'Direct Experience and Attitude–Behavior Consistency', pp. 161–202, especially 162–5 and 195–8; Eiser, *Cognitive Social Psychology*, pp. 51–3; and Baron and Byrne, *Social Psychology*, pp. 159–64.
54. Fazio and Zanna, 'Direct Experience and Attitude–Behavior Consistency', pp. 162–5.
55. Ibid, p. 165.
56. See John Sivacek and William D. Crano, 'Vested Interest as a Moderator of Attitude–Behavior Consistency' in *Journal of Personality and Social Psychology*, vol. 43, no. 2, 1982, pp. 210–21.
57. Fazio and Zanna, 'Direct Experience and Attitude–Behavior Consistency'. See also Eugene Borgida and Bruce Campbell, 'Belief Relevance and Attitude–Behavior Consistency: The Moderating Role of Personal Experience' in *Journal of Personality and Social Psychology*, vol. 42, no. 2, 1982, pp. 239–47, especially p. 246.
58. J. M. F. Jaspars, 'The Nature and Measurement of Attitudes' in Tajfel and Fraser (eds) *Introducing Social Psychology*, pp. 256–76, at p. 265.
59. Milton Rokeach, *The Nature of Human Values* (New York, 1973) p. 7.
60. Ibid, p. 122.
61. Ibid, p. 217.
62. A. R. Luria, *Cognitive Development: Its Cultural and Social Foundations* (Cambridge, Massachusetts, 1976). The book was first published in Russian as *Ob istoricheskom razvitii poznavatel'nykh protsessov* (Moscow, 1974).
63. Luria, *Cognitive Development*, p. 19.
64. Ibid, p. 133.
65. Caroline Humphrey, *Karl Marx Collective: Economy, Society and Religion in a Siberian Collective Farm* (Cambridge, 1983).
66. Ibid, p. 431.
67. Ibid, p. 441.
68. Ibid.
69. Alexander Zinoviev, *The Yawning Heights* (Harmondsworth, 1981) and *The Radiant Future* (London, 1981).
70. Aleksandr Yashin, 'Rychagi', in M. I. Aliger *et al* (eds) *Literaturnaya Moskva* (Moscow, 1956) pp. 502–13.
71. Robert C. Tucker, 'The Image of Dual Russia' in Tucker, *The Soviet Political Mind* (New York and London, 1963) pp. 69–90, especially pp. 88–9.
72. Ibid, p. 88.
73. Ibid, p. 89.

74. Yashin, 'Rychagi', p. 513.

75. Tucker, *The Soviet Political Mind*, p. 89. It is of interest to note the parallel comment of the psychologist, Serge Moscovici, on how the 'exceptional measures' resorted to by 'totalitarian governments' (and he evidently has the Soviet Union in mind, for he cites as his source the French edition of Zinoviev's *The Yawning Heights*) 'in the long run produce a split into an official and a real society, a generalized double talking and double thinking'. See Moscovici, 'Toward a Theory of Conversion Behavior' in Leonard Berkowitz (ed.) *Advances in Experimental Social Psychology*, vol. 13 (New York, 1980) pp. 209–39, at p. 212.

76. Too many to be answered in detail in this chapter.

77. Masaryk on *Thought and Life: Conversations with Karel Čapek* (London, 1938) p. 191.

78. Jon Bloomfield, *Passive Revolution: Politics and the Czechoslovak Working Class 1945–1948* (London, 1979) p. 116.

79. Vladimir V. Kusin, *The Intellectual Origins of the Prague Spring: The Development of Reformist Ideas in Czechoslovakia 1956–1967* (Cambridge, 1971) p. 7.

80. For its original formulation, se Jack W. Brehm, *A Theory of Psychological Reactance* (New York and London, 1966) especially pp. 116–19. For a summary of, and references to, the more recent literature, see Baron and Byrne, *Social Psychology*, p. 152.

81. Whether it holds good in a situation of massive social pressures of the kind operating in Czechoslovakia of the early 1950s remains a moot point, perhaps, but there is no lack of evidence of 'reactance' to propaganda in Eastern Europe (especially East-Central Europe) in more recent times.

82. *Akční program Komunistické strany Československa* (Prague, 1968) p. 62.

83. If we consider McAuley's 'devil's advocate' position that '*no* previous experience of democracy encourages democratic beliefs' (Chapter 2, p. 25) we should expect to find these beliefs to be particularly strong in Africa and in much of the 'Third World'. In few, if any, African countries which began their independent statehood with a democratic constitution and with political pluralism built into their institutional structures did these survive. Major (though by no means the only) factors here would appear to be precisely the lack of sufficient support from a dominant political culture for the immediate post-colonial political system and, in many cases, the existence of a fragmented political culture based upon tribal divisions.

84. See the Czechoslovak Institute of Public Opinion data set out in Brown and Wightman, 'Czechoslovakia: Revival and Retreat', in Brown and Gray (eds) *Political Culture and Political Change in Communist States*, p. 165.

85. Where the Communists were in a small minority, as in Poland and Hungary, spontaneous unrest could shake the systems, as it did in 1956, and but for the Soviet intervention, Hungary at least would have ceased to be a Communist system. In Czechoslovakia, where the Communists

were a significantly higher proportion of the population and where already before the February 1948 take-over, they had a mass base, including the support of a large section of the working class (even though Communists remained a minority of the population as a whole) change in the political system was much more dependent on change within the Communist Party itself.

86. The restriction on the number of 'glorious periods' which could be mentioned and the precise questions asked are noted in Brown and Wightman, 'Czechoslovakia: Revival and Retreat', pp. 164–5.

87. Ibid, p. 189.

88. R. K. Merton, 'Fact and Factitiousness in Ethnic Questionnaires' in *American Sociological Review*, vol. 5, 1940, pp. 13–27 (as cited by Schuman and Johnson).

89. Schuman and Johnson, 'Attitudes and Behavior', p. 195.

90. Baron and Byrne, *Social Psychology*, pp. 54–6.

91. Schuman and Johnson, 'Attitudes and Behavior', p. 201.

92. On political efficacy, see Ronald Inglehart, *The Silent Revolution: Changing Values and Political Styles Among Western Publics* (Princeton, New Jersey, 1977) especially pp. 305–6; Lester W. Milbraith, *Political Participation: How and Why Do People Get Involved in Politics?* (Chicago, 1965) especially pp. 56–61; and Robert A. Dahl and Edward R. Tufte, *Size and Democracy* (Stanford, 1973) especially pp. 41–65.

93. For some pertinent observations on the psychological dimension of this, see Paul, *The Cultural Limits of Revolutionary Politics*, pp. 278–81.

94. On this, see Vladimir V. Kusin, *From Dubček to Charter 77: A Study of 'Normalisation' in Czechoslovakia 1968–1978* (Edinburgh, 1978): and H. Gordon Skilling, *Charter 77 and Human Rights in Czechoslovakia* (London, 1981). For an application of the point to Soviet-type systems generally, see Zdeněk Mlynář, 'The Rules of the Game: the Soviet Bloc Today' in *The Political Quarterly*, vol. 50, no. 4, October–December 1979, pp. 403–19.

95. Martin Fishbein and Icek Ajzen, *Belief, Attitude, Intention and Behavior: An Introduction to Theory and Research* (Reading, Massachusetts, 1975).

96. J. Richard Eiser and Joop van der Pligt. 'Attitudes in a Social Context' in Tajfel (ed.) *The Social Dimension*, vol. 2, pp. 363–78, at pp. 364–5.

97. Ibid, p. 366.

98. Ibid, p. 365.

99. Mlynář, 'The Rules of the Game'.

100. Among other behavioural changes much remarked upon by Czechoslovak citizens today is the enormous growth in corruption in post-1968 Czechoslovakia as compared not only with 1968 but also with the pre-1968 period of Communist rule.

101. Samuel P. Huntington and Jorge I. Dominguez, 'Political Development', in Fred I. Greenstein and Nelson W. Polsby (eds) *Handbook of Political Science, vol. III: Macropolitical Theory* (Reading, Massachusetts, 1975) pp. 31–2.

102. Juan J. Linz, 'Totalitarian and Authoritarian Regimes', in Greenstein and Polsby, ibid, pp. 203–4.

103. Seweryn Bialer, *Stalin's Successors: Leadership, Stability, and Change in the Soviet Union* (Cambridge and New York, 1980) p. 192.
104. Ibid, p. 193.
105. Ibid.
106. Brown and Gray (eds) *Political Culture and Political Change in Communist States*.
107. Usually the reference is to a society conterminous with the boundaries of a state, though in the chapter on Czechoslovakia in *Political Culture and Political Change in Communist States*, which I co-authored with Gordon Wightman, we refer to 'the political cultures of Czechs and Slovaks' (p. 189) and in the present volume David Paul writes of 'Czechoslovak political culture, in both its Czech and Slovak variants' (p. 139).
108. Brown, Introduction to *Political Culture and Political Change in Communist States*, pp. 8–9.
109. White, *Political Culture and Soviet Politics*, especially ch. 6, 'The Impact of Marxism–Leninism', pp. 113–42.
110. See Geert Hofstede, *Culture's Consequences: International Differences in Work-Related Values* (Beverly Hills and London, 1980). Apart from the large number of countries included in the survey, Hofstede's work is impressively systematic in a number of other respects. The survey on which he bases his book was conducted *twice* – in 1968 and 1972. The size of the sample in each round of the survey was vast – about 60 000 respondents, of whom some 30 000 took part in both rounds. Most important of all, the respondents were the employees in different countries of the same large multinational corporation, with the exception of those from Yugoslavia (the one Communist country included) from where an import–export organisation, which among other things serviced and marketed the multinational's products in Yugoslavia, was included. Thus, with the exception of the Yugoslav firm (which had a different company structure), the respondents could be matched for occupation (as well as by sex and age) with a precision which is quite unusual. While it would be beyond the scope of this chapter to summarise Hofstede's findings on the values and perceptions within his forty countries which he considers along four major dimensions labelled 'power distance', 'uncertainty avoidance', 'individualism' and 'masculinity', the relevance of his work lies in the extent to which he is able to demonstrate great differences of national culture by holding other factors, which might be thought to be crucial, constant. His samples have the advantage of functional equivalence. While subsidiaries of multinational corporations are likely to be atypical for their country, this does not matter, Hofstede suggests, 'as long as they are atypical in the same way from one country to another' (p. 39). Among the pertinent conclusions Hofstede draws from his research is the point that 'culture affects in particular those ideas that are taken for granted without further proof because no one in our environment ever challenges them' (p. 323). Also of interest is his view that 'while economic evolution (modernity, differentiation) is an important dimension which is bound to be reflected in the evolution of societal norms . . . there is no reason why economic and technological evolution should suppress cultural variety' (p. 45).

Indeed, while 'technological modernization is an important force toward change which leads to partly similar developments in different societies . . . it does not wipe out differences among societies and may even enlarge them' since 'on the basis of pre-existing value systems societies cope with technological modernization in different ways' (pp. 343–4).

111. Hofstede, ibid, p. 38.

112. Ibid.

113. Dennis Kavanagh, *Political Science and Political Behaviour* (London, 1983) p. 58.

114. Cf. Gary K. Bertsch, *Nation-Building in Yugoslavia: A Study of Political Integration and Attitudinal Consensus* (Beverly Hills and London, 1971): and David A. Dyker, 'Yugoslavia: Unity out of Diversity?' in Brown and Gray (eds) *Political Culture and Political Change in Communist States*, pp. 66–100.

115. In *Political Culture and Political Change in Communist States* (p. 18) I noted that one of the themes worth a fuller treatment than could be accorded it in that volume was 'the relationship between the process of political socialisation and political culture' which, in turn, involved 'consideration of what are the major components of the *official* political culture'.

116. This perhaps applies only partially to the 'new man' literature which is not all equally authoritative. Some of it has, indeed, an official character, as, for example (if we take the Soviet case) *KPSS o formirovanii novogo cheloveka: Sbornik dokumentov i materialov (1965–1981)* (Moscow, 1982, 2nd edn). Certain other works on this theme may represent the views of individual scholars rather than an agreed view in the highest echelons of the Party responsible for ideology. At a level below this, Party intellectuals *compete* to influence the content of official doctrine. Even in the Soviet Union there is rather more diversity of published view on ideological questions than is commonly supposed (though less than, for instance, in Poland and Hungary and incomparably less than in the West). I have drawn attention to some of this diversity to be found in Soviet writing on politial concepts in my 'Political Power and the Soviet State: Western and Soviet Perspectives' in Neil Harding (ed.) *The State in Socialist Society* (London, 1984) pp. 51–103; and in 'Political Science in the Soviet Union: A New Stage of Development?' in *Soviet Studies*, vol. XXXVI, no. 3, July 1984, pp. 317–44.

117. W. E. Butler, *Soviet Law* (London, 1983) p. 205.

118. See, for instance, Philip E. Converse, 'The Nature of Belief Systems in Mass Publics' in Apter (ed.) *Ideology and Discontent*, pp. 206–61, esp. p. 215; and Robert A. Dahl, *Polyarchy: Participation and Opposition* (New Haven and London, 1971) ch. 8, 'The Beliefs of Political Activists', pp. 124–88, esp. 166–88.

119. Dahl, *Polyarchy*, p. 166.

120. Jack Gray, 'Conclusions', in Brown and Gray (eds) *Political Culture and Political Change in Communist States*, pp. 253–72, at p. 260.

121. As Robert E. Lane has put it: 'neither capitalism nor any other system can prepare socialists to convert an entire society into a working *community*'. See his 'Waiting for Lefty: The Capitalist Genesis of

Socialist Man', *Theory and Society*, vol. 6 (1978) pp. 1–28, at p. 18. In an interesting argument, however, Lane also suggests that if socialist man ever is to be created, it is likely to be on the basis of 'Western individualism', and that 'there is hope, but not certainty, that advanced capitalist society has shaped a personality that would fit, with transitional strain, the proposed socialist institutions' (ibid, p. 24).

122. The phrase is from Huntington and Dominguez. See note 101.
123. See notes 101 and 102.
124. See Archie Brown, Introduction to Brown and Gray (eds) *Political Culture and Political Change in Communist States*, at pp. 4–5; and Mary McAuley in Chapter 2 of the present volume, at p. 26.
125. For a scholarly study of the realities, as distinct from the stereotypes of Finnish–Soviet Relations, see Roy Allison, *Finland's Relations with the Soviet Union 1944–84* (London, forthcoming).
126. On affect and persuasion, see the references in notes 40 and 41.
127. See the references in notes 101 and 103.
128. See, for example, the works cited in Chapter 5, p. 113, notes 40–3.
129. These are partly, but only partly, overlapping categories. Some Slavophiles, but far from all, are also neo-Stalinists. Most Westerners are, to a greater or lesser degree, reformers, though the Slavophiles are attacked from orthodox Marxist–Leninist positions as well as from Westerner–liberal standpoints. For two very different evaluations of this significant division within the Russian political hierarchy and intelligentsia, see Alexander Yanov, *The Russian New Right* (Berkeley, 1978) and John B. Dunlop, *The Faces of Contemporary Russian Nationalism* (Princeton, New Jersey, 1983).
130. Nadezhda Mandelstam, *Hope Against Hope* (London, 1971) p. 96.
131. Archie Brown, 'Eastern Europe: 1968, 1978, 1998' in *Daedalus*, vol. 108, no. 1 (Winter 1979) pp. 151–74, esp. pp. 168–9; and Brown, *Soviet Politics and Political Science*, pp. 92–4.
132. Bialer, *Stalin's Successors*, pp. 145–6.
133. Klaus Mehnert, *The Russians and Their Favourite Books* (Stanford, 1983), p. 257. Mehnert adds 'The patriotism of the Russians, who constitute one-half of the Soviet population, is in my mind a factor of world political significance that I take seriously; it is shared by the men in the Kremlin and the people of Russia alike'. See also Robert C. Tucker, 'Swollen State, Spent Society: Stalin's Legacy to Brezhnev's Russia' in *Foreign Affairs*, vol. 60, no. 2, Winter 1981, pp. 414–35, at p. 432.
134. Nina Tumarkin, *Lenin Lives! The Lenin Cult in Soviet Russia* (Cambridge, Massachusetts, 1983) p. 266. See also Felicity Ann O'Dell, *Socialisation Through Children's Literature: The Soviet Example* (Cambridge, 1978) especially pp. 155–8 and 177–9; and John Morison, 'The Political Content of Education in the USSR' in J. J. Tomiak (ed.) *Soviet Education in the 1980s* (London and New York, 1983) pp. 143–72, esp. pp. 155–6.
135. That was also the rationale of Brown and Gray (eds) *Political Culture and Political Change in Communist States*; the relation of 'the national to the systemic' is further explored in a recent article by Stephen White, 'Political Culture in Communist States: Some Problems of Theory and

Method' in *Comparative Politics*, vol. 16, no. 3 (April 1984) pp. 351–65.

136. It was for this reason that I was happy to make extensive use in *Political Culture and Political Change in Communist States* of survey data made available to me by the Institute of Public Opinion of the Czechoslovak Academy of Sciences. The professional standards of that Institute were high and the surveys were conducted at times when respondents were likely (i) to have been thinking seriously about politics and history, and (ii) not to be afraid of revealing their preferences. The investigation of the relationship of Czechs and Slovaks to their history, moreover, dealt with and elicited answers to a number of questions of central concern to the student of political culture.

137. Again indigenous research within Eastern Europe and the Soviet Union can be of great help. I have in mind, for example, a major forthcoming study of value change in Hungary by a team of sociologists led by Elemér Hankiss.

138. For example, I do not find McAuley always as clear as she should be on two points: (i) that *evidence* for X may be distinguishable from *causes* of X as well as from the *definition* of X; and (ii) that it is oversimple to insist that if A is evidence for X, then one cannot use X to explain A. X may, after all, be independently establishable or supported by B, C and D as well as by A. While there is a *danger* of circularity in attempting to explain behaviour by reference to values and beliefs and then citing behaviour as evidence of the strength of particular values and beliefs, awareness of that danger need not drive one into the kind of *either–or* position which McAuley comes close to adopting (on, for instance, p. 20 of Chapter 2). Since, as I hope I have made sufficiently clear in this chapter, much political behaviour within Communist states cannot be seen as reflecting the values and basic beliefs of those concerned, one has to produce reasons why a particular pattern of political behaviour (such as that to be found in Czechoslovakia between January and August 1968) should count as evidence of a particular political cultural orientation (in this case pluralistic). There is much other evidence on the subjective orientations of Czechs and Slovaks to politics in 1968 – notably from surveys – on which I have relied, but given the removal of many of the sanctions against autonomous political behaviour it would be rather odd in these circumstances to ignore the *evidence* of the way people behaved during the 'Prague Spring' itself. That is quite distinguishable from *explaining* how the political culture came to be what it was by the second half of the 1960s in Czechoslovakia. Some of the causal factors necessary to an explanation of how that particular political cultural orientation was brought about have been discussed in this chapter as well as in Chapters 6 and 7. More generally, it should be clear from a reading of this book that the argument one sometimes encounters about whether a political culture is a dependent or an independent factor in political explanation is based upon the false assumption that if it is the one it cannot be the other. Political culture in general and values and basic political beliefs more specifically are clearly the product of political experience and it is possible, in principle, to explain how they have come to take the form they have. That in no way precludes their being part of

an explanation of political change consonant with such values and beliefs when constraints which have previously been placed upon their expression become less severe.

Index

absolutism, 67, 68, 76, 121
Adenauer, Konrad, 49
affect, 158, 186
Afghanistan, 86
Ajzen, I., 172
Albania, 31
Almond, G. A., 1, 2, 3, 4, 6, 7, 8, 74, 92
Andropov, Yu. V., 105, 106
anthropology, 1, 2, 5–6, 11, 74, 118, 149, 150–5, 156, 191, 193–4, 196
Aristotle, 1
Armenians, 50
Armstrong, J., 82, 91
Arnold, Matthew, 151, 152
attitudes, 11, 16, 20, 21, 29, 31, 46, 75, 135, 143, 155–73, 191, 195
Austria, 68, 69, 72, 73, 76
Austro–Hungarian Empire, 120, 121, 125
Avrich, P., 16
Azerbaijan, 31

Babel', I., 79
Bahro, R., 33, 36
Baltic States, 53, 54, 65
  Balts, 51, 53, 54, 55, 56
Banks, A. H., 69, 70
Barghoorn, F., 2, 71, 82
Barry, B., 26, 46, 74
Belgium, 69, 71, 72
beliefs, see values and political beliefs
Beneš, President Edvard, 125, 126, 127, 129, 138, 145
Berlin, Sir Isaiah, 85
Bialer, S., 174, 175, 176, 188

Bolsheviks, see USSR
Brezhnev, L. I., 64, 80, 86, 101, 104, 105, 106, 144
Brown, A. H., 1–12, 15, 19, 22, 23, 24, 25, 26, 34, 48, 100–14, 115, 119, 122, 137, 149–203
  see also Political Culture and Political Change in Communist States
Brown–Gray volume, see Political Culture and Political Change in Communist States
Brzezinski, Z., 81
Bukharin, N. I., 78
Bukovsky, V., 78
Burlatsky, F. M., 104, 107

Čapek, Karel, 117
Carr, E. H., 84
censorship, 17, 73, 79, 116, 180
Charles IV, King, 169
Charter 77, 136, 143
China, 27, 29, 35, 36, 77, 91, 108, 145, 161, 162
  Cultural Revolution, 27, 77, 158, 159
  mass line, 27, 31
Coleman, J. S., 1
collectivisation, 53, 89
Confucianism, 15
cognitive dissonance, 159, 163, 164, 196
Converse, P. E., 156
Cooper, J., 157
CPSU (Communist Party of the Soviet Union), 4, 30, 32, 35, 52, 55, 79, 124, 153, 179, 180
  Central Committee, 25, 110, 180, 188

CPSU – *continued*
  General Secrectary, 104, 105
  membership of, 50, 52, 53
  Twentieth Congress, 167
  Twenty-second Congress, 167
  Twenty-sixth Congress, 104
Croyle, R. T., 157
Cuba, 36, 63, 77, 91, 178
culture, 2–3, 14, 104, 157, 176,
    200–1
  anthropological conceptions of, 1,
    5–6, 74, 150–5, 191, 193
Czechoslovak Communist Party,
    124, 141, 165, 166, 167, 173,
    187
Czechoslovakia, 4, 8, 15, 25, 26,
    115–33, 134–48, 150, 161,
    164–73, 178, 184, 185, 186,
    187, 188, 190
  Action Programme (1968), 119,
    136, 137, 142, 168
  Agrarian Party, 139
  Czech Legions, 125, 145
  Czech/Slovak beliefs and values,
    4, 23, 24, 25, 29, 164
  democracy in, 27, 135, 170
  elections in, 165, 166
  First Republic, 8, 25, 115, 116,
    117, 119, 120–1, 124, 127,
    136, 137, 138, 139, 140,
    142, 165, 168, 169, 170
  invasion of, 141, 146, 171, 173,
    190
  L'udaks (Slovak Populists), 137,
    139
  National Socialist Party, 165
  Social Democratic Party, 165
  traditions, 115, 118, 128, 138
  see also Czechoslovak Communist
    Party, Prague Spring

Dahl, R. A., 182
Davies, A. F., 46
democracy, 36, 58, 105, 117, 135,
    136, 141–2, 170, 187
democratic centralism, 179
Denmark, 69, 72
dichotomous political culture, 11,
    176, 177

dictatorship of the proletariat, 105,
    179
dominant political culture, 11, 18,
    28, 29, 30, 31, 37, 45, 118,
    119, 120, 121, 156, 165, 166,
    173, 175, 176, 177, 178, 179,
    180, 181, 182, 183, 184, 186,
    188–90, 198
Dominguez, J. I., 2, 174
Dostoevsky, F. M., 189
Dubček, Alexander, 127, 129, 137,
    145
Dukes, P., 66, 67
Durkheim, E., 151
Dyker, D. A., 15

East Germany, *see* GDR
education, 41, 45, 51, 53, 54, 56,
    58, 68, 83, 89, 162, 172–3
egalitarianism, 32, 35, 39
Eiser, J. R., 172
élite political culture, 38, 168, 175,
    176, 177, 178, 183, 188
Engels, F., 33, 76, 79
Estonia, 4, 51, 52, 53, 55
Estonians, 51, 52, 54, 55, 56, 57,
    188
expectations, *see* political
    expectations

Fagen, R. R., 2, 3, 63, 77
fascism, 23
  see also nazism
'Fatherland war', *see* 'Great
    Patriotic War', Second World
    War
Fazio, R. H., 160
Ferro, M., 75, 76
Field, D., 19
Finland, 65, 69, 129, 187
'Finlandisation', 185
First World War, 69, 71, 75, 77,
    120, 138, 188
Fischer, G., 89, 90
Fishbein, M., 172
foci of identification and loyalty, 40,
    87, 101, 102, 178, 189–90
fragmented political culture, 11,
    176, 177, 198

France, 66, 67, 69, 70, 71, 72, 84, 144
franchise, extension of, 68, 69, 70, 71, 73

Geertz, C., 63, 152, 153
Georgians, 50, 101, 188
Gerlich, P., 69, 70
GDR (German Democratic Republic), 6, 31, 36
Germany (pre-1945), 23, 68, 69, 70, 72, 89, 124, 125, 126, 137, 141
Gierek, E., First Secretary, 81
Gitelman, Z., 101
Goodenough, W., 152, 153
Gottwald, Klement, 141, 190
Gourevitch, P., 128
Gransow, V., 6
Gray, J., 7, 15, 19, 24, 27, 30, 140, 182
    see also *Political Culture and Political Change in Communist States*
Great Britain, 7, 23, 68, 69, 70, 72, 76, 83, 90
'Great Patriotic War', 88, 103, 189
    see also Second World War
Great Proletarian Cultural Revolution, see China, Cultural Revolution

Hácha, President E., 126, 128, 141
Haimson, L., 75
Hapsburg rule, 121, 125, 128, 135
Havel, V., 123
Hegedus, A., 32, 33
Herder, J. G. von, 1
Herzen, Alexander, 93
Hitler, Adolf, 89, 101, 138
Hofstede, G., 176
Holy, L., 154
Hough, J. F., 78
Humphrey, C., 162, 163
Hungary, 15, 24, 27, 29, 31, 130, 143, 146, 161, 168, 170, 172, 175, 177, 186
Huntington, S. P., 1, 2, 174
Hus, Jan, 169

Husák, Gustáv, 123, 127, 141, 142, 146, 187
Hussites, 117, 145, 169

Iceland, 69
intelligentsia, 30, 31, 35, 38, 80, 103, 167, 168, 173, 175, 179, 189, 190
interests, 19, 33, 46, 47, 48, 50, 55, 56, 107, 116, 117, 120, 121, 127, 157, 160, 182
Israel, Soviet emigrants to, 22
Italy, 65, 69, 70, 72

Japan, 71, 145
Johnson, M. P., 160, 170
'Just Tsar', myth of, 16, 17, 19, 50, 74, 76, 102

Kádár, János, 158, 182
Kalensky, V. G., 104, 107
Kaplan, D., 5
Kavanagh, D., 177
Kazakhstan, 51, 53, 54, 56
Kazakhs, 51, 52, 53, 54, 55, 56, 57
Keesing, F. M., 153
Keesing, R. M., 153
Keynes, J. M., 185
Keyzerov, N. M., 109
kharakteristika, 55
Khrushchev, N. S., 36, 49, 101, 102, 103, 105, 127, 167, 182, 190
    era, 164, 187
Kirghiz, 56
Kirghizia, 162
Kolankiewicz, G., 15, 35
Komsomol, 104, 109
Kon, I., 82
Kopecký, V., 165
Kopelev, L., 32, 33
Kornberg, A., 69, 70
Kramář, K., 125
Kundera, M., 123, 138, 142, 143
Kusin, V. V., 165
Kutuzov, Prince Mikhail, 88, 181

Lambert, F., 15
Lane, Christel, 103
Lane, David, 79

LaPiere, R. T., 159, 160
Latvia, 31, 51, 52, 53, 55
Latvians, 51, 52, 54, 55, 56, 57, 188
Lazarsfeld, P., 1
Leach, E., 151
legend of 'Just Tsar', *see* 'Just Tsar'
legitimacy, 27, 28, 50, 59
Lenin, V. I., 1, 76, 78, 84, 87, 101,
    104, 105, 108, 154, 181, 189,
    190
Lenin cult, 87, 88, 189
Leninism, 81, 82
    see also Marxism–Leninism
Linton, R., 1
Linz, J., 174
Lipinski, E., 81
Lithuania, 31
Liu Shao-ch'i, 30, 64
Luria, A. R., 162
Luxembourg, 69

McAuley, M., 8, 13–39, 40, 41, 43,
    44, 46, 47, 48, 50, 53, 54, 64,
    73, 75, 83, 100, 140, 149, 150,
    157, 164, 165, 168, 170, 175,
    177, 178, 182, 183, 186, 187,
    192
Malinowski, B., 1
Mandelstam, Nadezhda, 188
Mann, M., 28, 35, 157
Manners, R. A., 5
Mao Zedong, 27, 158, 161, 181
'Mao Zedong Thought', 158
Marx, K., 33, 76, 79, 105, 181, 189
Marxism, 13, 33, 34, 64, 81, 82, 84,
    87, 183
Marxism–Leninism, 22, 29, 33, 41,
    45, 79, 86, 89, 109, 135, 158,
    178, 179, 181, 190
Masaryk, T. G., 34, 117, 119, 121,
    125, 129, 138, 165, 170, 190
Masarykism, 24, 165
mass political culture, 45, 92, 177,
    188
    see also dominant political culture
Maximov, V., 78, 87
Medvedev, R. A., 81, 89
Mehnert, K., 189
Merton, R. K., 171

Miller, J., 8, 40–61, 150, 157, 191
Mlynář, Z., 23, 24
Mongols, 65
Moore, B., 157
myth of the 'Just Tsar', *see* 'Just
    Tsar'

nazism, 23, 77, 101, 124, 126, 141
Netherlands, 69, 72
Nevsky, Alexander, 88, 181
'new man', *see* 'socialist man'
'new socialist man'/'person', *see*
    'socialist man'
Nohlen, D., 70
nomenklatura, 18
norms (standards), 152, 154, 161,
    162, 172, 177
Northern Ireland, 177
Norway, 69, 72
Novgorod, 65
Novotný, A., 146

O'Dell, F., 79
official political culture, 29–36, 92,
    103, 118, 119, 120, 121, 122,
    166, 168, 172, 173, 174, 175,
    177–81, 183, 186, 188, 190,
    201

'party saturation', 50, 61
Paul, D. W., 2, 8, 115, 116, 120,
    122, 124, 128, 129, 134–48,
    150, 171, 185, 186
peasants, 19, 30, 34, 65, 74, 76,
    102, 103, 179
Peroutka, F., 117
Persia, 57
Peter I (the Great), Tsar, 67, 84,
    85, 144
Pětka, 121
Pipes, R., 71, 81
Pithart, P., 121
Plato, 1
Pligt, J. van der, 172
pluralism, 78, 115, 116, 119–30,
    134, 136, 137, 138, 139,
    141–2, 166, 168, 170, 185–7,
    193, 198

Poland, 24, 27, 31, 35, 65, 81, 108, 129, 130, 143, 144, 146, 161, 168, 170, 172, 175, 181, 186
political behaviour, 3, 4, 14, 17, 21, 37, 41, 50, 58, 73, 80, 88, 107, 119, 135, 137, 150, 154, 155–73, 186, 191, 199, 203
political beliefs, *see* values and political beliefs
political culture
   definitions of, 2–3, 14, 40–1, 106, 107, 150
   methodological problems of, 1, 15–36, 47–50, 53–7, 191–2, 203
   scope of concept, 1–6, 37, 41, 62–4, 73, 74, 107–8, 118–19, 139–40, 149–51, 184, 193, 203
   Soviet use of concept, 8, 103–11
   transmission of, 23, 29, 48, 49, 83, 135, 142–3, 149, 167–8, 175, 183, 188–90, 192
   Czechoslovakia, 8, 115–30, 134–46, 164–70, 171, 172–3, 184–7, 190, 191, 203
   France, 139
   Hungary, 29, 186
   Japan, 145
   nazi Germany, 126
   Poland, 31, 181
   Soviet Union, 8, 18, 62, 78, 79, 88, 91, 162–4, 174–6, 181, 188–90, 202
   Tsarist (or pre-revolutionary) Russia, 15, 16, 37, 62–77, 81–3, 87, 90, 91, 102
   Yugoslavia, 177
Political Culture and Political Change in Communist States, ed. Brown and Gray, 3, 7, 14, 15, 16, 20, 23, 26, 27, 40, 45, 46, 50, 63, 65, 66, 169, 175
Political Culture and Soviet Politics, S. White, 3, 21, 22, 40, 62, 65, 66, 69, 70, 73, 75, 76, 79, 80, 90, 91
'political development', 1, 2, 5, 91

political efficacy, sense of, 117, 171, 173
political information, *see* political knowledge
political institutions, 18, 23, 31–2, 41, 73, 83, 84, 85, 137, 153
political knowledge, 17, 38, 40, 56, 100, 110, 114, 167, 172–3
political participation, 16, 29, 36, 38, 70, 71, 72, 106, 108, 110, 158–9, 196
political perception, 13, 15, 20, 23, 24, 25–9, 40, 41, 46, 48, 55, 58, 74, 145, 156, 157, 167, 186, 187
political science, 2, 5, 64, 88, 106, 109, 112, 134, 149, 155, 157, 173
   IPSA Congress 1979 (Moscow), 106, 116
   in USSR, 106, 107, 110
political socialisation, 34, 41, 45, 47, 48, 53, 100, 118, 156, 183–4, 186, 201
political symbols, 2, 182, 189
Portugal, 69, 70, 72, 76
Powell, G. B., Jr, 1
Prague Manifesto, 89, 90
Prague Spring (1968), 116, 127, 142, 168, 173, 187
Prussia, 67, 68, 76
Pskov, 65
Pushkin, A. S., 189
Pye, L. W., 1, 2, 3, 20–1, 26, 27, 63, 151

Rákosi, M., 182
'reactance', 166, 198
religion, 76, 83, 162–3
   Catholicism, 31, 181
   Islam, 52, 54, 57
   Protestantism, 52, 53, 54
Rieger, F., 125
Rokeach, M., 161
Romania, 31, 181
Rosenau, J. N., 124
Russians (ethnic), 51, 52, 53, 54, 55, 78, 89, 188

Sakharov, A. D., 78, 86
Scandinavia, 52, 54, 68, 76
Schapiro, L. B., 71
Schöpflin, G., 15, 29, 32
Schragin, B., 82
Schuman, H., 160, 170
Scotland, 83
Second World War, 49, 88, 100,
    101, 102, 103, 138, 141, 145,
    164, 181, 188
Seton-Watson, H., 73
Shakhnazarov, G., 107
Siberia, 162
Skilling, H. G., 8, 115–33, 134, 137,
    138, 140, 141, 150, 164, 168,
    169, 170, 171, 185, 187, 191
Slavophils and Westerners, 85, 86,
    188
Slovaks, *see* Czechoslovakia
Smirnov, V. V., 79, 107, 108, 154
social psychology, 1, 45, 109, 149,
    155, 156–62, 172, 173, 191–2,
    194, 195–6
social structure, 22, 102, 153
socialism, 24, 81, 85, 89, 90, 105,
    106, 108, 115, 146, 165, 179
'socialism in one country', 35, 85
'socialist man', 14, 29, 30, 33–4,
    100, 103, 104, 106, 140, 170,
    180, 182, 192, 201–2
Solomon, R. H., 2
Solzhenitsyn, A. I., 78, 86, 190
Soviet man, *see* 'socialist man'
Spain, 66, 69, 72, 76
Stalin, J. V., 20, 48, 49, 85, 88,
    89, 91, 100, 101, 102, 181,
    182
Stalin period, 36, 48, 49, 78, 100,
    101, 102, 161
Stalinism, 22, 23, 32, 48, 49, 79, 81,
    89, 90, 102, 120, 122, 123,
    127, 136, 188, 190
  purges, 103, 111, 167
Štefánik, M. R., 138
Stocking, G. W., 151
Stolypin, P., 68
structures of government, *see*
    Political institutions
Štúr, L., 138

survey data, 15, 18, 25, 28, 101,
    120, 130, 170–1, 191, 203
Suvorov, Prince Alexander, 88, 181
Švejkism, 129
Sverdlovsk, 110
Sweden, 69, 72
Switzerland, 70
Szelényi, I., 33, 34, 168

Tadzhiks, 50
Taras, R., 15, 35
Tigrid, P., 128
Tiso, Father J., 126, 128, 138, 141
traditional political culture, 15–20,
    25, 33, 44, 48, 49, 50, 91, 102,
    122, 145, 175, 181, 182
Treadgold, D. W., 73
Trobriand Islanders, 6
Trotsky, L., 85
Tucker, R. C., 2, 3, 6, 14, 34, 63,
    151, 163, 164
Turkey, 69, 71, 72, 76
Turkmen, 50
Tylor, E. B., 151

Ulbricht, W., 49
unified political culture, 11, 176,
    177
USA, 7, 22, 68, 69, 70, 71, 72, 76,
    90, 144, 157
USSR, 4, 6, 8, 18, 22, 28, 29, 31,
    35, 41, 50, 51, 52, 54, 62, 69,
    78, 80, 82, 86, 87, 88, 89, 91,
    100, 101, 103, 108, 110, 111,
    126, 141, 143, 161, 172, 175,
    187
  All Union Voluntary Society for
    the Preservation of
    Monuments of History and
    Culture, 83
  Bolsheviks, 17, 33, 36, 83, 84, 85,
    86, 89, 90, 182
  Buryats, 162, 163, 188
  Central Asia, 53, 65, 80, 162
  Congress of Soviets, 17, 75
  Constituent Assembly, 66, 75
  Constitution (1977), 100, 108
  Cossack lands, 65
  DOSAAF, 81

USSR – *continued*
    Duma, 65, 74, 75
    February Revolution, 89
    Mensheviks, 85
    Supreme Soviet, 83
    Tsarist Russia, 65–78, 79, 81, 82, 83, 100, 108
Uzbekistan, 55, 56, 57, 162
Uzbeks, 50, 56

values and political beliefs, 8, 11, 13, 14, 16, 20, 21, 23, 24, 26, 27, 28, 29, 31, 33, 34, 37, 46, 48, 49, 50, 56, 57, 58, 73, 79, 88, 100, 107, 119, 122, 123, 132, 142, 149, 155–73, 175, 177, 182, 183, 185, 187, 195, 203
Vanhanen, T., 72
Verba, S., 1, 2, 3, 41, 63, 74, 100, 151
Vlasov, General A., 89
Voinovich, V. N., 88

Warwick, P., 139
Weber, M., 92, 151, 153
Weimar Republic, *see* Germany
Wenceslas, Saint, 169

White, S., 2, 3, 6, 8, 15–18, 21–2, 33, 35, 36, 40, 48, 62–99, 100, 103, 150, 176, 181, 188, 189
    see also Political Culture and Soviet Politics
White Mountain, battle of, 128, 135
Wightman, G., 15, 19, 23, 24, 25, 34, 115, 119, 122, 137, 169
Willars, C., 128
Witte, Count S., 68
workers, manual, 23, 28, 30, 32, 34, 35, 75, 76, 80, 101, 102, 103, 104, 105, 116, 179
World War One, *see* First World War
World War Two, *see* Second World War

Yashin, A., 163, 164
Yugoslavia, 15, 27, 31, 130, 170, 172, 177, 178

Zanna, M. P. 160
Zaslavsky, V., 101, 102
Zeitlin, M., 63
Zinoviev, A., 102, 163
Zoshchenko, M. 82